Pacific Connections

AMERICAN CROSSROADS

Edited by Earl Lewis, George Lipsitz, George Sánchez, Dana Takagi, Laura Briggs, and Nikhil Pal Singh

Pacific Connections

THE MAKING OF THE U.S.-CANADIAN BORDERLANDS

Kornel S. Chang

UNIVERSITY OF CALIFORNIA PRESS
BERKELEY LOS ANGELES LONDON

University of California Press, one of the most distinguished university presses in the United States, enriches lives around the world by advancing scholarship in the humanities, social sciences, and natural sciences. Its activities are supported by the UC Press Foundation and by philanthropic contributions from individuals and institutions. For more information, visit www.ucpress.edu.

University of California Press
Berkeley and Los Angeles, California

University of California Press, Ltd.
London, England

Library of Congress Cataloging-in-Publication Data

Chang, Kornel S.,
Pacific connections : the making of the U.S.-Canadian borderlands / Kornel S. Chang.
p. cm. (American crossroads)
Includes bibliographical references and index.
ISBN 978-0-520-27168-5 (cloth : acid-free paper)
ISBN 978-0-520-27169-2 (pbk. : acid-free paper)
1. United States—Territorial expansion. 2. United States—Foreign economic relations—Pacific Area. 3. Imperialism. 4. Canada—Territorial expansion. 5. Canada—Foreign economic relations—Pacific Area. 6. Pacific Area—Foreign economic relations—United States. 7. Pacific Area—Foreign economic relations—Canada. 8. North America—Economic integration. 9. Globalization—Economic aspects—History. I. Title.
E179.5.C38 2012
973.1—dc23 2011053509

21 20 19 18 17 16 15 14 13 12
10 9 8 7 6 5 4 3 2 1

The publisher gratefully acknowledges the generous support of the Ahmanson Foundation Humanities Endowment Fund of the University of California Press Foundation.

CONTENTS

ILLUSTRATIONS

MAPS

FIGURES

TABLES

ACKNOWLEDGMENTS

It is with great pleasure and relief that I am finally able to thank the many people and institutions that have helped bring this book to the finish line. I want to start by thanking my teachers at the University of Chicago, where the book got its start. Thomas Holt taught me about the ways racism has operated in the modern world, and his commitment to deconstruct its corrosive logic has inspired many of the themes taken up by this book. From almost the very beginning, Bruce Cumings believed that I had something important to say. His faith has emboldened me to pose big questions and take chances with my writing. Kathleen Conzen patiently introduced a neophyte to the history of the North American West. Michael Geyer and Saskia Sassen taught me a great deal about the historicity and logic of globalization that have profoundly shaped my understanding about the development of the modern world. The camaraderie of Ellen Wu, Arissa Oh, Meredith Oda, Quincy Mills, Allyson Hobbs, Jason McGraw, and Albert Park who became friends and interlocutors enriched my Chicago experience.

From Chicago, I was fortunate to land at the University of Connecticut, where I found supportive colleagues in Shirley Roe, Frank Costigliola, Charles Lansing, Christopher Clark, Jeffrey Ogbar, Brendan Kane, Alexis Dudden, Nancy Shoemaker, Nina Dayton, Emma Gilligan, Melina Pappademos, Blanca Silvestrini, Cathy Schlund-Vials, Roger Buckley, Bandana Purkayastha, and Margo Machida. I want to especially thank Mark Overmyer-Velazquez who took a newly minted PhD under his wings and showed him the proverbial ropes. My current colleagues at Rutgers-Newark have contributed to the book in countless ways: Beryl Satter, James Goodman, Jan Ellen Lewis, Timothy-Stewart Winter, Ruth Feldstein, Susan

Carruthers, Clement Price, and Whitney Strub have offered suggestion, feedback, and encouragement for things big and small related to the book. I count myself lucky to be working among a talented and committed group of scholars at Rutgers. Thanks also to Dean Philip Yeagle for his enthusiastic support of junior faculty at Rutgers-Newark and Christina Strasburger, administrator extraordinaire, for her everyday support and encyclopedic knowledge of everything Rutgers.

I spent two enormously productive years at Yale University as the Ethnicity, Race, and Migration Postdoctoral Fellow. The program director, Stephen Pitti, was effusive in his support and has become a valued mentor and friend. The manuscript workshop Steve organized for me back in the spring of 2009 came at a critical juncture that helped me revise and expand the book. Time spent with Matthew Frye Jacobson, Ned Blackhawk, Mary Lui, Alicia Schmidt Camacho, and Kariann Yokota also made my time at Yale a thoroughly enjoyable one. At the Yale workshop, Richard White and Mary Lui gave the first draft of the manuscript a close read and provided invaluable suggestions on how to move forward. Moon-Ho Jung also participated in that workshop and then took on the unenviable task of reading the penultimate version of the book. Moon has gone above and beyond as an interlocutor and friend, giving more than generously of his time and insights—and the book is far better for it.

I am also grateful to David Roediger, Eiichiro Azuma, Paul Kramer, Lisa Lowe, Gary Okihiro, Henry Yu, Matthew Frye Jacobson, John Findlay, Mrinalini Sinha, Paul Sue, Adam McKeown, Bruce Nelson, Eileen Boris, Ann Fabian, and Chris Friday for helpful conversation and feedback on specific chapters and writings related to the book. Excerpts from the book were first published as articles in the *Journal of American History* and the *American Quarterly*. I would like to thank the publishers and editors of these journals for their permission to reprint them here. At the University of California Press, I'd like to thank my editor Niels Hooper for seeing promise in the project early on and for his steady hand throughout. Thanks also to Kim Hogeland, Kate Warne, and Michael Bohrer-Clancy for their help in shepherding the book through the production process and to Heather McElwain for her expert copyediting.

Research for this book has taken me far and wide, and I'm grateful to numerous librarians and archivists who helped me locate materials at the University of Washington Special Collections; University of British Columbia Special Collections; National Archives and Records Administration in

Washington, DC and the Pacific Northwest Region in Seattle, Washington; United States Immigration and Naturalization Service in Washington, DC; Library and Archives Canada in Ottawa, Ontario; Wing Luke Museum in Seattle, Washington; City of Vancouver Archives; Japanese-Canadian National Museum in Burnaby, British Columbia; Seattle Public Library; Simon Fraser University Archives in Burnaby, British Columbia; Densho Society in Seattle, Washington; Hoover Institution Archives in Stanford, California; and the British Library in London, England. A special thanks to Carla Rickerson, George Brandak, and Marian L. Smith for responding to my countless queries with patience and enthusiasm. I was fortunate to receive generous financial support from the Andrew W. Mellon Foundation, the Whitney and Betty MacMillan Center for International and Area Studies at Yale University, the Canadian Embassy, the American Historical Association, the Rutgers Faculty Research Grant Program, and the University of Chicago and the University of Connecticut History Departments.

I owe my greatest intellectual and professional debts to two people. I would probably not be a historian today (and this book wouldn't exist) if it weren't for Barbara Weinstein. Barbara was my first teacher, and it was her critically engaged teaching and scholarship that inspired me to be a historian in the first place. She also convinced me as an undergraduate that I would be happier (albeit poorer) as a history professor than as a lawyer. She was right on both accounts. Mae Ngai has contributed more to this book and my development as a scholar than anybody else. Having read and commented on the book more times than she cares to remember, Mae is probably happy (and relieved) to see the book finally in print. If there is anything interesting or smart in the book, it is probably due to her influence and model. It goes without saying any mistakes in analysis and interpretation are mine alone.

Finally, this book would not have been completed without the love of my family. My parents, Hyun Pyung Chang and Chun Young Rim, finally got used to their son reading books for a living though they had always preferred I take a "safer" professional route. I'm thankful for the big and small sacrifices they have made on my behalf. My sisters, Glory, Grace, Jin, and Min, my brothers-in-law Eugene Lee and Thomas Yu, and my father-in-law John Kim provided regular babysitting so I could work on the book, as well as timely diversions away from it. I am especially grateful to my mother-in-law Myong Hee Lee who took care of our infant twins on the days and nights I was commuting to Connecticut. As this book goes to press, I'm reminded of my late grandmother Kae Hee Lee who gave selflessly to everyone she encountered and was a model of human goodness. My children Kate and Carter didn't care one iota for the book, and for that, *appa* is grateful. My final and most important acknowledgment is saved for Laura Yon Kim who has known me and loved me far before this book (and hopefully long after it). Her partnership has meant more than she knows and so this book is dedicated to our life together.

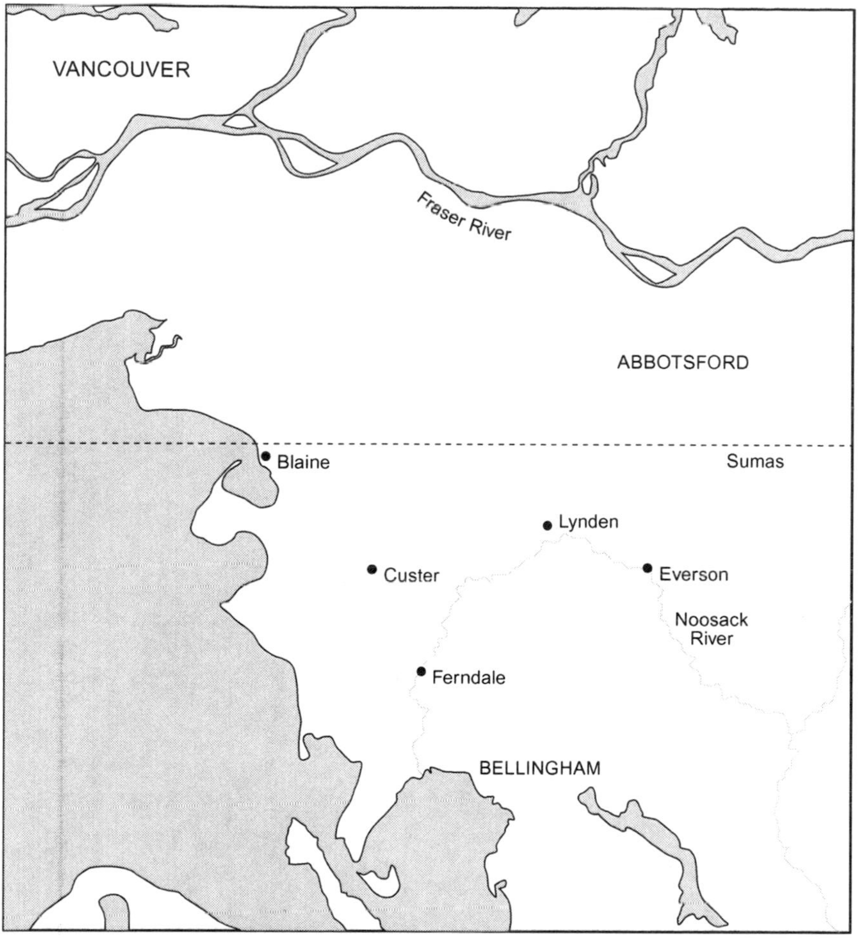

MAP 1. The Puget Sound and Surrounding Areas. Drawn by Melissa Mok.

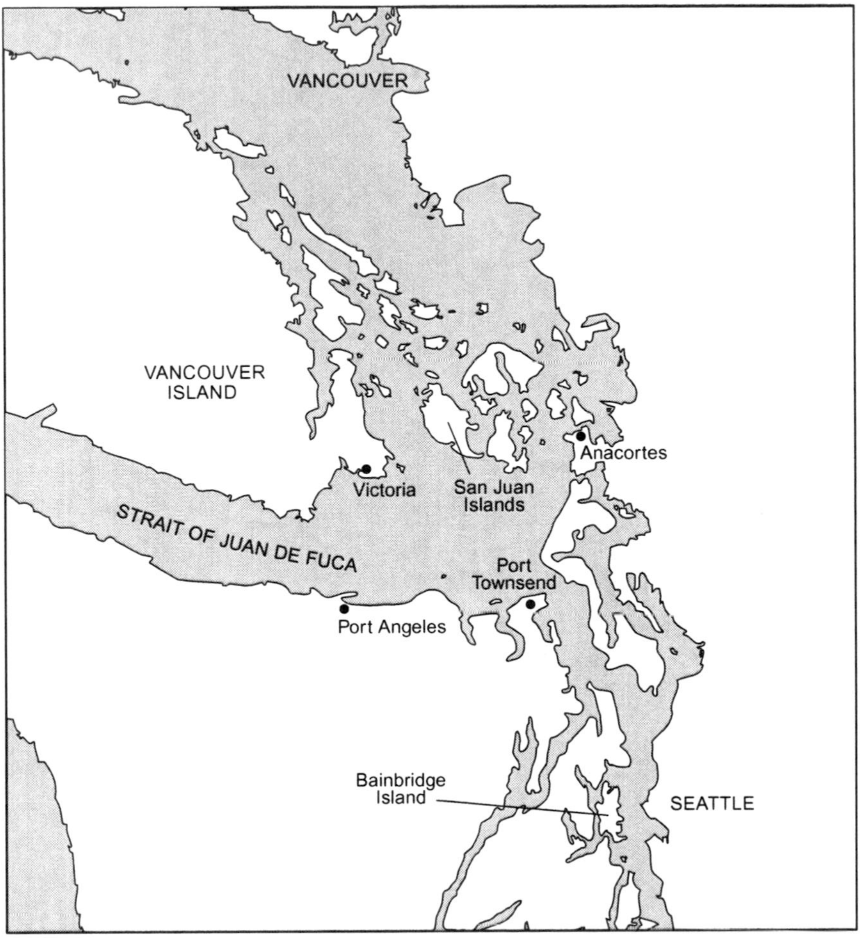

MAP 2. The Washington–British Columbia Boundary Region. Drawn by Melissa Mok.

Introduction

ON A CLEAR, LATE AUGUST afternoon in 1896, a large crowd gathered around the Seattle waterfront against the backdrop of a brilliant firework display, which illuminated the Pacific skies above them, giving the aura of a truly grand occasion. The throng came from all parts of the city, which included its leading citizens—the mayor, the president of the chamber of commerce, and members of the city council—who took their place at the head of the festivities nearest to the water's edge. A local reporter covering the pageantry noted: "The yells of thousands of people on the docks and the blowing of every steamship whistle for five miles along the waterfront, and the flaunting of innumerable flags to the breeze [that] celebrated the glad event and welcomed the Oriental visitor of the East to the Occident."[1] The "Oriental visitor" he was referring to was the *Mike Maru*, a transpacific steamship liner belonging to the Nippon Yusen Kaisha Company (NYK), which was making its inaugural voyage. Railroad mogul James J. Hill had recently entered an agreement with the Japanese steamship company establishing regular steamship service from Seattle to Hawai'i, Japan, China, Hong Kong, and the Philippines. For years Seattle leaders and boosters had pinned their hopes on becoming a bridge to Asia and the fabled China market. The landmark agreement between Hill's Great Northern Railway and the NYK, they thought, would finally make this dream a reality. With a twenty-one gun salute blaring in the background, the welcoming committee proclaimed Seattle the gateway to the Orient, the transpacific city where the Orient and the Occident, the East and the West, met and were to be united.

On a day when admiration for "the Orient" was running at a fever pitch, it was hard to believe that this very same port, only a decade earlier, was the site of a violent campaign to expel Chinese residents from the city. A few steps from where the cheering crowd stood to welcome the *Mike Maru* was where an angry white mob, almost exactly ten years earlier, forcibly held Chinese residents, while awaiting the ship that would deport them back to Asia. This campaign of forcible removal, called "abatement" by contemporaries, was inspired by the enactment of the Chinese Exclusion Act (1882), which enshrined into law the idea that the Chinese did not belong, which in turn legitimized the cries that "the Chinese must go." Indeed, white rioters, in justifying their actions, claimed that the Chinese posed a grave threat to the body politic. "All who have ever come into close contact with them are satisfied that they are not only a most undesirable but a positively dangerous class to any country having free popular institutions."[2] The expulsions, then, were seen as an act of self-protection, an effort to secure the racial and political integrity of the nation-state.

Exploring the contradictory impulses represented by these two moments and understanding how they came to mutually shape and define a region underpins this study of the U.S.-Canadian borderlands in the Pacific Northwest. Beginning in earnest with the nineteenth century, the imperatives of capitalist development and imperial expansion integrated this periphery into the world economy. As the region's vast natural resources came into range, foreign capital and labor rushed in to develop them. The rise and mix of extractive industries drew a diverse collection of people and cultures into contact through new systems of mobility and exchange. This polyglot assemblage, including Chinese merchant contractors, Japanese and European migrant workers, Anglo labor activists, and South Asian and white radicals, propelled the circulation of people, goods, and ideas across boundaries. This process—often captured loosely under the rubric of globalization—expanded the region's connections with the Pacific world, embedding it firmly within an imperial circuitry of migration, trade and communication in the late nineteenth and early twentieth centuries.

This book therefore re-imagines these ostensibly "Western" spaces as a critical intersection of colonialism and the Pacific world, where the American West, the Dominion of Canada, the British Empire, and Asia intersected and overlapped. Whereas Western historians have confined borderland studies to bi-national frameworks—as discrete and bounded spaces at the edge of two nations—my study offers a more expansive approach taking into account regions and historiographies beyond the Americas and, in doing so, re-orients borderlands history to the larger worlds of which it was a part.[3] The end of continental expansion did not signal the closing of the frontier, as Frederick Jackson Turner so famously declared, but instead extended its outer limits into the Pacific with Asia and the South Pacific re-imagined as the new "Far West."[4] Indeed, as Turner himself later acknowledged, beyond the West was the Orient, where "the long march of westward civilization should complete its circle"—or as historian Gerald Horne puts it, where "the frontier's closing encountered the dawning of a new age of imperialism."[5] Re-orienting the West and the history of the frontier toward the Pacific Rim allows us to complicate the Atlanticist perspective that dominates the writing of American history, opening new fields of vision in which encounters, interactions, and struggles in the Pacific as well as the Atlantic shapes the historical development of North America.[6]

But if the story of the U.S.-Canadian borderlands was about a world in motion, it was also a story about bordered polities and empires. Connections and transformations wrought by a globalizing world kindled a countermovement to solidify national borders among white settler societies in Canada and the United States, who together elaborated new forms of sovereignty in an attempt to control Asian migration across the Pacific and across landed borders in North America.[7] The multi-national effort at Asiatic exclusion codified immigration and boundary controls as rightful prerogatives of the nation-state, which in turn reconstructed racial and national borders through its practical enforcement. The historiography on modern borders in North America has focused largely on the U.S.-Mexico border, showing us how the racialization of Mexican immigrants variously as "illegal aliens" and "alien citizens" went hand in hand with state assertions of territorial sovereignty on the southern boundary.[8] In stark contrast, the boundary shared by Canada and the United States has been historically imagined as the longest unguarded border in the world, and thus rarely, if ever, problematized as site of contest or power.

Yet it was the struggle over Asian migration across the northern boundary that gave rise to the first sustained emphasis on border policing and surveillance in the Americas. By relocating the historical origins of the border from the southern to the northern boundary, this book shows how this process was transnational in scope, involving a contest over Asian migration that extended across the Pacific world. In doing so, my study highlights the contingent process of the territorial state, and considers the multiple and overlapping sites—the local, the national, and the imperial—that shaped its formation. By examining U.S. efforts to extend migration and border controls to Canada, Hawai'i, and the Philippines and British surveillance of imperial subjects in the North American West, my book demonstrates the ways border enforcement was inextricably tied to competing imperial projects in the late nineteenth and early twentieth century.[9] Following a spate of recent scholarship that shows the extent to which modernity was first worked out in the colonies—styled as "laboratories of modernity"—I argue that key surveillance principles and apparatuses of the modern state were forged in the crucible of empire.[10] Thus, even as the migration of people and capital across borders gave rise to a fluid regional world with shifting boundaries, Canada, Britain, and the United States sought to police such global flows through hardened borders, restrictive immigration laws, and state systems of surveillance and control.

These dueling impulses—to reach outwards, collapse boundaries, and integrate formerly disparate regions through boundless expansion, on the one hand, and to police movement across boundaries through bounded and delimited spaces, on the other—were formed dialectically constituting one of modernity's enduring paradoxes in which the global and the national were fashioned together.[11] In the Pacific Northwest, the tensions and contradictions arising from this global/local nexus were mediated and resolved, although never entirely, through the working and reworking of race. The imperatives of a "white man's country" that justified settler expansion and the exploitation of markets and labor abroad also at once rendered national boundaries at home inviolable and racially exclusive.[12] As one prominent western booster declared: "The Pacific Coast is the frontier of the white man's world, the culmination of the westward immigration which is the white man's whole history. It will remain the frontier so long as we guard it as such . . . Unless it is maintained there, there is no other line at which it can be maintained . . . "[13]

The territorializing processes of state formation and the de-territorializing prerogatives of capital were therefore inextricably intertwined, cohering into dual sides of an imperial project. As Amy Kaplan has explained: "The American Empire has long followed a double impetus to construct boundaries and patrol all movement across them and to break down those borders through the desire for unfettered expansion."[14] Following her insight, this book demonstrates how the quest for an

"Open Door" Empire in Asia—borrowing historian William Appleman Williams' evocative metaphor for U.S. imperialism—was coupled with a strategy of closure at home to form the double-edge of Anglo-American imperialism in the Pacific.[15] This double vision became constitutive of an imperial fantasy, one that performed essential ideological work on behalf of the empire.

However, if the dream of accessing lucrative markets abroad and delineating precise and stable borders at home was clear and unambiguous, the reality of empire was far more complex and messier. Operating on the edges of the imperium, American and British empire builders struggled with distance, their progress being impeded by a lack of ready access to capital and human resources. To overcome these limitations, they turned to Asian ethnic contractors, merchants, and smugglers, who facilitated exchanges and movements that were crucial to Euro-American imperial expansion in the Pacific. The empire, as Tony Ballantyne reminds us, was "a structure, a complex fabrication fashioned out of a great number of disparate parts that were brought together into a new relationship."[16] Asian intermediaries played a vital role in integrating these disparate parts into a functioning whole. In coordinating the flow of labor, capital, and goods across an empire that was spread across vast distances, they were the ones to maintain the lifeblood of the imperial system. As this suggests, despite their global pretensions, there was a wide gap between Anglo-American empires that were imagined as such and the reality of their capacity for such reach. The incorporation of an Asian middling elite into Anglo-American imperialism was a tacit acknowledgment of this reality.

But if their labor helped to propel the empire forward, their activities mobilizing people and resources also sparked wide-ranging struggles that would fragment, and, at times, undermine the imperial project. Thus, even as their transnational movements and practices more tightly bound the region into widening imperial circuits of power and culture, they also became, as historian Arif Dirlik points out, "a source of opposition and division economically, politically, and culturally" that lay to bear the "contradiction between the Pacific as Euro-American invention and its Asian content."[17] This contradiction would reveal the fissures between empire and nation, between an imperial impulse to incorporate diverse peoples and cultures, if always hierarchically and unevenly, and a nationalist envisioning for homogenous communities in which state and nation overlapped neatly, as Asian intermediaries organized an imperial system of mobility and exchange that challenged the imagined integrity of the nation-state. The development of modern border regimes should therefore also be seen in this light, as an effort to manage the at times conflicting interests of empire and nation. These tensions, moreover, created subversive opportunities for contract laborers, migrant smugglers, and radical activists.[18] Re-fashioning the networks that knit together the empire into pathways of resistance and avenues for negotiating Euro-American imperialism, these subaltern groups would pursue a transnational politics from below. The incorporation of this "Asian content," would, then, serve to both perpetuate and de-stabilize the empire, producing in the Pacific, a "radically unequal but also radically de-centered world."[19]

THE OUTLINES OF A PACIFIC WORLD

The transpacific connections and patterns of global exchange that grew out of Anglo-American ascendance to constitute the western U.S.-Canadian borderlands mapped onto coordinates of migration and trade first established by the Spanish Empire. That is, before the Pacific was an "Anglo-Saxon lake" it was a "Spanish lake."[20] The Manila galleon trade, which connected China, Spain, and its far-flung empire in the Americas through new trade and commercial networks, traced the outline of an emergent Pacific world beginning in the late sixteenth century. Vessels departed New Spain (what is today Mexico) with cargoes of manufactured goods, tools, munitions, and silver and returned from China with tea, silk, porcelain, and spices, stopping over in the Philippines in each direction and establishing for the first time "substantial and continuous trade across the Pacific Ocean."[21] Within this system of commerce, a powerful China—which was a regional hegemon in its own right at the center of a dynamic tributary trading system in Asia—figured prominently.[22] It was, after all, the desire for Chinese goods that propelled global trade in the early modern period. With the China trade serving as its structuring logic, Acapulco, Manila, and Canton emerged as intersecting nodal points in what historians consider to be the first global system of trade through which the Spanish and Chinese Empire expanded and grew rich. This far-flung trade network established some of the economic, political, and cultural relationships that gave the Pacific its initial configuration as a region.

By the seventeenth and eighteenth centuries, aspiring imperial powers contested Spanish dominance in the region. At first, this took the form of attacks on Spanish vessels associated with the Manila galleon trade as well as raids on Spanish settlements lying on the Pacific. Yet what started out as little more than a nuisance soon evolved into a more direct challenge to Spanish hegemony in the region as the Dutch, Portuguese, French, and the British all vied to expand into Asia and the South Pacific, seeking to exert influence in regions that were previously understood to be the exclusive sphere of the Spanish Empire. The British, in particular, pushed aggressively into the area, initiating exploratory campaigns—including the famous voyages of James Cook—that would eventually lead to the "discovery" of New Caledonia, Easter Islands, and the Hawaiian Islands, among other places in the Pacific.[23]

In the quest for new overseas markets and trade routes to Asia, opposing European rivals joined the Spanish in mapping, naming, and defining the area in their terms, imposing their vision of the Pacific in the process. In this regard the Pacific was more of an ideological construct than a spatial or geographic reality that reflected the conglomeration of discourses and ideas underpinning the strategy of empire. As Arif Dirlik has forcefully argued, "there is no Pacific region that is an "objective" given, but only a competing set of ideational constructs that project upon a certain location on the globe the imperatives of interest, power, or vision."[24] The Pacific, he insists, "is not so much a well-defined idea as it is a discourse that seeks to construct what is pretended to be its point of departure, a discourse that is problematized by the very relationships that legitimize it."[25] The various Euro-American formulations of the Pacific, as a "Spanish Lake," "British Lake," and, most recently, as an "American Lake," were, then, discursive strategies that sought to create a reality of what they purported to represent.

These Euro-American imaginings of the Pacific did go not uncontested, of course. Pacific islanders and other peoples native to the region challenged the notion of the Oceania as a vast, empty space bereft of "human civilization" prior to European "discovery," insisting that the Pacific was a place of human motion, creativity, and interconnections long before their arrival. In other words, they rejected the idea that the history of the region—that is a consciousness of the Pacific—only began or sprung up with Euro-American intervention. Understanding that to name and to narrate was to conquer and to dominate, the indigenous peoples of the Pacific put forth their own claims to the region, which, Tongan writer Epeli Hau'ofa envisioned as "a large world in which peoples and cultures moved and mingled unhindered by boundaries of the kind erected much later by imperial powers."[26] By doing so, Hau'ofa and other native critics of western imperialism offered an alternative genealogy of the "Pacific"—a world that was neither of colonizers and the colonized nor of centers and peripheries.

Still, as Dirlik himself readily acknowledges, European expansion gave rise to interactions and exchanges from which concrete relationships arose to endow the Pacific with a semblance of geographical or spatial unity. Indeed, the movements and the networks generated by western, and to a lesser extent, Japanese, imperialism integrated disparate spaces in the Pacific into a regional structure though, admittedly, one with fluid and shifting boundaries. The transpacific shuttle of people and commodities initiated by the Spanish galleon trade was made denser through a succession of foreign incursions that introduced new nodal points around which new circuits of trade, culture, and communication emerged. These linkages and transformations produced some of the world's first globetrotters: Chinese seamen sailing on the Manila galleon ships made their way to far-flung places in the Americas and the South Pacific; natives from Hawai'i and the Pacific Islands found themselves on American, British, and Russian vessels engaged in whaling and the fur trade; and locally extracted commodities such as silver, gold, fur, pelts, and sandal wood were traded across the Pacific. Not unlike the Atlantic, the histories of empires, regions, and nations around the Pacific were mutually imbricated through encounters generated by global migration, imperial rivalries, international trade, and cross-cultural interactions and exchange.[27]

The Pacific Northwest first became involved in this larger world—emerging as yet another link in the chain of an ever-expanding global economy—through the fur trade, which linked the region and its people to Asia, Hawai'i, and the Atlantic Northeast. Russian explorers initiated this process in the eighteenth century, when they happened upon the region while in search of the elusive Northwest Passage to China, and became aware of its economic potential. More specifically, they had discovered the commercial viability of sea otter pelt, finding that, as one of the few foreign items in demand in China, it could be exchanged for prized silks and spices. The fur trade established the structuring logic of the region, one that endured in the extractive economy of later years. Russian monopoly over the Northwest fur trade, institutionalized through the Russian-American Company, was quickly challenged by the Spanish, and later the British, the French, and the hard-charging Yankees. The modern Pacific Northwest, therefore, emerged out of intense imperial contest, as a product of foreign powers vying for control of the lucrative fur trade.

The land-based fur trade transformed this corner of the Northern Pacific into a contact zone in the eighteenth and nineteenth centuries, where foreign bodies, diseases, and commodities met and meshed with long established indigenous populations whose diverse and complex societies went back to at least 12,000 B.C.[28] With neither party possessing monopoly over violence and with their interests mostly aligning, early relations between Europeans and Native peoples in the Pacific Northwest were generally defined by negotiation and accommodation, punctured by the occasional outburst of violence. Within this framework of reciprocal relations, British, Russian, and French traders forged alliances with different Native groups based on terms of trade that were generally favorable to both sides.[29] This inter-cultural system of reciprocity was further cemented through sex, marriage, and the invention of fictive kin relations.[30] These encounters, moreover, produced new networks of economic and social relations that progressively wedded the region to a larger Pacific world. For example, migratory patterns established through the movement of Hawaiian and Pacific Island laborers, and commodity chains that made the Pacific Northwest a vital link in a mercantile nexus integrating the fur trade, whaling, and the China trade, brought the "Pacific" to the Northwest.[31]

As foreign encroachments intensified, indigenous peoples in the Pacific Northwest, who were by no means a monolithic group and thus had their own differences and divisions to contend with, responded with varying strategies of accommodation and resistance, ranging from securing alliances with Europeans through marriage to playing rival traders off one another to violent uprisings. In this context of competing imperial powers—one without a clearly established hegemon—these strategies, embodying Native agency, proved to be effective in keeping the Europeans at bay, at least for a time anyway. Gradually, however, foreign incursions, in particular, with the introduction of disease and guns, established what historical geographer Cole Harris has called a "protocolonial presence" in which the "balance of power" had "tilted inexorably toward" the Euro-American outsiders.[32]

With the ascendance of Anglo-American power in the mid-nineteenth century, this protocolonial presence gave way to a full-fledged colonial order. The Spanish, despite earlier claims to the region, failed to assert sovereignty north of California during this period and finally ceded existing claims to the United States in 1819.[33] Propelled by its growing investment in the fur trade, the United States established itself as a dominant power in the region.[34] The British, similarly, leveraged its commercial might, bolstered through the Hudson Bay Company, to beat out French and Russian rivals. Following several near confrontations, the two remaining imperial rivals came to an agreement in 1846, establishing the U.S.-Canadian boundary at the forty-ninth parallel. The fixture of national-state borders was followed by settlement and closure, processes that enabled Anglophone powers to consolidate colonial authority in the region. As sovereign power, with white settlers serving as its shock troops, reached deeper into the vast, hinterland spaces of the Pacific Northwest, it generated and sustained a geography of exclusion, where "the indigenous other would be tucked away, given as little land as possible, marginalized in its own territory."[35]

America's imperial forays into the region were part of an expansionist thrust that remade the Pacific into a vast American lake by the late nineteenth century, superseding the British, whose own imperial outreach led to the creation and development of the white settler outposts of Australia, Canada, and New Zealand and their subsequent integration into a larger Pacific world. This imperial drive was fueled by the growing belief that the destiny of the United States lay in controlling the Pacific. In this vision, the development of America's western frontiers and U.S. projections into the Pacific were closely linked, as the Pacific became a logical extension of Manifest Destiny. Not long after the signing of the Oregon Treaty, which set the Washington-British Columbia boundary in 1846, William Seward predicted that, "the Pacific Ocean, its shores, its islands, and the vast regions beyond will become the chief theatre of events in the world's greatest hereafter."[36] As Secretary of State, Seward pursued policies—acquiring Alaska from Russia in 1867 and following that up with the Burlingame Treaty with China the next year—that laid the foundation for U.S. dominance in the Pacific.

This imagining of America as a Pacific power was continued in the thought and practice of future U.S. statesmen and policymakers including Seward's protégé John Hay and future president Theodore Roosevelt, who were convinced that the "Age of the Atlantic is passing" and the "Age of the Pacific is here." These abstractions were given coherent form in the Open Door policy, which served as the guiding logic for a "New Empire."[37] As opposed to its imperial predecessors, which were territorially-based and, thus, predicated on the acquisition of formal colonies, this "New Empire" was about opening overseas markets, extending capitalist relations, and projecting power through commercial dominance. This did not preclude a territorial empire as attested by U.S. seizure of Hawai'i, Cuba, and the Philippines in 1898. However, in this imperial design, formal colonies supported and advanced the cause of an informal empire of capital by serving as stepping-stones to Asia and the China markets.

That the American empire was not an empire in the classic territorial sense—vacillating between "formal" (i.e. Philippines and Hawai'i) and "informal" elements (i.e. Chinese treaty ports)—has generated rancorous debate about its exact nature, from those claiming that the United States held no empire at all to those saying that it was an empire with no limits.[38] But as Ann Laura Stoler points out: "Oscillation between the visible, secreted, and opaque structures of sovereignty are common features [of imperial rule]."[39] The slippery logic and the seemingly contradictory character of U.S. empire building, she argues, reflected a concerted strategy of imperial rule, as part of a repertoire of colonial power and in this regard the American empire operated much like other modern empires, which "thrive[d] on such plasticities and reproduce[d] their resilience through the production of exceptions."[40] How these "oscillations" between territorial and nonterritorial expansion and between clarified and blurred imperial sovereignties depended "on moving categories, parts, and populations," and how they constituted the geographies, routes, and coordinates that integrated formerly disparate regions, communities, and peoples into an American empire that was seemingly everywhere and nowhere is a central concern of this book.[41]

TRANSPACIFIC BORDERLANDS AND BOUNDARIES

The political and spatial realignment and the integrative networks attending the formation of an American Lake progressively pulled the Pacific Northwest deeper into the orbit of the Pacific world. The history of U.S. expansionism is often split into two, distinct phases: continental expansion, on the one hand, and overseas empire, on the other, with Western historians studying the former and diplomatic historians and scholars of international relations researching the latter.[42] And while a few scholars have been able to bridge the fields by identifying important continuities between the two, most continue to analyze frontier expansion and overseas empire building as separate and relatively autonomous processes.[43] But we know, for instance, that the development of the North American West would not have been possible without overseas Asian labor and markets, which were made accessible and forced opened by Euro-American imperial incursions into East Asia and the South Pacific. As such, frontier expansion and overseas empire-building were inextricably intertwined—the development of one being utterly dependent on the other.

This book therefore approaches the western U.S.-Canadian borderlands from a Pacific perspective, delving into the myriad of worldly connections that brought the region into focus in the late nineteenth and early twentieth centuries. In mapping these connections, the narrative travels between locations tracking the pathways to and from the Pacific Northwest borderlands to distant and diverse places, from the sugar-cane plantations of Hawai'i to the hinterlands of the Canadian West, from the British Colonial Office in India to remote sites along the U.S.-Canadian boundary, where we will encounter overseas Chinese merchants starting businesses on the peripheries of empire; Japanese migrant workers eluding state borders to obtain jobs; and imperial agents tracking South Asian anti-colonial activists across the Pacific. Taking such an approach allows me to bring together the local sociopolitical relationships of a North American borderland with the transnational movements, networks, and discourses of a Pacific world.

Within this regional structure in which the global and the local were bound together, the port cities of Seattle and Vancouver served as the primary gateways between the Northwest borderlands and the Pacific world, constituting central nodes through which capital, labor, and commodities flowed in and out of the region. This book, then, unpacks the "bundles of relationships" that embedded the U.S.-Canadian borderlands in the Pacific world by tracing the local and global circulation of people, ideas, and material goods that transformed Seattle and Vancouver into Pacific Rim cities in the late nineteenth and early twentieth centuries.[44] This study is not, however, a detailed urban history of either city. Rather it focuses on each city's role as an imperial hub for the myriad movements and relationships that connected its surrounding hinterland world of labor and extraction (associated with railway construction, logging, fishing, and mining) to an outside world of trade and commerce. Historians have identified the dialectical relations between city and country, and more recently between city and suburb, to great effect, unearthing previously hidden connections between those spaces.[45] I propose here, albeit in a limited fashion, to extend these spatial dialectics to the city and the world, showing how Seattle and Vancouver emerged as global cities in the late nineteenth and early twentieth centuries.[46] Asian merchants, labor contractors, transportation agents, and immigrant smugglers within these two cities performed key intermediary functions, mediating movement and exchange between the city and the hinterland, between the city and world, and between the periphery and the center. "In this way," as historians Michael Geyer and Charles Bright write," "they were the ones to produce the resources for global integration, creating in the process a more integrated world, albeit not exactly as Western imperialists had intended." By highlighting the multiple and varied ways these Asian go-betweens engaged "Western power in complex patterns of collaboration and resistance, [and] accommodation and cooptation," this book shows how the Pacific Northwest, rather than being a spatial-geographical given, was animated by border-crossings of various kinds.[47]

These border-crossings set off an intense contest in which the forces of globalization and nationalization collided. The U.S.-Canadian boundary became the primary site of this struggle with Asian ethnic labor recruiters, white labor activists, East and South Asian migrants, and local civil servants locked in protracted struggle over the permeability of the border. The rapid circulation of people, goods, and resources kindled a countermovement to harden national borders in the Pacific Northwest even as these movements integrated the region into a larger Pacific world. The border emerged from expanding imperial relations and struggles to demarcate the boundaries of a "White Pacific" in which race and empire was instantiated in and through space and geography.[48] The extension of U.S. commercial and political power into the Pacific introduced new problems of unregulated mobility and movement for the modern state, which prompted new strategies of state management and control in turn. Policing America's Empire involved the construction of transpacific borders, which defined an outer limit against the encroachment of an Asia-Pacific world while simultaneously consolidating a territorial boundary between Canada and the United States.

By extending U.S. history to Canada and the Pacific, my study offers the first sustained account of the double movement—border-crossings that drew previously disparate communities into contact, on the one hand, and the racial and national borders that were constructed in response, on the other—that defined the Pacific Northwest borderlands in the late nineteenth and early twentieth centuries. The quest for boundless markets and growth and the simultaneous emergence of increasingly bounded nations were not antithetical historical developments locked in a zero-sum relationship, as some scholars have contended, but instead they were mutually imbricated processes. The chapters that follow, then, is about how the western U.S.-Canadian borderlands evolved in the context of a larger Pacific world, describing how the region emerged from the dialectics of globalization and nationalization, mobility and immobility, and inclusion and exclusion.

The book begins with the role of Chinese merchant contractors in the development of the Pacific Northwest, showing how they facilitated the region's transition from a gold-rush society to a diversified resource-based colony with an incipient settler society. Beginning in the late nineteenth century, the Pacific Northwest underwent a period of rapid economic expansion with resource extraction and railroad construction leading the way. Overseas Chinese, flowing through the widening networks of labor and capital produced by Euro-American imperial expansion into the Pacific, supplied the labor force to energize economic development and growth in this corner of North America. Chapter 1 looks at how Chinese merchants, who themselves arose from the ranks of migrant labor, seized on openings arising out of capitalist development and imperial expansion to construct a transnational system of labor recruiting. In furnishing overseas labor, and later opening overseas markets, these select immigrants became incorporated into a managerial elite, functioning as critical intermediaries in a budding empire of capital. The chapter concludes by examining how white racial hysteria, in the aftermath of passage of the Chinese Exclusion Act, produced the first modern border scare in the United States.

In the wake of Chinese exclusion and the anti-Chinese riots, the region's industrialists and entrepreneurs turned increasingly to Japanese merchants to meet their labor needs. As I discuss in Chapter 2, Japanese labor-supply firms including the Oriental Trading Company and the Furuya Company expanded on migratory links first established by the Chinese by producing circuits of labor in and through America's newly acquired empire in the Pacific. More specifically, it looks at how Seattle-based Japanese merchants combined multiple and overlapping imperial spaces to defy and evade state power across the Pacific, coalescing around Japan, Hawai'i, and Western Canada and the United States. In mapping this far-flung geography of labor alongside the movement of goods, the first two chapters show how the exploitation of Asian labor and the opening of East Asian markets went hand in hand in the colonial development of the Pacific Northwest.

Chapter 3 focuses on the anti-Asian politics and agitation of white Euro-American and Canadian workers in the Pacific Northwest. It reveals how riotous working-class activism and the Pacific Northwest story of Asians as the "indispensable enemy" was part of imperial movements that connected proletarian racism in the Washington-British Columbia borderlands to like movements in Australia, New Zealand, and South Africa. By re-locating the process of white-working class formation to a transnational context, this chapter bridges the intellectual divide between critical whiteness studies on one hand and colonial and postcolonial studies on the other, and in doing so, shows how white identity was a product of inter-colonial exchanges that spanned the Pacific world.

But if a Pacific world of migration figured prominently in anti-Asian labor politics, emerging as a space for transnational whiteness, Chapter 4 examines how it also spawned radical movements as white and South Asian activists attempted to wage transnational campaigns around anti-racism and anti-colonialism. For white labor leaders associated with the Industrial Workers of the World (IWW), the Pacific provided a crucible for imagining a radical Asian manhood worthy of class inclusion and solidarity. Paying especially close attention to the discursive strategies that the IWW employed to incorporate Chinese, Japanese, and South Asian workers into the labor movement, this chapter explains why these efforts to achieve interracial unity ultimately failed. Similarly, some of India's most radical nationalists, organizing and traveling across revolutionary circuits across the Pacific, transformed the borderland spaces of the Pacific Northwest into a hotbed for anti-colonial insurgency. South Asian revolutionaries exploited the fluidity of the border to disseminate and circulate anti-British literature, smuggle arms and explosives, and recruit members on both sides of the border. This chapter focuses on these radicals, their ideas, and their political struggles, showing how they profoundly shaped and were shaped by movements being staged across the Pacific world.

Chapter 5 examines how anxiety over illegal Asian migration and insurgent radicalism gave rise to national and imperial systems of surveillance and control. The United States, the Dominion of Canada, and the British Empire joined forces to create a dense, multi-state policing and intelligence apparatus by which to regulate the movement of Asian migrants, gather information on their communities, and thwart the circulation of subversive politics, which generated new geographies of exclusion in turn. The border was therefore elaborated against the racialized figures of the illegal Asian immigrant and the menacing South Asian insurgent in a process in which the boundaries of race and nation were mutually constructed in the Pacific Northwest. This process brought various state officials, imperial agents, and departments together as part of an inter-imperial border enforcement regime.

State intervention may have ushered in an era of the border, when the movement of Asian migrants was highly restricted and regulated, but it still left open the door to commercial exchange and flows of goods and capital to and from Asia. In the epilogue I return to the central contradiction that defined the Pacific Northwest borderlands, revealing how dreams of fabled Asian markets continued unabated in the wake of solidifying borders as the pursuit of greater economic integration and intercourse with Asia stood alongside a deep and abiding disdain for Asian bodies. Thus, the proliferation of border controls and immigrant regulations was, paradoxically, accompanied by a dramatic expansion in trade and commercial relations between the North American West and the Asia-Pacific Rim.

This is a story, then, of the contradictory coexistence of globalization and nationalization, of the ways these two powerful forces at once collided and merged in the Pacific Northwest borderlands, which brings us back to the two scenes on the Seattle waterfront paired in the opening. The hero's welcome for the *Mike Maru* and the campaign for Chinese expulsion were inextricably intertwined in a dialectical process in which the deterrorializing forces of globalization and the territorializing processes of national-state formation developed in tandem to spawn diverse and divided societies in the Pacific Northwest. It was thus a world in motion amidst a world of borders, brought into existence by transnational trade and cosmopolitanism as well as racial pogroms and the border patrol in which the global and the national were mutually constituted.

ONE

Brokering Empire

THE MAKING OF A CHINESE TRANSNATIONAL MANAGERIAL ELITE

IN 1862, CHIN GEE HEE began a journey that would take him from his rural village in Guangdong province, China, to the various frontiers of the North American West. Inspired by the dream of "Gold Mountain"—the ubiquitous myth that spurred the mass movement of Chinese to the Anglophone settler world in the mid- and late nineteenth century—Chin Gee Hee joined the California gold rush with the hopes of striking it rich. Upon his arrival he headed straight to the foothills of the Sierra Nevada where visions of gold-paved streets quickly yielded to the harsh reality of labor and toil. After six years, Chin Gee Hee gave up on mining and criss-crossed the North American West, bouncing from one seasonal job to the next. He eventually left the world of migrant labor for good to become one of the leading merchant contractors in the Pacific Northwest. Commodifying the transpacific spaces that he had once traveled and traversed, Chin Gee Hee helped develop an international market in labor that connected rural villagers in southern China to the railways, mines, fisheries, and mills in Washington, Oregon, Montana, and Alaska.

At first glance, Chin Gee Hee's personal journey would seem to recycle the conventional beginnings of early Asian American history, of gold rushes and railroads. But these dominant narratives of Chinese migration to North America, which are almost always framed in terms of its significance to national history—as part of the "winning of the West" or the unification of an internal marketplace—fail to capture the far-flung connections and broader histories that made Chin Gee Hee's life possible.[1] His mobility and movement and those of his contract laborers followed the multiple pathways spawned by empire. By the mid-nineteenth century, China was the site of intense imperial rivalry, the center of competing Euro-American colonial projects in the Pacific and Indian Oceans. The "opening of China" signaled a crucial moment in the history of Western expansion, as the dream of tapping the fabled China markets, centuries in the making, finally appeared to be in reach.[2] But markets were not the only enticement; Western imperial powers were also lured by China's seemingly inexhaustible supply of laborers. In 1852, U.S. Secretary of State William H. Seward insisted that the "North American continent and Australia are capable of sustaining, and need for their development, five hundred millions," but their populations were "confined to fifty millions," meanwhile, lying in Asia were "two hundred millions of excess."[3] The abolition of chattel slavery made the question of who would furnish the labor in the mines, plantations, fisheries, and woods of colonial America, Africa, the Caribbean, and the Pacific more than a mere abstraction.

As Euro-American powers reached deeper into China, searching for new sources of labor as well as new markets for their goods, the country and its people became increasingly integrated into an imperial circuitry of trade, migration, and communication. The imperial enterprise hinged on its ability to move people and goods across vast expanses of space and time, to fill gaps and needs in distant parts of empire. The functioning of the empire, as one scholar points out, "was dependent on these intercolonial exchanges."[4] In the Pacific Northwest, imported Chinese labor was critical to the region's development, having built the infrastructure—railway lines, streets, and ditches—that powered an extractive economy there. The commodities that their labor helped produce were, in turn, sold internationally with China serving as a vital foreign market, one that was forcibly opened under the terms of an Anglo-American "Open Door" policy.

The connections that gave rise to the migration of Chinese laborers to the Pacific Northwest were, then, the product of networks created by empire that connected frontier expansion in the North American West to Western imperialism in Asia and the South Pacific. Chinese migration did not, of course, begin with the "treaty ports"—the Chinese had a long tradition of mobility and moving abroad as strategies for social mobility, and family and kin survival—but western encroachments intensified and accelerated the process, producing widening channels through which Chinese migrants would flow to the hinterlands of North and South America, Africa, Asia, and the South Pacific.[5]

These imperial networks were not, however, solely the handiwork of Euro-American colonizers. Their organization and maintenance required the assistance of native middlemen, the incorporation of a transnational Chinese managerial elite into empire building. In the Pacific Northwest and elsewhere, a Chinese mercantile elite played a crucial role in establishing imperial nodes and facilitating traffic across them as they distributed migrant workers to sites of labor scarcity and opened Asian markets for Western goods. In circulating overseas Chinese labor, and as protagonists in the opening of East Asian markets, Chinese merchant contractors like Chin Gee Hee performed concrete work on behalf of the empire, mediating the flows and exchanges that energized colonial development in the North American West and across the Pacific.

But if they served as agents of empire, by extending the reach of U.S. and British imperialism into China, and Asia more broadly, they simultaneously undermined the colonial project by organizing subversive forms of mobility that challenged national-state sovereignty and by appropriating "barbarian" methods to enhance their individual positions and their nation's position within this imperial formation. As Michael Geyer and Charles Bright forcefully argue, "imperialism was also able to exist because Indians, Egyptians, Argentines, Chinese, Persians, and Africans helped make it happen, and not simply as lackeys and dupes but pursuing strategies of renewal that synchronized in the web of European-dominated global regimes."[6] These cross-cultural collaborations and alliances were therefore highly contradictory and fraught with tensions, falling into the netherworld between collaboration and resistance.

This chapter explores two exemplars of this Chinese transnational managerial class whose lives and fortunes were intimately bound up with Anglo-American imperial expansion in the Pacific Northwest and across the Pacific. Chinese middlemen Chin Gee Hee of Seattle and Yip Sang of Vancouver played profoundly important roles in greasing the proverbial wheels of imperial commerce, managing the international linkages and labor and capital flows that integrated the British and U.S. empires in the Pacific. By tracing the ways leading Chinese middlemen made the empire and how the empire, in turn, made Chinese middlemen, this chapter resituates immigration history within the multiple and overlapping histories of frontier expansion, the globalization of capital and empire, and the territorializing process of state formation in Canada and the United States.

IMPERIAL PROJECTIONS AND FRONTIER DEVELOPMENT

Starting with the maritime fur trade in the eighteenth century, Euro-American entrepreneurs and traders had searched for ways to extract, commodify, and profit from the vast natural resources of the Pacific Northwest. Early travel writings chronicled the immense potential of the region, opening this remote corner of the northern Pacific to Euro-American exploitation and expansion. In one such account, written in 1857, James Swan observed that "its numerous and inexhaustible mines of bituminous coal, its quarries of marble and sandstone, its rich gold and lead deposits, and its unrivaled water privileges offer great inducements to the capitalist, whether as manufacturer, trader, or ship-owner." All that these pristine lands and this untapped natural wealth needed, he argued, were "men and means."[7] The railroad magnate James J. Hill later remarked similarly that the region "has within itself an abundance of wealth, in the water, in the fields, in the mines, and her forests," contending that the "permanent and great prosperity will come through the development of these resources."[8]

This vision of exploiting and settling the Pacific Northwest started to become a reality with breakthroughs in transportation and communication during the late nineteenth century. The technological revolution that accompanied the construction of the Canadian Pacific Railway (C.P.R.), extending from Montreal to Vancouver in 1885, and the Great Northern Railway, connecting St. Paul to Seattle in 1893, paved the way for large-scale extraction and production of natural resources in the Pacific Northwest. The C.P.R. opened a north-south feeder line from Vancouver to Seattle shortly thereafter, integrating these frontiers into a binational borderland economy. The railroad companies also began to provide regular steamship service to transpacific ports in China, Japan, Hong Kong, and the Hawaiian Islands. The interlocking network of railroads and steamships linked the region to the rest of the continent and to more distant markets around the world. "Modern invention found the ocean a barrier and made it a highway," is how one early Washington settler put it.[9] This conquest of distance enabled resource exploitation and production to accelerate rapidly during the late nineteenth and early twentieth centuries. As a result, the region's identity became associated with that of a colonial hinterland, a place known to extract and furnish raw materials for more advanced economies on the East Coast and across the Pacific, an empire of extraction.

By the turn of the century, Washington State was one of the nation's leading producers of several key natural resource–based commodities. The logging and milling industries benefited overwhelmingly from the arrival of the railroads. Prior to the completion of the northern transcontinental railroad in 1893, Washington was average among states in the union in timber production, manufacturing about 160 million board feet of timber per year. By 1910, however, the emerald state produced over four billion board feet of timber per year, an output that led the nation. Logging and milling companies emerged as the state's leading employers, with their payrolls accounting for more than 50 percent of all salaries and wages in Washington State prior to the First World War.[10] Salmon canning also developed into an important extractive industry during the late nineteenth century. In 1877, canneries on the Puget Sound packed about 5,000 cases of salmon. Two decades later, there were sixteen canneries on the Puget Sound packing almost a million cases of salmon to sell on markets at home and abroad.[11] The state's rapid commercial expansion was accompanied by a demographic surge led by immigrants. Between 1900 and 1910, fueled mainly by the infusion of people from outside the state, the population of Washington State doubled—a growth rate six times that of the national average.[12]

Global capitalism encroached upon and transformed British Columbia as well, placing its equally rich natural resources in reach of the world economy. As it was the case with Washington State, railroads fueled the growth and the development of the region's far-flung hinterlands. Between 1900 and 1913, revenues from commercial timber rose from $136,000 to more than $2 million per annum. Commercial fishing also emerged as an important industry in British Columbia. There were close to eighty salmon canneries in the 1890s, mostly located on or around the Fraser River. Although the salmon runs proved to be highly unpredictable, British Columbia canneries still managed to pack more than a million cases of salmon valued at close to $5 million in 1897. Forestry and salmon canning, along with mining, constituted British Columbia's economic base.[13] The total value of the region's output from manufacturing, forestry, mining, fishing, and agriculture went from a little over $8 million in 1881 to over $22 million in 1891 and almost quadrupled to $84 million in 1901.[14] Here, too, a settler society began to take root as a diverse array of immigrants began to pour into the province. At the turn of the twentieth century, four out of five residents in British Columbia were new arrivals.

In 1907, Daniel Lincoln Pratt, writing for *The Westerner*, paid homage to the region's rapid growth, extolling the "big undertakings" and the "large scale" of industrial development in the Pacific Northwest. Since the railroad was considered the harbinger of modernity and industrial progress, Pratt focused on the fact that "there are more miles of new railroads planned for the State of Washington than any other in the union" and that "Oregon, Idaho, British Columbia, and Montana are also being crisscrossed and belted by steel rails" to predict that the region stood on the brink of a mighty economic expansion.[15] Yet, the scene in Seattle and its surrounding hinterlands in 1873—the year of Chin Gee Hee's arrival—was of a sleepy backwater mired in muddy flats, impassable roads, and thick forest cover that hardly portended a thriving extractive economy that would reach across the Pacific. Indeed, what was to become the premier city in the Pacific Northwest was little more than a tributary at this time, outfitting the logging and mining camps in its surrounding hinterlands with supplies it received from San Francisco. This is to say that the settlement and exploitation of the region was neither preordained nor natural, the rhetoric of boosters notwithstanding: There were railroad tracks to be laid down, rivers and lakes to be connected, and hills to be shaved, before the region's vast natural wealth could be tapped and consumed by global capitalism. Indeed, the exploitation of nature would require a commensurate exploitation in people: "The handling of picks, the digging of ditches, [and] the swinging from nine to ten hours a day of a heavy shovel" involved "rough, strenuous labor on the part of many thousands of men," as one industrialist put it.[16]

Fortunately for developers, just as they were beginning to pour capital into the region, Euro-American imperial incursions into Asia spun new global circuits of labor and capital through which overseas Chinese were channeled across the Pacific. Following the First Opium War in the 1840s, the Ch'ing dynasty, under duress from Western imperial powers, signed a series of unequal treaties opening southern China coast ports to foreign capital.[17] In carving up China into spheres of influence, Western imperial powers were not only interested in opening overseas markets but also in locating new sources of labor for their newly acquired colonies. As Philip Kuhn explains, "the settlement forced by Britain on the Qing government established a framework of special privilege for Westerners in China-coast ports, where labor recruitment was then able to flourish largely unhampered by Chinese laws."[18] China made an additional round of concessions on this score at the end of the Second Opium War. In 1866, Britain and France signed the Chinese Labor Immigration Agreement, which permitted foreign emigration agencies to recruit laborers in coastal Chinese ports. Not to be left out, the United States negotiated the Burlingame Treaty two years later, which regularized Chinese immigration to America.[19]

In this reconfigured China, politically and spatially realigned by Western imperialism, the "treaty ports" and the colonial hubs of Hong Kong and Macao emerged as important new nodes through which Chinese migrants would flow to new destinations both inside and outside of the British imperial system. The labor trade that emerged at these sites was organized by Chinese merchant companies, the *Jinshanzhuang,* or Gold Mountain firms, which collectively gave rise to a transnational network of creditors, merchants, and laborers that were bound together by ties of kinship and native place. Native participation in this commerce would result in the systemization of Chinese migration, the creation of a permanent infrastructure that would ensure the perpetual migration of Chinese across the Pacific. Within this system, Hong Kong emerged as the central node for Chinese migrating to the Western Hemisphere.[20]

The primary, though by no means exclusive, method by which earlier Chinese migrants came to the American West was through the credit-ticket system. This labor migration system was embedded in international trading and credit networks and native-place associations stretching across the Pacific. Creditors and transportation brokers in Hong Kong provided Chinese migrants with the cost of passage to the United States and then transferred or sold the debt (including interest) to affiliated companies and associations in San Francisco. Upon their arrival, Chinese merchants furnished the newcomers with lodging, food, supplies, and jobs. In between were passage brokers who facilitated the transaction from one side of the Pacific to the other. The functioning of this complex system of mobility and exchange rested on its ability to ensure that laborers repay their creditors. As historian Madeline Hsu and others have shown, it ultimately worked because their debt was guaranteed "not by contracts but by relationships based on kinship or native-place ties," and thus the indebted Chinese migrant was accountable not only to his creditor but to a much wider (and more intimate) web of relationships.[21] Some migrants found ways to circumvent the credit-ticket system by raising funds on their own, typically from family or kin members, who viewed the advancing of this money as an investment.[22] All told, close to 40,000 Chinese laborers came to California during the gold rush of the 1850s through one of these methods.[23]

The initial wave of Chinese laborers to the Pacific Northwest came by way of California, drawn by the discovery of gold deposits on the Columbia and Fraser Rivers in the 1850s and 1860s.[24] Reproducing scenes from the early gold rush in California, thousands of Chinese miners migrated northward to work on claims left behind by white miners in British Columbia and Washington Territory. In 1879, the *Washington Standard* wrote: "From the old abandoned gold fields of California to the icy streams of the Cariboo, they are literally taking the country." "The Chinese," the paper reported, "never let up when they once fairly settle down to business in the gold diggings. Years ago, white men rushed to the Fraser mines, and as they thought, exhausted them. Chinamen followed hard after them, as usual, and found good paying diggings where white miners could not or would not live; as characteristic of the race, they are still in the business"[25] This short account captured the basic contours of the Chinese immigrant experience in the North American West: Excluded from the mainstream of frontier life, they performed tasks undesired and left behind by white Euro-Americans.[26]

Yet, among these migrant workers emerged a select number of Chinese who would go on to become powerful merchant contractors in the leading cities of the Pacific Northwest. Exploiting the transpacific connections generated by imperialism and by rapid frontier expansion, these laborers-turned-merchants established new niches within an international system of movement to produce and sustain a steady stream of Chinese migrants to Pacific Northwest long after the Gold Rush was over. Bilingual and bicultural, this Chinese middling elite straddled two social worlds, mediating (and profiting from) the geographical and cultural gulf separating them.[27] The ability to expertly move human bodies and goods across borders made them indispensable. On these imperial peripheries, far removed from the centers of power, where services and transactions of this sort were conducted through more formalized structures and institutions, the marginal man went on to become a powerful middleman.[28]

CONSTRUCTING IMPERIAL CORRIDORS

In Place du Canada in Montreal stands a statute of John A. Macdonald facing west. Unveiled in 1895, it was to serve as a tribute to the first prime minister of the Dominion of Canada, for his visionary leadership in expanding Canada and unifying its disparate provinces. This iconography of national origins illustrated how a bold visionary willed a nation into being. But what is forgotten in this nationalist telling was that Macdonald's vision for a united confederation was part of a larger imperial vision that saw "the great task of welding the scattered provinces of Canada" as "only forging the initial link in that mightier chain to unite the Motherland with Canada, the Orient and Australia on the all-red line of Empire."[29] In this rendering, the nation was merely a stepping stone to an empire. The lynchpin to this grand imperial scheme was the Canadian Pacific Railway (C.P.R.), what would become the Dominion's first transcontinental railroad. "Establish an unbroken line of road and railway from the Atlantic to the Pacific through British territory," wrote Macdonald's close friend and ally, Edward Watkins. "For Japan, for China, for the whole Asiatic Archipelago, and for Australia, such a route must become the great highway to and from Europe." Pushing Macdonald's vision of a "Greater Britain on the Pacific," Watkin declared that "whatever nation possesses that highway must wield of necessity the commercial spectre of the world."[30]

The physical task of fashioning these important sinews of empire was performed by imported Chinese labor and there was perhaps no single individual more responsible for assembling this vital overseas labor force than Vancouver's Yip Sang. The fantasy that envisioned the transcontinental railroad as an integral part of an imperial network that would extend the Dominion's reach into exotic, far-flung markets in Asia was initially frustrated by acute labor shortages. In 1881, British Columbia had fewer than 50,000 residents, many of whom were unaccustomed or unwilling to perform industrial wage labor.[31] A project of this scale would therefore require a massive infusion of outside workers. The C.P.R., like every other railroad company in the North American West, would come to rely almost exclusively on overseas Chinese migrants.[32] As superintendent of the C.P.R.'s labor supply company, Yip Sang would recruit thousands of Chinese laborers to help build the most powerful transportation system on the planet. Yet, in doing so, he and his overseas Chinese laborers became unwitting participants in opening their homeland to further Western penetration, constructing the very imperial technologies by which it was made possible.

Yip Sang had migrated to San Francisco in 1864, lured, like so many of his contemporaries, by dreams of gold. He was nineteen years old at the time and had lived his entire life until then in the southern Chinese province of Guangdong. Born to a poor family, and having lost both his mother and father at a young age, Yip Sang seized on the opportunity to migrate, seeing it as one of the few chances to improve his life fortunes. In San Francisco, Yip Sang first worked as a dishwasher, cook, and cigar roller, before panning for gold. In 1881, he hitched on the wagon trail to the Yukon gold fields. He would ultimately make his fortunes not from gold however, but by commodifying the labor and mobility of his overseas compatriots. In Vancouver, Yip Sang landed employment with the Canadian Pacific Railway's labor supply firm, where he started as bookkeeper. He quickly graduated to timekeeper, and then to paymaster, before being promoted to company superintendent.[33] At the time of his promotion, the C.P.R. was just starting construction on the western sections of its transcontinental railroad.

Company executives initially tried to meet their labor needs by attracting white European immigrants. Company agents and officials, with assistance from Western boosters, emphasized the Eden-like qualities of the Pacific Northwest and held out the promise of upward social mobility. Yet, despite these efforts, the number of Euro-American and Canadian newcomers failed to keep pace with the company's seemingly endless labor needs. White labor recruits also proved to be less than dependable as workers. Henry Cambie, a surveyor and engineer for the C.P.R., described the first group of white men that the company imported from California in 1880, as the "most useless lot of broken down gamblers, barkeeps, and etc., ever collected in one place."[34] As a result, the railroad giant turned to an alternative source of unskilled labor, namely overseas Chinese, to solve the perennial problem of labor scarcity. As one leading industrialist acknowledged: "It is altogether clear and evident to the manufacturers, contractors, and railroad builders who must have certain sorts of labor accomplished that the Orientals are the only ones who will attempt it."[35]

At the outset, the white labor suppliers for the C.P.R. focused on local and regional markets in their recruiting efforts, sending company emissaries across the border into Washington, Oregon, and California, where they siphoned hundreds of Chinese laborers from U.S. railroad companies. As one C.P.R. manager recalled, their American labor supplier, "[Andrew] Onderdonk picked up a few China gangs in 1880, from the Northern Pacific Railway in Oregon, and some in 1881 from the Southern Pacific Railway in Southern California, the latter whom had among them some trained gangs of rockmen, as good as I ever saw."[36] In a classic case of how colonial labor was used to energize the development of multiple, and sometimes competing, imperial spaces, capitalists and their labor suppliers disregarded national boundaries, drawing upon a labor pool that cut across the U.S.-Canadian frontiers. This method of recruiting, however, proved to be ineffectual for the time being; it would have to wait until Chinese middlemen took over the role exclusively and built a transborder labor network for it to generate a more consistent flow of Chinese laborers across the border. As C.P.R. officials noted, "by the end of 1881 these, all told, amounted to only about 1,500 men, or less," which fell well short of meeting the company's growing labor needs.

When Yip Sang came into the role of superintendent a year later, he dramatically expanded the geography of the company's labor recruiting system by going directly to the source. Being familiar with cultural practices and customs, having access to immigrant networks, and understanding the working of government bureaucracies on both sides of the Pacific, he was able to organize Chinese labor migrations from abroad. Yip Sang chartered C.P.R. ships to contract and import thousands of men from China's countryside, focusing his efforts on his home region on the Pearl River Delta. The transpacific passage from China was treacherous, exacting a terrible cost on its human cargo. Ten percent of the laborers the C.P.R. brought over from China in the winters of 1881 and 1882 died soon after their arrival. As one C.P.R. official recalled, "They came in the winter, had long and rough passages and the men were kept below most of the time, with closed hatches and bad ventilation. They arrived in B.C. in April, apparently well and in good condition, but in a short time a large number developed scurvy."[37] More men died during the harsh winter months when the Chinese were forced to make due in makeshift tents in subfreezing temperatures because the company failed to build enough cabins. According to some estimates, two Chinese laborers died for every mile of track built.[38] Despite the enormous human losses, the C.P.R. still found the use of Chinese labor the most cost-effective way of addressing the company's labor needs.[39] Yip Sang went on to employ and supervise some 7,000 Chinese workers between 1881, and until the last spike was driven into the ground.[40]

At the completion of the C.P.R., Yip Sang departed for China, making his triumphant return home as a Gold Mountain success story. His departure may have also been hastened by the passage of the Chinese Immigration Act, which was signed into law shortly after the transcontinental railroad was completed in 1885. The law imposed a $50 head tax on Chinese migrants, which was designed to discourage their immigration to Canada. The timing of the head tax was not coincidental. Canadian Prime Minister John Macdonald wanted to ensure the completion of his pet project before appeasing white supremacists on the west coast with anti-Chinese legislation.[41] Macdonald's instrumental attitude toward Chinese immigrants was the prevailing one among the region's ruling elite, whose tolerance of Chinese immigrants did not go much beyond the utility of their labor, thus making them disposable at a moment's notice. "The truth that Oriental labor has become a necessary thread in the Northwestern industrial fabric is too manifest to be avoided." But, if this was a truth, as booster Daniel Pratt posited, it was also a truth that only "a limited immigration of Oriental labor is very desirable."[42]

Back in his home village in south China, Yip Sang cemented his new elite status by marrying additional wives, siring more children, and engaging in a number of philanthropic projects. Perhaps growing restless with the routine of village life, Yip Sang returned to Canada with his family after three years. In 1888, he opened the Wing Sang Company, which imported and exported Chinese goods and contracted migrant labor. His earlier relationship with the C.P.R. helped him launch his labor-contracting business. Using his former contacts, Yip Sang secured the coveted position of Chinese passenger agent for the C.P.R.'s steamship lines. In 1891, the C.P.R. agreed to provide regular mail service between Hong Kong and Britain via Vancouver. The company's new fleet of transpacific ocean liners—the *Empress of China,* the *Empress of Japan,* and the *Empress of India*—provided regular passenger service soon thereafter. As the firm's new Chinese passenger agent, Yip Sang almost at once gained control over the entire Chinese migrant traffic between Vancouver and East Asia. His rise to prominence would, therefore, be built on the pathways and connections traced by his imperial patron, the C.P.R., which integrated the borderland economy of the Pacific Northwest into transpacific commerce and markets in the late nineteenth and early twentieth centuries.

Yip Sang's imported Chinese laborers would help facilitate the region's transition from gold rush society to industrial economy. With the basic infrastructure of the emerging economy in place, which earlier Chinese laborers had a big hand in constructing, their manpower would now be needed to commodify the region's vast natural resources—to extract, package, and bring to market, that is. Recognizing the pivotal role Chinese labor played in the region's development, one booster wrote in 1907: "the West, in a way, owes a degree of gratitude to Chinese labor, which has in a number of instances met a crucial need at a time when lack of laborers would have been disastrous."[43] Similarly, Everett Deming, manager of the Pacific American Fishing Company in Washington, acknowledged in 1902, that, "If there had been no Chinese the salmon canning business would not have been conducted on so big a scale."[44]

As this suggests, the task of transforming the hinterland spaces of the Pacific Northwest into a productive empire of extraction required a specific

FIGURE 1.1 Portrait of Yip Sang, 1890. University of British Columbia Library, Rare Books and Special Collections.

type of workforce, one that operated on logic different from either the plantation societies of the American South or the industrial centers on the Atlantic seaboard. In the Pacific Northwest, employers sought laborers whom they could quickly mobilize during peak seasons and dispose of just as quickly at season's end. Conducting business in geographically remote areas, the region's capitalists found that they could not meet their labor demands by recruiting from the local populace alone, and high competition among the various seasonal industries only exacerbated the problem. The harvest season for salmon and hops, for example, coincided with the months the railroad companies required additional section hands.

This is where Chinese labor contractors like Yip Sang came in. Indeed, the value in using someone like Yip Sang, according to historian Gunther Peck, lay precisely in his ability to "organize labor markets at sites of labor demands, creating truly disposable workforces that could be mobilized from remote corners of the earth to equally remote industrial islands at the drop of the hat."[45] In the case of Yip Sang's contract laborers, theirs was a global mobility organized across the Pacific only to be fixed to isolated hinterland corners upon their arrival in the North American West. What Yip Sang and other Chinese labor contractors were providing, ultimately, then, was not only their ability to fuel and foster mobility across great distances but also their capacity to discipline that mobility, to lock migrant workers firmly in a place. The power of the contractor therefore rested on his ability to calibrate mobility and immobility simultaneously.

Chinese labor contractors were also attractive to western firms because all the responsibility, inconvenience, and liability involved in employing and maintaining a sufficient supply of unskilled workers fell on the contractors themselves. The contractor, for example, assumed all financial risks stemming from hiring too few or too many laborers. Additionally, the passage of contract labor laws in the United States and Canada made it illegal to import overseas laborers under contract and thus corporations were eager to transfer any potential legal liability to these middlemen. Furthermore, Chinese contractors were able to furnish laborers who were willing to work for less—anywhere between one-quarter to one-third less wages in most cases—compared to white laborers for the same job.

Applying the skills he had acquired earlier as C.P.R.'s main labor supplier, Yip Sang quickly rose to the top of the labor-contracting world. As the Chinese passenger agent for the C.P.R., Yip Sang had subagents stationed in cities across the Dominion, including in Victoria and Montreal, as well as ports of call in South China: Hong Kong and Shanghai, among others. In addition to advertising the C.P.R.'s steamship services in these cities across the Pacific, Yip Sang and his agents recruited Chinese migrants for contract labor. In this way, this one-time migrant laborer was able to establish Vancouver as a groove within a global system of movement: a "local specialization," as historian Adam McKeown calls it, that made transnationalism possible.[46] Operating out of Vancouver's Chinatown, on 51 East Pender Street, Yip Sang routed migrants from across Canada and across the Pacific to productive sites in the region's hinterlands and beyond. His corporate clients included salmon canneries, lumber mills, and railroad companies.[47]

Like other labor contractors, Yip Sang profited from this arrangement by imposing an elaborate system of fee for employment, transportation, and housing, which were deducted directly from workers' paychecks. The Wing Sang Co. generated additional revenue streams by provisioning workers with

FIGURE 1.2 Chinese workers at the Marble Bay Mine, Texada Island, British Columbia, April 1912. University of Washington Libraries, Special Collections, UW 5761.

supplies and goods and by charging them for services bound up with native place, including mailing and translating letters and transferring remittances on behalf of its workers. The firm therefore profited from its contract laborers both as consumers and as producers. Yip Sang used his gatekeeping powers as the exclusive Chinese passenger agent for the C.P.R. to ensure that all laborers paid their debt in full before being permitted to depart for China. If the Sam Kee Company, Yip Sang's main competitor, serves as any kind of guide, Chinese laborers, on average, handed over roughly a quarter of their earnings to their contractors to pay for food, supplies, and other commissary services.[48] In 1907, the Wing Sang Co. was one of only four Chinatown businesses to post revenues of $150,000 or more.[49]

Yip Sang eventually leveraged labor contracting to build other facets of his firm's business, which included real estate, shipping, and trading. For example, in 1904, he led a Chinese merchant group to buy and develop the Canton Alley complex, a row of storefronts and buildings running south of Pender Street that would become the center of commercial life in Chinatown.[50] The Wing Sang Co. owned and managed a number of tenements in the complex, which the firm used to house and provision immigrant workers.

The company also imported general merchandise from China and Japan, and owned and operated multiple fisheries off the coast of Vancouver Island to start an international trade in dry-salt herring.[51] Turning himself into an international businessman, Yip Sang created overseas markets for the latter by working closely with business partners in Hong Kong, Shanghai, Kobe, and Osaka. To get a rough sense of the size of the business the firm was doing, the Wing Sang Co. shipped 1,000 ton of dry herring in 1919, with a market price of $35,000.[52] By the 1920s and 1930s, the firm was trading dried herring and canned fish from British Columbia on an even larger scale.[53]

The Wing Sang Co.'s diverse portfolio of labor contracting, international trading, and real estate and business investments required careful coordination and management. Each spring, the firm brought over laborers, silk, rice, tea, and other goods from China and Japan. Chinese migrants went to meet the high labor demands of the peak summer season, a portion of them being diverted to the firm's fish-packing plants in Nanaimo and on Nanoose Bay off Vancouver Island, while imported goods were sold to Chinese and white residents as well as tourists who shopped in Vancouver. At the end of the season, the firm shipped canned salmon and dry-salt herring as well as returning Chinese migrants to Asia.[54] The seasonality of the extractive economy meant that if Chinese migrant laborers wanted to visit China, they did so in the winter months when jobs were scarce. This cycle of comings and goings repeated itself each spring.

Yip Sang's integrated business model was the imperial logic writ small, in which the exploitation of foreign labor and the opening of overseas markets went hand in hand with Asian migrant bodies coming in one direction and the commodities that their labor helped produce going in the other, across the Pacific. Incorporating far-flung regions and new products into his business portfolio made Yip Sang one of the most powerful merchants in Vancouver. Indeed, when he died in 1927, his vast merchant-contracting empire was linked to trading, credit, and labor markets across the Pacific world. But if these accumulated connections enriched Yip Sang (as well as other Chinese middlemen), they also diversified the region's international links that made empire possible as more and more commodities from British Columbia and other parts of the Dominion found their way to Asian markets. "Vancouver is now the recognized gateway between East and the West," the Governor General of Canada Earl Grey declared, "the gateway through which the double streams of commerce between the Occident and the Orient, and between Britain and the self-governing nations of New Zealand and Australia will flow in ever increasing volume, until Vancouver shall become, perhaps, the first and most important port in the world." The life of Yip Sang was, then, a story about how a Chinese managerial elite made the empire and how the empire made a Chinese managerial elite.

THE RACE TO THE CHINA MARKETS

The belief that economic salvation would come through access to the China markets was gospel to white settler societies across the Pacific world, sparking a global competition to be the first to Asia.[55] "The trade of China, which is for the most part in British hands, is now estimated at $130,000,000 annually, and it can securely be said that it is yet in its infancy. The development of this vast empire has but begun, and, though the China trade has been the stake for which nations have waged wars through a dozen centuries, it is as nothing compared with what it will be in the near future."[56] In the Pacific Northwest, the emergence of Seattle directly challenged Vancouver's imperial aspiration to be the "gateway to the Orient." Staking Seattle's claim to the title was Washington pioneer Frederic James Grant who insisted in 1890 that, "The teeming millions of the Orient are, for all purpose of trade, Seattle's near neighbors." He boldly predicted that the "China of a quarter of a century hence will be a land rendered accessible by railroads, and the Chinese will be larger consumers of American wares and fabrics." Seattle and the Puget Sound more broadly, he contended, would be the "chief beneficiaries of Oriental trade," which "has rendered rich and great every city through which it has flown, from Venice and the Hanse towns to London and Amsterdam."[57]

No one wanted to beat Vancouver, and the Dominion, more broadly, to the China markets more than James J. Hill. The Canadian-born Hill was the visionary and architect behind the twin railroads of the U.S.-Canadian borderlands: the C.P.R. and the Great Northern Railway. He was a firm believer in the transforming power of the railroad, considering it the means by which the promise of modernity would be realized in the North American West. Like his sprawling railroads, Hill's investments, alliances, and rivalries spanned nations and industries crisscrossing the North American frontiers. In this regard, Hill was a quintessential capitalist, chasing profits and building empires on both sides of the international line. Fittingly, historian Beth LaDow calls Hill a "hybrid" because he "crossed the border to great effect," and thus it was impossible to tell with him "where the Canadian stopped and the American began."[58]

Yet, as the only original member of the C.P.R. syndicate unceremoniously dumped from the company's board, Hill was set on beating his former business associates to Asia. As a scion of the Canadian railroad giant, he was infatuated with the myth of boundless China markets. "If you go back into the commercial history of the world you will find that the people who controlled the trade of the Orient have been the people who held the purse strings of nations."[59] He remained committed to this vision long after leaving the C.P.R. in 1883, carrying it with him across the border to Seattle, where Hill found a community of like-minded men who shared his vision in which trade with the Orient was thought to be the rightful, even natural, preserve of the "commercial people" of the Pacific Northwest. As his lawyer Thomas Burke remarked, "The Pacific Ocean, which alone separates us is our common frontier. Nothing could be more natural than that a commerce should spring between the countries served by that great highway."[60] In what might be considered an earlier version of what Bruce Cumings has called "rimspeak," this discourse constructed the Asia-Pacific as a virgin economic frontier ripe for Euro-American capitalist penetration.[61]

Understanding very well that the fortunes of the city were bound up with gaining access to the China markets, Seattle's elite rallied around the cause of bringing Hill's transcontinental railroad to the emerald city, reaching agreement with the railroad magnate in 1890.[62] In one of his famous stump speeches, Hill promised city leaders that he would "reverse the immemorial course of trade eastward over the seas, and turn it from the Suez to Seattle."[63] His Great Northern Railways and steamships eventually connected locally produced commodities—wheat, lumber, minerals, and fish—to external markets, which in turn stimulated investment and settlement. Hill generated streams of profit by bundling transportation, land, and trade together. "When we built the Great Northern Railway to the Pacific coast," he recalled in 1897, "we knew that it was necessary to look to Asia for a part of our traffic."[64] Thus, even as he was rapidly extending his commercial empire across the Great Plains, Hill had his eyes squarely on Asia, imagining it as the next frontier of capitalist development. Unlike another famous imperialist, Hill didn't view the end of continental expansion as signaling the "closing of the frontier," framing a narrative of American exceptionalism, but rather he saw it as merely another stage in the unfolding of world history that would reach its apogee when the promise of the China markets would be fulfilled through Western expansion in which Western civilization would finally come full circle.[65]

But the kind of integration that would give Hill's business the global breadth and reach that he craved and one that could transform Seattle into a major hub for transpacific commerce required tight coordination and synchronization of a range of transnational processes. As it was the case with their competitors to the north, the C.P.R. and Vancouver, respectively, Hill's Great Northern and Seattle's ruling elite would come to rely on versatile Chinese intermediaries to meld disparate points in the Pacific Northwest and across the Pacific into global circuits of mobility and exchange. In 1890, Thomas Burke brought one Chin Gee Hee to the attention of his ambitious patron. Chin Gee Hee had arrived in San Francisco in 1862, as part of the California gold rush. He spent the next several years bouncing back and forth from mining towns in the Sierra Nevada Mountains. However, like Yip Sang, who arrived two years later, Chin Gee Hee's plans took a detour when he migrated northward from California to the logging town of Port Gamble, Washington, in the late 1860s. And like Yip Sang, he would amass wealth and power by energizing the mobility and movement of Chinese migrants across the Pacific and across the North American West.[66]

Chin Gee Hee relocated to Seattle in 1873, joining the Wah Chong & Co. as a junior partner. The move was made at the urging of his friend and future mayor of Seattle, Henry Yesler, who convinced him of the city's commercial potential. The Wah Chong & Co. was the first wholly Chinese-owned company in Seattle. Chin was placed in charge of the firm's labor-contracting business, and in this role he worked tirelessly to drum up demand for Chinese laborers with mine owners, railway foremen, and farmers in Seattle's immediate hinterlands.[67] Chin Gee Hee sought to capitalize on the dramatic growth in labor demand generated by the region's transition to an industrial-extractive economy. His efforts turned the company into one of the leading labor suppliers in the Pacific Northwest. The firm's contract workers could be seen working in almost every corner of the territory, building roads and streetcar lines in Seattle, logging and milling on the Puget Sound, and picking fruit and hops in the Yakima Valley.

But, by far and away, Chin Gee Hee's largest and most important clients were the railroads.[68] In 1882, the Northern Pacific Railway employed 15,000 Chinese workers in Washington Territory (and another 6,000 in Montana and Idaho) to construct its line through the Pacific Northwest, and although exact numbers are hard to come by, it's probably safe to assume that the Wah

FIGURE 1.3 Studio Portrait of Chin Gee Hee, Seattle, 1905.
The Wing Luke Museum.

Chong & Co. supplied a fair share of the total as the leading labor supplier in the Puget Sound district. In fact, the Northern Pacific made Chin Gee Hee the general passenger agent for its railroad (and later steamship) lines ending in the Puget Sound, which gave him access and control to a steady source of Chinese migrants. The grading, drilling, and demolition performed by his laborers, at the rate of around a dollar per day per worker, helped the Northern Pacific complete the western sections of its railroad, reaching the Puget Sound in 1887. His services were highly valued because, in addition to furnishing laborers, Chin Gee Hee provisioned workers with supplies from his merchant business, handled payroll for them and dealt with all issues related to wages and payments, and provided a loyal cadre of Chinese foremen to enforce workplace discipline—labor contracting from soup to nuts, if you will.[69] His firm, of course, exacted a fee for each of these services, subtracting them from workers' wages.

FIGURE 1.4 Chinese workers clearing snow from railroad tracks, 1886. Heavy snowfall sometimes buried tracks so deep that rotary snowplows could not operate. Then it was necessary to employ shovel gangs to clear tracks. University of Washington Libraries, Special Collections, UW552.

The labor needs of the railroad giant continued to take priority even after its completion. In a letter written to the general manager of the Northern Pacific in 1895, Chin Gee Hee requested "that you inform me at your earliest convenience for the reason that the season of the year is now approaching when there is considerable demand for our men on farms and in fishing industries and while of course this will not entail any inconvenience to you, it means some little expense to me should they become scattered before you need them." However, he was quick to note, "that this is a matter for my own look-out as of course I will furnish the men promptly whenever called for."[70] When Chin Gee Hee left the Wah Chong & Co. to start the Quong Tuck Company in 1889, he performed the same dual roles for the Great Northern, serving simultaneously as labor broker and passenger agent for its transpacific railroad and steamship lines in Seattle. Needless to say, the patronage of these behemoth transportation companies was crucial to Chin Gee Hee's rise as a successful middleman.

Chin Gee Hee furnished large quantities of imported Chinese workers from southern China and from neighboring states and territories. The first direct ship route from Seattle to China was established in 1874, allowing Chin Gee Hee to directly tap the Chinese countryside for migrant labor.

In 1870, the census reported 33 Chinese people residing in King County and 234 Chinese people in total in Washington Territory. Six years later, officials recorded 250 Chinese in Seattle and perhaps another 300 or 400 transient Chinese in the territory. Other estimates put the number much higher, as much as five times higher in some unofficial tallies.[71] The transpacific links constructed by transportation giants Northern Pacific and Great Northern only served to thicken the migrant movement between Seattle and China. Chin Gee Hee combined the growing number of overseas Chinese with migrant workers he recruited from California, Oregon, and Montana. The completion of the Central and Union Pacific Railroads in California was a big boon in this regard. It left thousands of Chinese railway laborers with skills in grading, boring, and demolition searching for employment. The ever-vigilant businessman, Chin Gee Hee was quick to identify an opportunity and so he sent labor agents to California to recruit the unemployed railway hands to the Pacific Northwest.[72]

The passage of the Chinese Exclusion Act in 1882, however, made the task of contracting Chinese laborers a far more difficult and complex affair for Chin Gee Hee and other Chinese labor contractors in the United States. The law, which prohibited overseas Chinese laborers from migrating to the United States, severely hemorrhaged their labor supply with the number of Chinese laborers entering the country plummeting following its enactment. Between 1883 and 1888, less than a 100 Chinese laborers entered the United States annually, whereas almost 16,000 Chinese laborers had entered the country in the previous ten years, and total Chinese immigration to the United States during the 1880s dropped by 50 percent from the previous decade.[73] The labor supply problem was further exacerbated by the anti-Chinese riots of 1885, having led to the expulsion of Chinese residents in Seattle, Tacoma, Olympia, and Portland.

In response, Chinese merchant contractors like Chin Gee Hee became experts at negotiating and contesting political and legal boundaries in North America. They provided fraudulent documents and certificates, coached prospective immigrants for entrance interviews, and created new identities and statuses for overseas Chinese laborers seeking entry into the United States.[74] In doing so, Chinese labor contractors resisted and profited from the new legal regime of Chinese exclusion, simultaneously. In the Pacific Northwest, authorities singled out Chin Gee Hee's Quong Tuck Company for being one of the worst violators of the new law. "In immigration matters, this firm, it is understood, are a lot of grafters, doing their blood-sucking from their own people, who come into and depart from this country. The principal trade-business of this firm is furnishing papers to Chinese."[75]

The U.S.-Canadian border became a major venue for these clandestine activities. Indeed, cross-border migrant smuggling became the primary way to fill the gap created by Chinese exclusion. "The business of running Chinese," as one Washington newspaper reported, "from Victoria, British Columbia, into the United States is a well organized business, as much so as any legitimate branch of trade." "Chinese merchants in Portland, Oregon, in Seattle, and other Sound ports in Washington Territory and Victoria, British Columbia, furnish the cast, and white men transact the business."[76] U.S. Customs officers stationed in the Puget Sound district corroborated these journalistic accounts. "From Victoria, B.C. to these canneries [on the Puget Sound] the Chinese are brought over night, during the fish season. They are put to work by the contractor, where they remain until the season is over, when they make their way to Seattle, or other American ports."[77] The Quong Tuck Company was believed to be the worst of the lot. "There is no doubt that the immigration officials will experience a great deal of trouble from this Chinese firm and perhaps at no place will they have to keep a closer watch than on them."[78]

While Chin Gee Hee left no paper trail of his clandestine activities, for obvious reasons, we can reconstruct the basic mechanics and patterns of his cross-border migrant trafficking by drawing on newspaper accounts, government reports, and oral testimonies about Chinese merchant smuggling, more generally, in the Pacific Northwest. For Chinese merchants in the region, western Canada was viewed as the last bastion of Chinese migrant labor. This was the case because the Dominion, despite strident protesting from its west coast residents, had yet to enact law to restrict Chinese immigration to Canada. That would have to wait until 1885, and even then, it wasn't outright exclusion but instead new legislation simply required Chinese immigrants to pay a head tax, initially, of $50. Chinese merchants in Seattle, Portland, and other Northwest cities were quick to exploit the opening in Canada to circumvent Chinese exclusion in the United States. The first step under this scheme was to have overseas migrants, whose ultimate destination was the United States, routed to Victoria, first. Beginning in 1882, tramp steamers carrying Chinese passengers started to come in greater numbers to British Columbia: the *Euphrates* with 600 Chinese on board arriving from Hong Kong, the *Escambia* with 902, the *Suez* with 890, and the *Strathairly* with 1,056.[79] As a result, the port city on Vancouver Island experienced a record influx of Chinese immigrants in 1882 and the first half of 1883.[80]

From there, border guides, or runners—a motley collection of whites, Chinese, and indigenous people—conveyed Chinese migrants across the border, both by land and by sea. "The numerous islands in Puget Sound at the head of the Strait of [Juan de] Fuca, lying on both sides of the suppositious line separating the two countries, offer special facilities for the operations of smugglers who . . . have little difficulty in crossing the line with cargoes of opium and its smokers, land both in the hidden recesses of some American Chinatown."[81] During an 1890 Congressional hearing on smuggling on the Puget Sound, one Chinese merchant confirmed the practice, testifying that, "I have never smuggled, but have heard it stated that for $20 a head Chinamen can be gotten from British Columbia." He added that, "It is common report that Chinamen are smuggled across the line."[82] All throughout this period, white and Chinese smugglers were being prosecuted and convicted for attempting to import Chinese migrants from British Columbia. In 1904, for example, white smugglers, Thomas and Anderson, were convicted and sentenced to one year in the penitentiary and ordered to pay a $1,000 fine for trying to smuggle in fourteen Chinese from across the border.[83]

Once a Chinese migrant safely made it across the border, he typically spent a couple of days at the merchant's store, before being sent to a work site in the hinterlands. "Chinamen would be in the store Monday who would not be there Wednesday," William Daly recalls. "It was common knowledge when I was a boy that they engaged in activities they didn't advertise. I think they found work for those that were brought in illegally." "They had their own underground," the long-time Port Townsend resident explained.[84] We know that the three-story brick building from which Chin Gee Hee operated his storefront during the day also furnished residential housing. We also know that some of his laborers used the store's address as their mailing addresses, making it very likely that Chin Gee Hee housed migrant laborers temporarily in the building—among them, laborers who had just arrived from Canada. If he ran into any legal problems on any of this, Chin Gee Hee had some of the best white lawyers in Seattle standing by to protect his firm's interest and legal standing.[85] It may explain why, despite widespread suspicion that his firm was engaged in illicit activities—on a large-scale, it seems—Chin Gee Hee and his company were never formally charged.

Yet as much as Chin Gee Hee and other Chinese merchants tried to devise new methods and develop ever more intricate schemes to elude state regulations, their labor-contracting businesses eventually succumbed under the impact of the Exclusion Act. By the turn of the twentieth century, fewer than 4,000 Chinese were in Washington State, making their population less than half the size of the Japanese population, who, as the newest Asian immigrants, were beginning to supplant the Chinese in a number of different industries.[86] By 1907, as one observer put it, "the story of the Orientals in the lumber industry [was] almost wholly a story of the Japanese."[87] As this suggests, the legal regime of Chinese exclusion, paradoxically, helped to both make and unmake Chinese labor contracting in the late nineteenth century.

Facing a diminishing supply of Chinese laborers, Chin Gee Hee turned away from labor contracting and focused on international trade and commerce instead. The leading men of Seattle had always envisioned a dual role for the Chinese entrepreneur: a middleman who could broker trade and commerce between Seattle and Asia, as well as secure overseas laborers who would transform the city into a strategic nodal point in the transpacific economy. Under this arrangement, a Chinese managerial regime was incorporated into America's "informal" empire in which middling men like Chin Gee Hee functioned as crucial go-betweens, facilitating the global flows and exchanges energizing an "Open Door" empire.[88] The Quong Tuck Company eventually expanded into Asia, opening branch offices in Hong Kong, China, and Japan with Chin Gee Hee himself relocating to the southern Guangdong province in 1904. White supremacy may have circumscribed the lives of most Chinese migrants but it didn't stop Chin Gee Hee from translating his bicultural and bilingual skills into financial and cultural capital, albeit as something as a perpetual outsider.

Chin Gee Hee's main collaborator on promoting trade with Asia was his long-time patron James J. Hill, who was constantly searching for ways to fill his train cars to capacity, especially traveling westbound. As his biographer notes: "To Mr. Hill an empty car was a thief."[89] A way to remedy this problem, he thought, was to connect the commodities produced in the American heartland to overseas markets in Asia, which would enable frontier commerce and international trade to develop in tandem. But it would mean integrating two distinct commercial systems: one on the continent, and one overseas. To link the two, thereby capturing Asian trade traffic for his Great Northern Railway and Midwestern farmers and producers, Hill partnered with the Nippon Yusen Kaisha (NYK) shipping line in 1896, on a joint venture to provide regular steamship service between Seattle and Japan, China, Hong Kong, and the Philippines.

For his first overseas trade venture, Hill had the quixotic idea of transforming the hundreds of millions of Chinese rice eaters into bread eaters.[90] In one of his famous county fair speeches to Midwestern farmers, he proclaimed, "Our white bread is like the lotus; no nation that once eats it will change to a poorer diet. I will make wheat flour as cheap as rice for the millions of the Orient, and our farmers will profit by a new demand."[91] In lieu of the agreement with NYK, his Washington State representative, Thomas Burke, lobbied Seattle officials for proper facilities—grain elevators and warehouses—to store and ship wheat while his other partner in this endeavor, Chin Gee Hee, pitched the product to Chinese merchants in Seattle and Portland, showing them how bread can be made from wheat flour, and even left behind Chinese language instruction manuals for them. With Hill's assistance, Chin Gee Hee made his first shipment of flour in 1897. By 1902, the Puget Sound was the largest flour-exporting port on the Pacific coast, exporting close to 1.3 million barrels.[92] Hill would soon add cotton, lumber, and salmon among the staples being exported to Asia.

As Chin Gee Hee spun wider webs of relationships of commerce across the Pacific, accumulating great wealth in the process, his ambitions grew further still. Sparked by grand dreams of transforming the site of his home village into a hub of maritime traffic thick with commercial activities, he sought to invigorate Taishan County with foreign trade and investment. In 1904, he relocated to Guangdong province, hoping to do for his home province what Hill, Burke, and others had done for Seattle. Having observed the development of the emerald city firsthand, Chin understood if his homeland was to benefit from international trade he would have to create transportation links to connect its untapped interior markets with the wider world economy. Benefiting from the high tide of Chinese nationalism at the turn of the twentieth century, Chin Gee Hee collected almost $3 million (Chinese) in subscriptions from overseas Chinese investors in the North America West, Hong Kong, and Singapore to build an integrated railroad network in the southern Guangdong province.[93]

Chin's former patrons in Seattle were eager to lend their financial and technical expertise to his ambitious endeavor. "Judge Thomas Burke and J. J. Hill of the Great Northern Railroad arranged for me to be given a trip over some of the principal railway lines of the country," Chin Gee Hee recalled; "That was my opportunity to add to my knowledge of railroad construction." Paying homage to the transpacific bonds that made his career as an international businessman possible, he wrote, "Could I ever be what I am if it wasn't for Seattle men?"[94] James J. Hill even assisted Chin Gee Hee in locating financial backers for his project in Canada and the United States. His support for a railroad project a half a world away was undoubtedly self-interested, driven by an obsessive pursuit of the China trade. Despite the enormous hype surrounding it, the promise of the China markets had eluded Hill up until that point. The factors that had hindered trade between China and the United States since the early nineteenth century—political instability, lack of infrastructure, antiforeign hostilities, and an impoverished countryside—continued to frustrate American investors and traders almost a century later.[95] The movement to boycott American goods in 1905, which drew a broad coalition of Chinese in protest over the treatment of Chinese immigrants in the United States, was symptomatic of some of these problems.[96] The China market thus proved more myth than reality, accounting for only 2 percent of America's total foreign trade in 1900.[97] Nevertheless, Hill had high hopes for Chin's new railway project, seeing it as a sign of progress, another step in opening China's countryside to American goods and services.

Chin's plans for a railway-led development that would transform his Taishan home into a maritime hub in the image of Seattle collapsed slowly over the course of the first two decades of the twentieth century. During its construction, Chin was forced to make costly concessions to local landowners, warlords, and bureaucrats, which exhausted precious resources and time. Moreover, in a region that produced little in the way of exportable goods, he had trouble generating freight traffic for his railway. Beset with these problems, Chin's ambitious railroad project languished in Guangdong province. Authorities eventually ousted Chin Gee Hee and seized control of his railway in 1926.[98] Chin was forced to retire to his home village, where he died shortly thereafter. Lest it be assumed that Chin's railroad debacle was an isolated case of an incompetent businessman, the American China Development Company, founded by a group of Pacific Northwest businessmen and backed by the likes of Edward H. Harriman, J. P. Morgan, and Jacob H. Schiff, also failed miserably in its bid to bring the railroad to China during this period.[99] Chin's failure, along with those of other entrepreneurs, demonstrated the limits of the China market at this time. The obstacles posed by political instability and underdevelopment in the Chinese countryside proved far more formidable than the most ardent China market enthusiasts wanted or cared to admit.

The combined efforts of merchants, smugglers, and migrants to subvert law and sovereignty in the Pacific Northwest generated a fierce public backlash, which brought with it a new consciousness of state territoriality. Indeed, it was starting with the mid-1880s, amid rumors of a highly organized Chinese smuggling ring operating along the U.S.-Canadian boundary, that the border began to become more than an abstraction. The *West Shore*, for example, reported alarmingly that the "Canadian border is the one now offering the easiest opening for the guileless Mongolian." Citing the fact that the "Canadian Pacific railroad runs parallel the border from the Pacific to Lake Superior," it noted that there "are many places along the route where a crossing can be made by a person willing to spend the time and money necessary to effect it." But "it is on the Puget Sound where this illegitimate business has become a science."[100] Frederick Grant, the editor of the Seattle *Post-Intelligencer,* explained similarly that, "After Congress had passed a restriction act, little was done to make its provisions effective. The meager appropriations to secure the enforcement of the law made it a dead letter and a mere farce, so far at least as Washington Territory was concerned." The trafficking of Chinese migrants, therefore, went "practically unhindered" and a "systematic business was conducted in smuggling them in, which the insufficient force of custom house officials was unable to suppress."[101]

As this suggests, the law to restrict Chinese labor migration to the United States had created unintended problems and consequences for the modern state. The U.S. architects of the Chinese Exclusion Act never anticipated that excluded Chinese laborers would exploit the nation's landed borders to gain unlawful entry into the country. The federal government initially assigned the task of enforcing the exclusion laws to the U.S. Customs Service, which up to that point had no prior experience in immigration matters. Within this department, the government created an official position known as the "Chinese inspector," who was responsible for screening Chinese immigrants entering the United States. In the Pacific Northwest, this small cadre of inspectors determined the eligibility of Chinese immigrants seeking admission, primarily in Seattle and other seaports, while leaving the border unguarded. Although first made aware of the problem of illegal Chinese border crossers in the 1880s, U.S. Customs inspectors cited limited resources as the primary reason for the lack of proper border enforcement.[102]

The situation was not much different on the Canadian side. Apart from the occasional sighting by the North-West Mounted Police, movement across the U.S.-Canadian boundary went virtually unregulated. At this time the Mounties were more concerned with the movement of indigenous groups and radical labor activists than with Chinese migrants.[103] There was good reason for this: In Canada, after all, Chinese immigrants found it less trouble to pay the head tax than to attempt more clandestine means of illegal entry. This policy difference—with Canada instituting a poll tax as opposed to outright exclusion—decisively shaped the directional flow of illegal Chinese immigration in the Pacific Northwest, where it ran from north to south or from British Columbia to Washington, for the most part.

But how was it that Canada, a white settler society that was equally bent on excluding Chinese immigrants, came to pass less draconian measures than the United States? This discrepancy can be explained by the different degrees of sovereignty accorded to the two polities at this time. Canada was a self-governing white settler colony and as such could make and pass laws provided that they were not in direct conflict with the crown's laws and interests. In the case crown officials deemed a law *ultra vires*—that is, repugnant to English laws and interests—the law was nullified. Unfortunately for white nativists in British Columbia, the more draconian anti-Chinese measures—for example, an outright ban on Chinese immigration—fell into this category. Having a keen interest in deepening commercial ties with Asia, the crown wanted to maintain cordial relations with China. British officials believed that an overt act of discrimination on the part of one of its dominions would interfere with this important crown objective.[104] This pattern, in which white settlers passed restrictive immigration legislation only to see it nullified by the metropole, was, therefore, repeated throughout the Anglophone settler world, in New Zealand, South Africa, and the Australasian colonies, where white settlers and crown officials sparred over the power to control Asian immigration.[105] In this regard, the United States' exclusion law was exceptional among white settler societies in the 1880s but only for a limited time. Through the persistent efforts of white settlers, the various dominions of the British Empire would pass more restrictive laws by the early twentieth century, establishing border control as a rightful prerogative of a self-governing polity, as the different white settler societies competed to see which one could pass the most stringent anti-Asian measure.

Among the constituencies that were especially scandalized by news of illegal Chinese immigration were the white workingmen of the Pacific

Northwest. Having successfully lobbied for the Chinese Exclusion Act in 1882 and the Foran Act in 1885, the latter prohibiting the importation of foreign contract labor, the white working class were led to believe that the problem of "coolie" labor was a thing of the past.[106] It was hence not long before white labor activists, mainly associated with the Knights of Labor, linked the plight of the workingman to the problem of illegal Chinese immigration. "During the construction of the Canadian Pacific railroad," one local observer recalled, "large numbers of Chinamen had been at work in British Columbia"; however, "on the completion of that work they were discharged and crossed into Washington territory, congregating principally at Seattle, Tacoma, and Olympia," and "their presence swelled the number of Chinese laborers at these points and furnished to anti-Chinese orators additional arguments to excite the laboring element of the population."[107]

Allegations that the Chinese defied the nation's immigration laws only to become "willing tools" of "tyrannical employers" fueled overlapping feelings of racial resentment and class oppression among the white workingmen in the region. In this narrative, Chinese contractors were especially vilified as degraders of labor. "[The] long established practice on the part of the companies to hire Chinese workers through a system known as the contractor system, in which a worker must depend on the contractor for his means of livelihood during those months of the year when the canneries are not operating has resulted in grinding the worker to an extreme degree of servility to his master contractor."[108] In the age of emancipation, relations between worker and capitalist were now supposed to be based on voluntary exchange, guaranteed by the contract.[109] The Chinese labor-contracting system, white labor activists charged, fostered subservience and thus violated the core principle of free labor: economic independence.[110] The labor newspaper, the Seattle *Union Record,* was of the opinion that there is "strong support" for the "assertion made that Asiatic immigration is not really free immigration, but that the men are brought here by the crowd of contractors who farm their labor out."[111] Such accounts gave credence to the ubiquitous charge that the Chinese were "coolies," as opposed to "free" immigrants, brought into the country under a system of coercion.[112]

These charges galvanized disparate white workers into a social movement and facilitated the emergence of a highly racialized working-class consciousness in the Puget Sound district. Modeling themselves after labor demagogues in San Francisco, the Knights of Labor, led by Daniel Cronin, mobilized the working-class in Tacoma, Seattle, and Portland by calling for

Chinese expulsion. As historian Carlos Schwantes writes: "As organizer for the Knights of Labor in Washington Territory, Cronin exploited the discontent caused by hard times and seemingly overnight transformed a faltering, intimidated band of workers into a militant and idealistic brotherhood widely believed to number several thousand."[113] Anti-Chinese racism, in other words, furnished the basis for the first instance of labor organizing in the Pacific Northwest.

The anti-Chinese agitation in the Puget Sound was part of a wider movement to "drive out" Chinese from towns and cities all across the Western United States that included expulsion campaigns in California, Oregon, and Washington during the mid-1880s.[114] These pogroms, called "abatement" by contemporaries, were inspired by the enactment of the Chinese Exclusion Act. By enshrining into law that the Chinese did not belong, the act encouraged exclusion by any means necessary. In Seattle, Cronin convened an anti-Chinese Congress in September 1885, where he announced that all Chinese residents of Washington had until the first of November to leave the city. If the Chinese failed to comply, the Congress threatened to have them forcefully removed. Prior to this edict, the *Seattle Daily Call,* voice of the Knights of Labor, made the case for vigilante justice, arguing that the Chinese, in choosing to reside in the country unlawfully, had "forfeited the protection of our laws."[115]

By November 1885, the Congress authorized local coordinating committees in Tacoma and Seattle to assemble workingmen for the purpose of gathering the remaining Chinese, and escorting them to the nearest railroad station or harbor for transport outside the region. In Tacoma, a vigilante mob led the two hundred remaining Chinese residents to the Northern Pacific station, several miles outside of the city limits. These working-class insurrections led to confrontations with law and order groups, backed by the commercial elite who feared that the social disorder and chaos would sully the reputation of their cities, and threaten future investment and development in the region. Thomas Burke, Henry Yesler, and Chin Gee Hee were central figures in the opposition to the mob and led efforts to diffuse the crisis. In his call for help to the Chinese consul in San Francisco in 1885, Chin Gee Hee described a dire situation: "Chinese residents of Tacoma forcibly driven out yesterday from two to three hundred Chinese now in Seattle imminent danger local authorities willing but not strong enough to protect us we ask you to secure protection for us."[116] The class conflict resulted in bloodshed as workers clashed with home guards deputized by the territorial governor. The federal government eventually stepped in, dispatching troops to the area, which brought an end to the violence.

But just as the intervention of federal troops was quelling the racial upheavals on the Puget Sound, anti-Chinese hysteria across the border in British Columbia was beginning to gather momentum. In November 1886, on the one-year anniversary marking the anti-Chinese riots in Seattle and Tacoma, the Vancouver and Victoria assemblies of the Knights of Labor issued a joint resolution pledging that they would resist the "increase of Mongolian competition to citizen labor," and would do so by an "active and persistent action against all persons who continue to encourage or employ Chinese." True to their word, later that month, the Knights of Labor instituted a formal boycott against merchants and storekeepers hiring or conducting business with the Chinese. The group enforced this strategy by employing a rather simple scheme: "When a business man created one of these offences he found a big black 'x' painted on the sidewalk in front of this store or office when he went to his place of business in the morning, and the initiated understood that store or office, as the case may be, had to be boycotted for supplying Chinese."[117] Several hundred local businesses and residents signed pledge cards vowing that they would neither employ nor sell to members of the Chinese community. Nevertheless, these anti-Chinese boycotts failed to achieve the goal of eliminating "coolie" labor from the province, as larger corporations and government institutions continued to recruit and employ Chinese laborers for their private businesses and public works projects. Consequently, the Knights of Labor, including labor activists "hailing from Seattle, Tacoma, and other Sound cities," resorted to the "Tacoma method"—the extralegal measure adopted earlier by their working-class brethren across the border.

Their final ultimatum unheeded, several hundred workingmen converged upon the Brighouse estate near Granville Street to force the Chinese laborers working for the C.P.R. to board a waiting steamship liner back across the Pacific. To discourage the Chinese from entertaining any thoughts of returning, the mob demolished the work camp, leveled their living quarters to the ground, and set their goods and supplies ablaze. "It was a weird scene to those standing on the bluff and looking down at the shed, inside of which were burning the bundles of clothing and bedding which were thrown down the hill from time to time whenever the fire grew dim," one participant later recalled. "At intervals no sound was heard but the crackling of burning wood, the flames from which were quite brilliant and the smoke from the surround fires dense, the whole making a spectacle not to be forgotten in the annals of the province."[118] The agitators then proceeded to False Creek the next day, where they expelled the eighty-six Chinese fishermen there in exactly the same manner. The provincial constables eventually brought the anti-Chinese mob under control, but restored order only after several days of heavy rioting and violence.

The ruling elite in British Columbia insisted that the acts of lawlessness were the work of a "small mob chiefly of American anti-Chinese agitators, among whom it was reported were a number of San Francisco sand lotters, at which city and other U.S. coast cities serious anti-Chinese riots had recently taken place."[119] Such analysis of the riots was not surprising, given the British-Canadian propensity for scapegoating "lawless" Americans for acts of social disorder in their western provinces.[120] Yet, in this case, the agitation in Vancouver and Victoria did appear to have a strong resemblance to the anti-Chinese disturbances across the border in Seattle, Tacoma, and Portland a year earlier. Indeed, the similarities were stark; they shared the same organizational roots, methods, and goals, providing some credence to the contention that the "ruffians and hoodlums" across the border were behind the riots in British Columbia.

However, attributing the labor unrest solely to "American" agitators ignores the complex histories of transience and movement that defined transnational working-class politics and culture in the Pacific Northwest. In this fluid borderland region, white labor activists were constantly on the move, organizing and agitating on both sides of the border. "The fact that the dividing line between Canada and U.S. is a frontier rather than a border is indicative of the ease citizens of either country could cross and recross," one labor leader explained. "Consequently, organizers, both for unions and for radical groups, were free to come and go."[121] In doing so, anti-Chinese activists were merely following the well-worn paths of the workers they were seeking to organize. As Canadian unionist Harry Cowan recalled, "Subsequently to the anti-Chinese movement in Vancouver large numbers of workingmen kept coming and going. Work in this city was good, but it was better across the line in the neighboring state of Washington, where higher wages were the rule."[122] The constant movement and the common cause against Chinese labor served to obscure national distinctions in a frontier with porous boundaries.

The massive disturbances resulting from the unanticipated flow of Chinese migrants prompted the United States to seek the collaborative assistance of their northern neighbors in rooting out what they believed to be a social problem common to both nations. As reported by a Dominion official in the foreign ministry, "The United States Minister called at this Office today and spoke to me respecting the exclusion of Chinese subjects from the United States. The Chinese, he said, were in the habit of using Canada as a stepping stone to enter the territory of the United States and his government would be glad if the Canadian government could give their assistance in preventing this practice."[123] With this exchange, a long, productive, and yet at times, contentious partnership over the issues of unauthorized Asian immigration and border management was born.

The U.S. Immigration Service, in what was known as the "Canadian Agreement," extended its bureaucratic powers and laws beyond its own borders. While the arrangement went through several revisions during the 1890s and 1900s, the core of the agreement was to have all U.S.-bound Chinese immigrants traveling through Canada directed to designated ports along the Canadian border, where they would be subject to U.S. immigration protocol and standards, before being allowed to proceed to the United States. Upon passing inspection, Chinese immigrants received certificates of admission, which they then presented to border authorities on the U.S. side. The intent behind these measures was to "establish the same level of control over Chinese immigration through Canada as it had over Chinese sailing directly into the United States," with the goal of preempting illegal cross-border migrations.[124] Historian Erika Lee argues this was part of a larger strategy that "centered on border diplomacy based on a historically amicable diplomatic relationship and a shared antipathy for Chinese immigration."[125]

However, efforts to solve the problem solely through diplomatic channels ran up against the subversive mobility of Chinese immigrants who were intent on circumventing the international agreements designed to keep them out. Devising new cross-border migratory strategies and networks, the Chinese contested the policies of "border diplomacy," forcing the state to come up with different tactics and approaches for enforcing the northern boundary. The Canadian Agreement—the diplomatic solution to the problem of Chinese migration—had major flaws, which the Chinese were quick to exploit. It failed to account for the Chinese already residing in the region, and, more importantly, for newly arriving immigrants who were increasingly claiming British Columbia as their final destination, paying the poll tax, and then surreptitiously crossing the largely unguarded border into the United States. This issue would later become a source of tension between the neighboring nations. An often-heard complaint within official U.S. circles was that "British Columbia gets the money and we get the Orientals."[126] Thus, despite their diplomatic accords, the problem of illegal Chinese migration across the U.S.-Canadian border persisted. The United States, therefore, while continuing to cooperate with Canada over the issue of unauthorized Chinese border migrations, developed a parallel system of policing and surveillance to detect and apprehend illegal Chinese border crossers in the Pacific Northwest. As this suggests, border enforcement strategies were fluid as the state reacted and revised their policies according to shifts in Chinese migration patterns in a cat-and-mouse-like game.

As we have already seen, Chinese merchant contractors played a major role in creating and sustaining the cross-border traffic of unauthorized Chinese immigrants. Working through previously established channels used for the cross-border smuggling of opium and fish, these merchants now utilized these routes for the new trade in human contraband.[127] Consider the following cross-border smuggling scheme arranged by Seattle-based Chinese merchants in 1900:

> Acting on information already gained, C. K. and Colonel Hill left Blaine, Washington, for the farm of Hop Lee, located some 9 miles from Blaine, and in B.C., and near the small town of "Cloverdale." [Hop Lee] was in the smuggling of Opium, and Chinese, that he made his farm, a depot for the Chinese to rest in, until their contractors could secure their landing, by guiding them over the border. That he had then, some 40 Chinamen, waiting to be landed, in this way. That these Chinamen belonged to Toy Wing, Wong Good, Yong Goon, and Goon Me Kan, smugglers who reside in Seattle, when at home.[128]

In another scheme, authorities reported smugglers exploiting the waterways of the Puget Sound to bring in illegal immigrants. "One Mar Get, residing at Port Townsend, and conducting the firm of Wing Sing Co. has been steering contraband Chinese through Coupeville, and sending them to this city by the steamer *Fairhaven*."[129]

The *Seattle Union Record* complained bitterly about illegal Chinese immigration across the U.S.-Canadian border. "The Chinese cheerfully pay the Canadian poll tax of $50, but 90 percent of them do not stay more than a week, but go immediately to the other side of the line, where by law their entrance is barred."[130] "Orientals go back and forth practically unmolested," and consequently "more Orientals get into this country through Puget Sound ports than all of the rest of our coast combined." The labor newspaper opined that "if the authorities at Washington lived up to the spirit, as well as the letter of the law they would have hundreds instead of a half dozen customs officers in the Puget Sound district."[131] On the other side of the border, *The Province* reported similarly that there "appears to be, to say the least, an impression prevailing among the Chinese scattered along the border line from the Rockies to the coast that papers issued to them in either Canada or the United States entitle them to pass out of one country into the other and return when they feel like it." The Vancouver paper exhorted Dominion officials to "put a stop to [this] promiscuous maneuvering."[132] In 1902, the U.S. Immigration Service announced that the "Canadian border has become the most prolific field for the introduction into the United States of the Chinese coolie."[133]

Lacking the manpower and resources to address the problem at the point of entry, U.S. Customs inspectors responded by scrutinizing the status of Chinese laborers in the interior of the state. They conducted unannounced inspections and raids of canneries, laundries, merchant stores, and other major business operations suspected of employing illegal Chinese. The passage of the Geary Act in 1892, which required that all Chinese laborers possess a certificate of residency or be subject to deportation, made such a border strategy possible.[134] A sign of a weak regulatory state, however, one that lacked a formal apparatus for border management, this ad hoc strategy yielded mixed results, at best. For instance, on a typical tour in 1898, U.S. immigrant inspectors paid visits to salmon canneries in Anacortes and Fidalgo Island, reviewing several hundred Chinese certificates in the process, but were unable to make a single arrest.[135] The reason for this may be explained by Inspector Fisher's findings in a subsequent visit in the fall of 1899. When making a similar tour of canneries in Fairhaven and Whatcom, he discovered that the Chinese knew of his inspection a week prior to his arrival. Chinese cannery workers had developed a communication network for sharing information and tipping off fellow workers to potential inspections and raids. Inspector Fisher was informed that "they were on the watch for him, and the first call that he made, word was sent to all other Canneries, and the Chinese hid themselves by opening up the floor and sliding down the piling, to the water below where they remained until after the Inspector's departure."[136] The irony, of course, was the more proficient the Chinese (and later the Japanese and South Asians) became at eluding the law and the boundary, the more the state intruded into their lives, as more powerful exclusions and more sophisticated techniques of border control would be introduced in their stead.

• • •

Taken together, the various exclusion laws, head taxes, and border controls led to the declension of Chinese migrant labor, paving the way for a new class of ethnic middlemen and labor brokers in the Pacific Northwest borderlands. While Chinese merchants continued to furnish workers, especially in British Columbia where less draconian measures were passed, their diminishing labor supplies simply could not keep pace with the industrial expansion taking place across the Pacific Northwest. The Japanese would ultimately fill the labor vacuum left in the wake of Chinese exclusion, becoming the region's main source of foreign labor by the turn of the twentieth century. Their arrival, however, was not a simple story of immigrant succession, for it coincided with the inauguration of America's territorial overseas empire and the emergence of modern Japan upon the world's stage. The increased movement of Japanese migrant labor to the region was part of larger flows of people, goods, and ideas introduced by imperialism and geopolitics through which hitherto disparate nations, communities, and individuals were integrated into the circuitry of the Pacific world.

TWO

Contracting Between Empires

IMPERIAL LABOR CIRCUITS IN THE PACIFIC

IN 1906, EXECUTIVES FROM THE Oriental Trading Company huddled in their Seattle office to come up with a response to the new restrictions on Japanese emigration imposed recently by the Meiji government. Over protests from mercantile houses in Japan and the United States, the Japanese government had made the decision to limit the number of laborers leaving for America to two hundred per month. As one company executive pointedly noted: "This number will hardly more than suffice to maintain the present supply of Japanese in this country."[1] With the decline in overseas Chinese labor, the Japanese had become the labor of choice in the Pacific Northwest. But the new Meiji regulation threatened to choke the labor supply from Japan. Faced with this challenge, company executives turned their eyes to Hawai'i, where they saw tens of thousands of Japanese laborers available for the taking. Having undergone inspection when they first arrived from Japan, Hawaiian Japanese were not subject to the rules or protocols of either the U.S. Immigration Service or the Meiji state and could therefore come freely to the continental United States. Knowing this, the Oriental Trading Company decided to charter the steamship *Olympia*, which after discharging company cargo at San Francisco, made its way to Honolulu, from "whence she will sail on or about March 7th with not less than six hundred Japanese laborers who will be equally divided between the Great Northern and Northern Pacific Companies."[2]

For much of the second half of the nineteenth century, Hawai'i stood at the nexus of two competing empires in the Pacific, where American westward expansion collided and overlapped with a Japanese eastward advance. For U.S. expansionists, Hawai'i was a key link in an imperial chain at the end of which laid the fabled China markets. President Grover Cleveland articulated this vision in his address to Congress in 1886, when he declared: "those Islands, on the highway of Oriental and Australasian traffic, are virtually an outpost of American commerce and a stepping-stone to the growing trade of the Pacific."[3] In Japan, the ruling elite, as historian Eiichiro Azuma explains, imagined Hawai'i as part of a "transpacific eastward expansionism focused on emigration-led colonization . . . envisioning the conquest of the overseas hinterlands through the transplantation of Japanese masses."[4] Indeed, Japan's "manifest destiny" lay east, spurring the mass migration of Japanese laborers to Hawai'i and the Pacific coast of North and South America in the late nineteenth and early twentieth centuries.

The executives of the Oriental Trading Company developed a labor recruitment strategy at the interstices of these two alternatively competing and cooperating empires in the Pacific, by integrating disparate points mapped by imperial expansion into a system of labor circulation. So much has been written about how the colonies were incorporated into America's Open Door Empire as stepping-stones to Asia and the mythical China markets.[5] But far less attention has been paid to the ways colonies were structured as nodes within an imperial system of labor transfer and exchange that were just as crucial to imperial expansion in the Pacific. If exploiting the colonies for the benefit of the metropole was the sine qua non of empire, then the circulation of imperial labor between the colonies and between the colonies and the mainland constituted the lifeblood of the system.

The Seattle-based Oriental Trading Company put some of the networks in place that would knit the colonies into a series of interlocking labor markets. Across them flowed Hawaiian Japanese whose migration and settlement on the islands were originally spurred on by Meiji visions of an emigration-led colonization but who were now being imported to energize the development of the North American West. Supplanting the Chinese, overseas Japanese merchant contractors reconfigured the imperial circuits through which immigrants and goods moved across the Pacific, and, in doing so, helped to coordinate and synchronize the transnational processes that made empire possible.

COMPETING FOR HEGEMONY IN THE PACIFIC

In 1900, the illustrious diplomat and long-time editor of the *New York Herald Tribune,* Whitelaw Reid felt it safe to declare the Pacific the exclusive preserve of the United States. "Practically we own more than half the coast on this side, dominate the rest, and have midway stations in the Sandwich and Aleutian Islands. To extend now the authority of the United States over the great Philippine Archipelago is to fence in the China Sea and secure an almost equally commanding position on the other side of the Pacific—doubling our control of its and of the fabulous trade the Twentieth Century will see it bear." "Rightly used," Reid wrote, "it enables the United States to convert the Pacific Ocean almost into an American lake."[6] This bold proclamation was made shortly after America had seized Hawai'i, Guam, Wake Island, and the Philippines (along with Cuba and Puerto Rico) to form a string of "stepping stones across the Pacific to a boundless maritime empire."[7] These colonies acting as links to the China markets were jealously guarded by an overlapping archipelago of military bases—inspired by the ideas of influential naval strategist Alfred Thayer Mahan—that stretched from the Puget Sound to Pearl Harbor to Manila.[8] Despite rhetoric to the contrary, the United States would not hesitate to use force to maintain its Open Door policy in China and to protect its imperial interests in Asia, more broadly.[9]

Yet, at the same time that leading American statesmen were declaring supremacy in the Pacific, Japan was quietly building their own empire in the western Pacific basin. Since being opened under the threat of gunpoint by Commodore Matthew Perry in 1853, Japan's ruling elite had worked feverishly to protect the nation's sovereignty and territorial integrity against further Western encroachment. According to historian Walter LaFeber, Japan was driven to imperialism by "the well-justified fears that Westerners were creeping uncomfortably close to the home islands, and that these outsiders intended to dominate Japanese trade."[10] Thus, in the name of national protection, Japan joined the global scramble for empire, creating a defensive perimeter out of colonial outposts that included Hokkaido, Okinawa, Taiwan, and Korea. In doing so, Meiji Japan established itself as a regional hegemon with a periphery to call its own.

The nation expanded its empire in 1905, when it netted the southern half of Sakhalin and South Manchuria as a protectorate as part of the settlement ending the Russo-Japanese War. By 1911, a rising Japan was able to negotiate out of the humiliating, unequal trade agreements that Western imperial powers had forced upon the country decades earlier. Yet, despite their competing imperial aspirations in the Pacific, the United States and Japan maintained a tenuous peace for much of this period, as the two emerging powers grudgingly recognized each other's imperial claims in the region. In 1905, for example, under the secret Taft-Katsura agreement, the United States acknowledged Japan's control over Korea and, in exchange, Japan accepted U.S. imperial presence in the Philippines.[11] In agreeing to the "mutual responsibilities for elevating the level of civilization in Korea and the Philippines under their separate tutelage," as historian Yukiko Koshiro writes, "Japan's responsibility toward Korea and America's 'White Man's Burden' toward the Philippines coexisted in Asia and the Pacific."[12]

But the one site in the Pacific where the imperial contest between the United States and Japan threatened to boil over was Hawai'i. Since the 1880s, both nations had their eyes on the islands, hoping to bring them under their respective sphere of influence. For the United States, its interest in Hawai'i was both commercial and geostrategic in nature, coveted for its sugar industry and as a coaling station in the mid-Pacific. With regards to the latter, the annexation of Hawai'i was seen as vital to strategic sea power, a position in the Pacific from which the United States could project its maritime empire into Asia. On the other side of the Pacific, the Meiji elite, likewise, viewed the Hawaiian Islands as an outpost from which to extend Japanese trade and emigration beyond Asia. By the early 1890s, more than 20,000 Japanese were in Hawai'i, which became a source of anxiety for the vastly outnumbered whites on the islands.

Japan's designs on Hawai'i were part of what historian Akira Iriye called a "peaceful expansionism" in which emigration and colonization were tightly bound. Like the United States, Japan, seeking to expand into places outside of its immediate reach—North and South America, and Hawai'i—pursued an informal empire, which entailed "the creation of Japanese communities overseas as centers of economic and social activities closely linked to the mother country."[13] In an earlier era, the Japanese ruling elite had considered immigrants a national liability, believing that the mass migration of society's lower strata would undermine state efforts to project an image of modernity and progress to the Western world. While this concern, driven largely by class bias, never completely disappeared from elite Meiji circles—it would be reignited with the outbreak of anti-Japanese agitation on the west coast of North America—the view that immigrants could serve the interest of the nation and the empire eventually prevailed, helping to ease restrictions on their outbound movement. Indeed, as Iriye has written, "Japan's self-perception as an overseas settler and colonizer gave an ideological impetus to thousands of men to leave the country."[14] This slightly more inconspicuous strategy of empire building was also seen as a way to relieve social tensions in the countryside wrought by Meiji's intensive modernization program. The new frontiers of Japanese emigration and settlement would, then, include islands and territories in the mid-Pacific and North and South America.

U.S. expansionists exploited the specter of Japanese hegemony in the Pacific to push for annexation, justifying it as a preemptive action to forestall Japanese takeover of the islands. Attempts to annex Hawai'i, however, drew loud protests from Japan with some members of the Meiji government deeming it an act of war. Some of their worries centered on the discriminatory treatment of Japanese subjects on the islands. In 1897, the white oligarchy in Honolulu exacerbated these concerns when it turned away two shiploads of Japanese immigrants. The immigration question brought to the fore by Japan's emigration-led expansionism would put the Meiji government in a tight spot time and time again, with it having to choose between protecting its national prestige (and its countrymen from discrimination) and scaling back its expansionist agenda outside of Asia. In Hawai'i, a more direct confrontation was averted when a crisis closer to home forced Japan to reluctantly cede the islands to the United States in 1898.[15] But the contest over Hawai'i would not be easily forgotten by either side, setting the stage for a future confrontation between the two Pacific powers.

Japanese merchant firms like the Oriental Trading Company in Seattle enriched themselves by operating and navigating between these two converging empires. Overseas Japanese merchants were envisioned as the "shock troops" of Japan's "peaceful expansionism" in Asia and across the Pacific, expected to populate overseas land with Japanese immigrants, open new foreign markets for Japanese products and goods, and build new commercial networks for the benefit of the metropole.[16] On the Pacific coast of North America, these mercantile colonialists formed "what was to become the core of urban Issei leadership."[17] Yet, at the same time Japanese merchant firms like the Oriental Trading Company in Seattle were the vanguard of an emigration-led expansionism for Japan, by importing and settling immigrants in the North American West and by promoting commerce and trade between Japan and North America, the immigrants they contracted and the commercial networks they helped build also simultaneously fueled the capitalist development of the American West and helped open overseas Asian markets to American goods and commodities.

The Chinese Exclusion Act and the departure of Chin Gee Hee prompted railroad mogul James J. Hill to search for an alternative source of labor as well as a new middleman to procure it. Hill initiated this process in 1893, when he sent company emissaries to survey economic prospects in East Asia. Their reports indicated that Japan, and not China, represented the most viable field for the "Oriental trade." In a span of fifty years, since Western powers had forcefully opened the island nation to the world, Japan had undergone a rapid industrialization that became the marvel of the world. This development was tracked closely on the Pacific Rim, especially in port cites competing for the Asia trade. In 1903, Seattle treasurer William Farrand Prosser wrote admiringly: "The extraordinary transformation of Japan from an obscure and unknown people to the position of a power with whom all modern nations having business in the east must take account, is one of the wonders of the nineteenth century." Buoyed by the fact that the export trade had grown almost sixfold in the Puget Sound since the Great Northern established its western terminus there, Prosser declared Seattle the "natural and logical gateway" for the new trade and commerce with a rapidly rising Japan.[18]

This newfound interest in Japan coincided with the decline of Chinese labor contracting, and thus Japan was looked to not only as a potential overseas market but also as a possible new source of labor. During the interim, Hill's Great Northern had experimented with Italian and Greek immigrants but company executives were not especially satisfied with their performance, recycling old complaints about the unreliability of white immigrant labor. The company was presented with an alternative when Japanese immigrants started to arrive in larger numbers at the end of the nineteenth century. The first Japanese to the Pacific Northwest came as stowaways and sailors. As an early Issei immigrant Toyokichi Matoba recalled, "The Japanese worked without pay on ships crossing the Pacific with the understanding that they were to enter Canada to Vancouver. There was no immigration office in Vancouver and the police was lax about these things."[19] Other early Japanese immigrants, not having worked out such agreements, resorted to "jumping ship" when the vessel they were working on made calls at port cities in the Pacific Northwest. "[W]hen his ship landed in Seattle, they said that they needed workers," Betty Morita Shibayama recounted, "So my grandfather jumped ship."[20] These random cases of immigration eventually gave way to a more sustained movement of Japanese. Between 1898 and 1908, over 20,000 Japanese immigrants entered Washington State and British Columbia.[21] Japanese migration to the region was part of a larger pattern of movement, inspired by the goals and policies of an expansionist Japan. Following a short probationary period experimenting with the new arrivals, Great Northern officials decided to make the Japanese the mainstay of their labor force on lines running from St. Paul, Minnesota, to Seattle, Washington. In correspondence with firm executives in 1900, Superintendent Russell Harding wrote: "I am glad the Japs are turning out so well, and am getting to believe with you that we better place our main reliance on them and have nothing to do with Italians or outside labor."[22]

To tap overseas Japanese labor and markets, now thought to be crucial to the expansion of his commercial empire, James J. Hill worked out a partnership with merchant contractor Charles Tetsuo Takahashi and his Oriental Trading Company in 1900. As the new company middleman, Takahashi filled the position formerly held by Chin Gee Hee. He stepped into the role just as the firm was about to extend its global reach. The year Takahashi came aboard, James J. Hill founded the Great Northern Steamship Company, with a market capitalization of $6,000,000. His ambitious plan for "a system of transportation by land and by water which would reach from New York to Yokohama and Hongkong"—one that would allow him to reign over a truly global empire—was met with skepticism even among his most ardent supporters. As his lawyer Thomas Burke recalled, "As the details of the project were laid before me, the boldness of the conception and the colossal character of the undertaking made me think that the author was dreaming." Yet, presiding over the unveiling of the Great Northern steamship S.S. *Minnesota* in 1903, the largest cargo carrier yet to sail under an American flag, Burke pointed out that Hill's grand vision "proved to be no idle dream." "The important event of the launching of the Minnesota impresses me like the fulfillment of a prophecy, or the realization of the wonderful dream," he marveled.[23]

As an extension of his railroads, Hill's new steamship lines extended the frontiers of the American West to East Asia and the South Pacific, linking the region and its hinterlands with new overseas immigrants, markets, and territories. The opening of Asian markets and the development of the American West went hand in hand in the mind of this empire builder. This belief flowed organically from Hill's philosophy of development, which saw economic growth (and profits) coming from the combination of trade, transportation, and land. He envisioned bringing in immigrants to settle and work the region's hinterlands; their labor, in turn, would produce market surpluses to be sold abroad, which would be carried to outside markets through a network of transport that some of these very same immigrants would help build. In this integrated system of mobility and exchange, opening new markets in Asia was a way to extract maximum value from the natural resources of the Pacific Northwest. In combining people and goods from Manila, Shanghai, Hong Kong, Honolulu, Yokohama, and Nagasaki, this linked system of commerce fashioned some of the very threads by which these disparate sites became woven into an empire of capital.

This sprawling transpacific commerce that integrated geographically dispersed people and regions demanded a high degree of coordination. The firm therefore employed a network of intermediaries who could facilitate traffic between the different nodes in the Pacific. These new middlemen were responsible for maintaining a constant flow of people and goods—the lifeblood of the imperial system. There was perhaps no more complex task, none riddled with as many obstacles, as the trade in Japanese migrant labor. Japanese merchant contractors confronted this challenge, which included government restrictions on both sides of the Pacific, by innovating on traditional importation models. Adding new links to a linear scheme that connected the site of labor demand directly with the site of labor supply, they developed global labor circuits that channeled the flow of Japanese contract laborers across multiple national and imperial boundaries.

THE ORIENTAL TRADING COMPANY

The Seattle Oriental Trading Company emerged at the cutting edge of this development, reflecting the shift from an ad hoc to a more formal labor recruiting system. Founded by Japanese immigrants Charles Tetsuo Takahashi and Ototaka Yamaoka, the firm was established in 1898. As it was the case earlier with Chinese merchants, English language skills and general knowledge of the Anglo-American legal system, especially as it pertained to business contracts, were prerequisites for Japanese immigrants seeking to become labor contractors. Takahashi first immigrated to Washington as a student-laborer, working part-time and attending school during his off-hours. The U.S.-educated Takahashi became the company's primary representative and spokesperson, initiating business contacts, drafting and negotiating contracts, and managing everyday relations with corporate clients. Yamaoka, on the other hand, worked behind the scenes to acquire and manage the company's most important asset: immigrant laborers. Recruiting immigrants from Japan was an especially complex task because, even after the liberalization of Japanese emigration laws in 1885, the Foreign Ministry maintained strict guidelines for Japanese laborers seeking to obtain a passport. Contractors faced a complex maze of government regulations and bureaucrats in seeking to import Japanese labor. Being well connected to local officials in Japan, Yamaoka was well suited for the task.[24] Through a sophisticated system of financial kickbacks and falsified documents, Yamaoka was able to successfully recruit laborers from Japan.[25] He acquired thousands of Japanese immigrant workers for the firm through this method. Takahashi, as the face of the company, and Yamaoka, as labor procurer behind the scenes, made quite the formidable team and profited enormously from the partnership.

The Oriental Trading Co. received its first break in December 1899, when Takahashi obtained an exclusive agreement with the Great Northern to furnish Japanese laborers for section work in the Pacific Northwest. The imminent departure of Chin Gee Hee, combined with the ever-diminishing number of overseas Chinese immigrants, meant that railroad mogul James J. Hill needed to look for alternative sources of low-cost labor. The Great Northern had initially experimented with Italian and Greek immigrants but increasingly showed preference for Japanese labor as it became available. As one company executive opined: "Personally I prefer Jap section laborers to any others that we have had during the last three years, as they are certainly more reliable than either Greeks, Italians or white labor generally and seem to be peculiarly adapted to ordinary section work." This preference for Japanese labor, however, had less to do with productivity and more to do with cost efficiency. Takahashi calculated the annual savings to the company to be in the range of $300,000. "Suppose this difference of 20 cents amount to a sum of 20 × 25 (days worked per month on an average) × 7 (number of months worked) × 8000 (number of workers)." The Great Northern would "have sustained a loss of $291,000.00 this year by the employment of the said Europeans, and would have gained same amount, had the Japanese labor been used."[26]

The competition for Great Northern's lucrative contract was fierce as labor contractors lined up to make their bid. The partners of William Remington and Hifumi Kumamoto and their firm Tacoma Construction and Maintenance Company aggressively pitched to become Great Northern's

FIGURE 2.1. Japanese American workers on railroad tracks. University of Washington Libraries, Special Collections, UW11552.

labor supplier. In his bid, Remington portrayed himself as a patron of Japanese immigrants and represented them as a docile workforce that he expertly controlled. "I have been handling this labor for a number of years on the Oregon Short Line and they have demonstrated their ability to equal any labor in track repairs and laying of steel. I handle the pay-rolls, saving you much clerical work; have my own interpreters and a sufficient number of English speaking Japs so your Section Foreman, Road Masters, and Superintendents will have no trouble in making their wants known."[27] Although the Great Northern finally settled on the Oriental Trading Company to be their exclusive labor supplier, not all was lost for Remington and Kumamoto; in fact, they successfully outmaneuvered their main competitor to acquire the rights to furnish Japanese laborers for the other giant railroad company in the region: the Northern Pacific Railway (N.P.R.). The two labor contracting firms continued to battle over Japanese migrants and corporate contracts well into the 1900s.

To satisfy the enormous labor needs of the Great Northern, Takahashi and Yamaoka had to find an efficient way to link the labor supply in Japan to the myriad sites of labor demand in the American West. In their earliest attempt to do so, the firm partnered with one of the numerous emigration companies that started to appear in the major port cities of Japan at the turn of the twentieth century. In 1900, the Oriental Trading Company submitted a request for 2,500 laborers to the Shin Morioka Company, one of the emigration firms authorized by the Japanese Foreign Ministry to submit requests for passports. W. M. Nice, commissioner appointed by the U.S. government in 1900 to investigate Japanese immigration, described their inner workings in his report. "These companies have offices at all important emigration centers," he explained. "All advertise more or less in the newspapers for contract laborers, designating them to go to Hawai'i, Peru, Mexico, and that in a general way they advertise through circulars, pamphlets, and by means of traveling solicitors for emigrants going to the United States."[28] Once companies met their labor quota, 2,500 in the case of the Great Northern, they submitted applications for passports, which had to include a legal contract showing the terms of their employment as well as a guarantee of a paid return passage to Japan. Nice was critical of these companies for colluding with private interests to "take advantage of the law." "[They are] very closely connected through the brokers and hotel keepers," he asserted, "and it is hard to draw a line of separation of interests." Such official criticisms, along with the growing social unrest over the influx of Japanese immigrants on the Pacific coast of North America, prompted the Foreign Ministry to temporary ban outbound immigration in 1900. Applications submitted by the Shin Morioka Company on behalf of the Oriental Trading Company were therefore denied.

Frustrated in its dealings with ineffectual middlemen and intransigent government bureaucrats, the Oriental Trading Company devised a plan to circumvent this system all together. Shortly after the prohibition was announced, Yamaoka departed for Japan to open branch offices in Yokohama, Wakayama, Kobe, and Hiroshima. He managed and oversaw the company's labor-recruiting efforts in these Japanese port cities that included placing ads in newspapers, disseminating pamphlets and circulars advertising employment opportunities, and dispatching agents to cities and countryside, where they recruited laborers for the Great Northern.[29] In doing so, Yamaoka had simply taken over the functions that were previously outsourced to the emigration company. His agents furnished would-be immigrants with forged passports, which he obtained through his political connections; money to avoid being rejected as a public charge; and steamship tickets to travel to North America. In 1900, the firm purportedly sent four thousand Japanese to the Pacific Northwest through "Yamaoka passports," accounting for almost all the Japanese immigrants entering the region that year.

Awaiting immigrants on this side of the Pacific was Yamaoka's partner, Charles Takahashi, who assigned each immigrant to a section crew and had them shipped to one of Great Northern's railroad construction camps the moment they came off the ship. Oral histories reveal that deception and coercion were often involved in the recruiting process. Issei immigrant Kichisaburo Ishimitsu recalled that when he along with a number of Japanese immigrants agreed to company terms, it was with the understanding that they would be going to San Francisco. His group, however, was shipped to Seattle instead. He recounts: "We were put into the train which was run onto a siding in Ballard, but the next morning the expected engine didn't come. Among us was one fellow who had graduated from junior high school and could understand a little English, and he asked the white man about things. The white man told him that this train was bound for the railroad section gangs in Montana. Realizing that we had all been taken in, we made a big fuss." When the group resisted going to Montana, they were met with force. "We tried to appeal to the Consulate in Seattle, but when we went out onto the siding, two police guards threatened us with pointed revolvers."[30] Similarly, Issei Uhachi Tamesa recollected two occasions, "where from ten to fifteen men were complaining that this was not what was promised and were refusing to get on a train for Montana."[31]

When immigrants finally arrived to their assigned site, Takahashi relied on a cadre of loyal foremen to impose company authority and discipline. They communicated and enforced company policies and were in charge of getting the most out of the newcomers. In the highly competitive business of labor contracting, the foreman was also responsible for protecting the firm's new laborers from rival firms, who frequently sent agents to raid their work camps, enticing laborers with promises of higher wages. "During the last year W. H. Remington, who has been supplying Japanese labor for the N.P.R. Co., has used every endeavor to interfere with the Oriental Trading Co.'s men employed upon your line." Takahashi went on to complain bitterly about what he considered to be the underhanded tactics of his main rival. "More than once our gang of men struck by the malicious influence of the N.P. contractor's agents who intruded into camps in disguise, instigated them to quit work and come to N.P. lines; disbandment followed and abduction of them was committed by agents."[32]

FIGURE 2.2. Japanese American workers, possibly logging crew. University of Washington Libraries, Special Collections, UW11556.

To exert further control over his immigrant labor force, Takahashi designed a scheme in which the firm withheld 10 cents per day from each worker and returned the withheld amount in the form of a season ending "bonus." In reality, however, it was a ploy to discipline the mobility of his contract laborers. Clarifying the firm's bonus system to a Great Northern executive, Takahashi explained: "The so-called 'bonus' really means 'hold back' of 10 cents per day out of wages actually earned by the men who work during the term, however, with the condition if they voluntarily leave the service before the end of the term, they shall lose the compensation." Takahashi was unabashedly forthcoming about its true aim: "We schemed this bonus system merely for the purpose of holding the men till the end of the working season. We call it 'bonus' but not 'hold back' simply to avoid the bad sound and ill feeling among the men."[33]

From 1900 onward, the Oriental Trading Co. supplied the Great Northern with thousands of Japanese laborers annually, the bulk of the railway's workforce west of St. Paul, Minnesota. All told, the firm supplied roughly 15,000 laborers between the years of 1899 and 1908. The Japanese railroad workers they contracted were paid between $1.00 and $1.10 per day, depending on the season. In return for their employment, the firm subtracted a fee of 10 cents per day in addition to cost of supplies, lodging, and other commissary services. In 1900, for example, Takahashi and Yamaoka recruited and acquired close to 3,000 laborers for the Great Northern, generating more than $70,000 in revenues for the company from employment fees alone.[34] The firm created additional revenue streams by marking up prices for food and provisions by 30 percent or more.[35]

THE NEW INDISPENSABLE ENEMY

The growing influx of Japanese immigrants generated by Takahashi's labor contracting quickly came to the attention of the public. Albert Johnson, who would later become the chair of the House Committee on Immigration and Naturalization and chief architect of the National Origins Act of 1924, cut his teeth on Asiatic exclusion while reporting on Japanese immigration for the *Tacoma Daily News* in the late 1890s and early 1900s. With the assistance of an informant in Victoria, British Columbia, Johnson was able to "receive the first information as to the number of Japanese coolies arriving" in the region. The headline of one his numerous dispatches from 1900 read: "(SPECIAL DISPATCH)-PASSED IN AT 10 A.M. S.S. TACOMA WITH 1,763 JAPANESE COOLIES ABOARD."[36] "This was the beginning of my campaign for restricted immigration," Johnson recalled. "How could I have imagined that in 1912—14 years later—I would be elected to Congress, with restriction of immigration as the chief plank in my platform?" Albert Johnson's life and career reflected just how much the issues of Japanese immigration and settlement would come to dominate local politics in the Pacific Northwest.

The white working-class response to the new pattern of Asian migration was to fasten the old rhetoric of cheap foreign labor, which they had assigned previously to the Chinese, onto the Japanese newcomers. The Western Central Labor Council in Seattle, for example, vilified the new immigrants as "pauper aliens" who were "contracted for and hired for work on railways and diverse places to the detriment of American workmen."[37] But if the Japanese were "pauper aliens," they were also different from the Chinese "coolie" in that, as citizens of a rapidly developing Japan, they also raised the menacing specter of the "yellow peril." The concern always with Chinese labor was that they would degrade white labor through attrition, by being able to survive on subhuman wages and conditions. Japanese immigrants, on the other hand, evoked anxiety of being eclipsed by a more competitive, more vigorous race, which, in turn, cast doubts on white racial superiority.[38] These racial anxieties only grew in the aftermath of Japan's stunning victory over Russia in 1905, signaling the first time in the modern era a traditional European power was defeated by a non-European power in the field of battle. The *Seattle Union Record* wrote dramatically: "The greatest struggle free labor ever had is approaching in America, and the preliminary brunt of the fight will be borne by the white laborers of the Pacific coast in competition with the Japs who are now being dumped upon our shores by unscrupulous corporations with the consent and through the aid of a plutocratic administration."[39] White labor leaders and activists alternated between these two discourses of the Japanese immigrant—as cheap foreign labor, on one hand, and as a kind of super competitor, on the other—not necessarily seeing them as contradictions.

Given the effectiveness of the anti-Chinese crusades in previously galvanizing the workingmen of the region, some white labor activists actually welcomed the influx of Japanese immigrants, viewing it as an opportunity to reinvigorate a racialized class consciousness against a new indispensable enemy. As one union leader opined, "This Japanese question, in the final outcome, will prove to be one of the best things that ever happened to labor. It is destined to make workingmen conscious of the political power they have. Years may elapse before this result is attained, but it is written in the book of destiny that labor is coming into its own."[40] This seemed to hold true in places like Everett, Washington, which was "fast coming to the front as a union town," with "anti-Japanese agitation the chief incentive," according to one white labor activist.[41]

Reviving old methods of social protest, white workers took to rioting and mob violence to express their discontent of this latest incursion of Asian immigrants. In 1900, for instance, racial hostilities involving white and Japanese laborers erupted in one of the railroad construction camps near Hillyard, Washington. As the *Spokesman-Review* reported, racial tensions had been brewing for some time: "[W]hite laborers and machinists of Hillyard have taken a dislike to the Japs and have frequently abused them, throwing rocks and pieces of coal into the cars occupied by the Japs."[42] One hot summer day in 1900, these tensions spilled over with white workers threatening to "clean out the whole Jap crowd." The white mob quickly realized however, that the Japanese had no intention of retreating quietly. "In the center pit of the round house where the fight waged hottest the white men seemed to be getting the worst of it until they were reinforced." In similar fashion, albeit with less resistance, the white mining community across the border in Atlin, British Columbia, also rioted against the Japanese, forcing the new arrivals out in May 1902. "About 150 miners did the trick: This may not be according to the law, but it is a very effective way of settling the Oriental cheap labor question."[43]

In their fight against this new wave of Asian immigrants, the white working class was not limited solely to extralegal measures to gain redress for grievances. Collaborating with new allies in the U.S. Immigration Service, white labor leaders brought state power to bear on the problem of overseas Japanese immigration. Commissioner General of Immigration Terence Powderly, formerly Master Workman of the Knights of Labor, in response to the growing alarm over Japanese immigration, expanded the force of immigration inspectors in the northern Pacific region in 1900 and established tighter controls over the U.S.-Canadian border.[44] In 1903, he was succeeded by Frank Sargent, who, like his predecessor, had close ties to the labor movement as the former president of the Brotherhood of Locomotive Firemen, and was therefore, sympathetic to the cause of Asiatic exclusion. In an interview with the *Seattle Union Record*, the general commissioner of immigration duly noted his allegiances: "For sixteen years it was my business to voice the opinions, the necessities of the laboring men of the United States and to endeavor to protect interests and elevate them."[45]

Over time a symbiotic relationship developed between organized labor and the U.S. immigration service in the Pacific Northwest district. Labor groups supported the fledgling bureaucracy by lobbying for increased government funding and an expansion of administrative and enforcement powers. In a formal letter to the state's congressional delegation, delivered in 1900, the Western Labor Council demanded that the U.S. Treasury Department "enlarge the force of immigration inspectors on the Puget Sound."[46] That same year, the *Seattle Union Record* called on the federal government to place "hundreds of customs officers on duty in the Puget Sound District," arguing that the "present force is entirely too small to prevent smuggling and so long as it is not increased the government is at least censurable for neglect."[47]

In return, local immigration authorities focused their efforts on curbing Japanese immigration, the latest threat to white labor. In the absence of formal exclusionary laws, officials carved out Japanese migrant illegality from existing statutes within U.S. immigration law. A government report in 1900, alluding unknowingly to the activities of the Oriental Trading Company, indicated that, "some individual or corporation is engaged in importing large numbers of Japanese laborers to work on the railroads of the Northwest." These Japanese migrants were in violation of contract labor laws and as such subject to deportation. "The plan is cunningly devised and persistently, accurately, and, so far, successfully carried out. . . . That several thousand laborers have been imported under an evasion of the law is not doubted."[48] In 1900, the U.S. Immigration Service in Seattle and Vancouver joined forces with local unions to crack down on Japanese contract labor. For its part, the Western Labor Council formed a committee dedicated to investigating violations of the Foran Act (1885) and agreed to forward their findings to the Seattle immigration office.[49]

As the leading employer of Japanese immigrants in the Pacific Northwest, James J. Hill and the Great Northern came under a barrage of criticism from the white labor movement. Unions and various labor organizations accused him and his lawyer Thomas Burke of degrading white labor through their importation of foreign Japanese labor. The *Seattle Union Record* scathingly editorialized: "Who is it that benefits by the importation of Oriental labor? The only gainer by this influx of Eastern labor is the monopolist, and the immediate beneficiaries here on the coast are the great railroad companies."[50] The struggle over Japanese contract labor invoked a *Herrenvolk* republicanism in which free white labor believed they were under siege from both above and below.[51] James J. Hill countered these charges through the editorial pages of Seattle's major dailies, over which he held considerable influence. In an editorial he penned for the *Seattle Post-Intelligencer*, for example, he represented the Japanese as model employees who posed no sort of threat to the white workingman. "We have found the Japanese clean, faithful, and respectful workmen and have no complaint to make regarding him. I do not think that there is the slightest danger of the aliens now in the West cutting any figure in labor circles."[52]

LABOR SUPPLY WOES

Despite supplying the Great Northern with thousands of Japanese laborers annually, for which it was impugned, the Oriental Trading Company still fell short of satisfying the company's labor demands. In

1903, Great Northern executives expressed frustrations with the inability of Takahashi's firm to adequately fill the company's ever-growing labor needs. "The Great Northern Railway company has during the past year, as you know, suffered considerable inconvenience because of your inability to furnish us with the number of laborers required in carrying on our work. We could use permanently from four to five thousand men as laborers along our line and if a plentiful supply were available we would use Jap laborers farther East than is now the case."[53] Company executives had little idea of the myriad boundaries—legal, political, and cultural—Takahashi and Yamaoka had to negotiate and contend with in bringing overseas Japanese laborers to the Pacific coast. They believed, rather unrealistically, that the firm would eventually no longer need the services of the Oriental Trading Co., and predicted that the company would assume the responsibilities of labor recruitment and management in the near future. "The contract that I have just negotiated with them will be a long step towards a direct control of the Japanese laborers by our own people; and I think by the end of another year we will be almost ready to get along without the Oriental Trading Company."[54] Another company manager similarly opined, "I believe we can get Japs on our own account now as well as the Trading Company can, and make fluctuations in rates of pay to meet conditions as they arise."[55] This optimism was, however, not rooted in reality. The Oriental Trading Company went on to furnish the majority of Great Northern's labor force for the next decade. In fact, the firm serviced the railroad's labor needs, albeit in much lower numbers after 1908, until the Second World War.

The labor supply problem grew worse for the Oriental Trading Co. in 1904. In response to the outbreak of the Russo-Japanese War, the Meiji government began to conscript all able-bodied Japanese men for active military duty. Concerned that the nation's young men were emigrating overseas to evade military service, the Japanese Foreign Ministry stopped issuing passports as a wartime measure. In North America, nationalist organizations and groups urged their compatriots to return to Japan to fight on behalf of their homeland, although it was unclear how many migrants heeded their calls. To make matters worse, just as the supply of laborers dwindled, the demand for labor grew. By 1904, the Oriental Trading Co. required almost double its usual number of Japanese workers, having finally wrested away N.P.R.'s contract from Remington's labor-supply company.[56] And while Takahashi certainly welcomed the financial benefits of the deal, the company regarded their new agreement with the N.P.R. as something of an albatross, especially in these times of acute labor shortages.

Compounding his problems, Takahashi also had to deal with the rising discontent coming from his own laborers, and, thus, he was faced with pressure not only from above (from his corporate clients) but also from below. The so-called "bonus" system he schemed, which was designed to retain laborers through the work season, proved to be ineffective, and, in some cases, provoked resistance. The company's arbitrary system of withholding wages, along with its usury charges for provisions and supplies, caused Japanese workers to revolt in certain work camps. As one Great Northern official reported: "Our roundhouse men on the Montana Division not only threatened to, but did leave the service of the company until they were assured they would not have to work for the Oriental Trading Company. They alleged as a reason that the Oriental Trading Company deducted $2.50 from them each pay day, which they would not stand for."[57]

The "bonus" inducement, moreover, did little to stop Japanese section hands from leaving their positions before the end of their contracts. During the peak summer months, canneries, fisheries, and commercial farms in the Pacific Northwest offered substantially higher wages than the Great Northern. As one company executive observed in 1906:

> Owing to the great development and the prosperity in the North West, the wages for the common laborers are in the highest ever known during the last ten years. The sawmills in the Pacific Coast are paying from $1.80 to $2.00 per day for the Japanese laborers, the farmers along the line pay $2.00 with the board, the construction work on C.M. & St. Paul pays $1.75 in Montana and eastern Washington, the demand for Jap laborers are so great that they will employ all the Japanese laborers they can get.[58]

This situation prompted Great Northern executive G. T. Slade to lament that "many opportunities present themselves to Jap laborers to engage in occupations paying a higher rate of wages."[59] Company records reveal that a significant portion of their Japanese labor force took advantage of these opportunities. In 1905, more than half of the eight hundred Japanese track workers in the Cascade and Spokane districts forfeited their summer "bonuses" by leaving their jobs before the end of the work season.[60] While most Japanese workers surrendered their "bonuses" quietly, others began to organize more systematically to abolish the system. In 1907, Katsunari Sasaki organized close to seven hundred Japanese railroad laborers to protest the "custom of contractors to withhold 10 cents a day until their Japanese employees have worked six months."[61] His labor organizing also helped to secure a raise for Japanese railway workers with their wages going from between $1.00 and $1.25 to $1.50 per day that year.

The Oriental Trading Company used political channels on both sides of the Pacific in the hopes of boosting the company's labor supply. As president of the Japanese Association in Washington State, Takahashi met with Japanese Minister of Foreign Affairs, Baron Komura, and the rest of the Japanese delegation, who were visiting the Pacific Northwest to survey the conditions of the overseas immigrant community there in 1905. "Upon the return of the party from the east I again took up this whole matter with them, and they were very much surprised to see the attitude of this country towards our people, and the vast opportunities which are here afforded for development work in every line of our natural resource."[62] Takahashi hoped that the experience would lead Komura, a distinguished diplomat and a leading figure within the Meiji government, to take up his cause when he returned to Japan. In Japan, Yamaoka tried to tap his personal connections with bureaucrats in the immigration department to further lobby for the liberalization of immigrant regulations. For his part, James J. Hill made personal overtures to both the Japanese ambassador in Washington, DC and the State Department to encourage the migration and settlement of Japanese immigrants in the United States.[63]

Yet for all their behind-the-scenes machinations, their combined efforts bore few tangible results. By the early 1900s, the anti-Japanese movement had coalesced into a potent political force, which it wielded to make demands for Chinese-style exclusion. The Meiji government, sensitive to the rising tide of anti-Japanese sentiment on the Pacific coast of North America, was careful not to further exacerbate the situation. Fresh off its impressive victory over Russia in 1905, Japan hoped to gain recognition as a legitimate world power. Fearing that its immigrant subjects might expose the country to national humiliation, thereby undermining its greater national aspirations, the Japanese Foreign Ministry instituted a policy in 1906, where only two hundred Japanese laborers were permitted to leave the country each month, which quickly reversed the lift on the wartime immigration ban. Unlike China, Japan, as an independent, sovereign power, used the levers of a centralized state to try to protect its subjects abroad though one could argue that it hardly made a difference in the way they were treated, at least in the North American West.

Having exhausted the supply of immigrants in the labor markets in Japan, the Oriental Trading Co. increasingly turned to alternative sites for recruiting migrant workers. Takahashi's initial response to labor shortages was to send company emissaries into the neighboring states of Montana, Idaho, Utah, and Oregon, and across the border into British Columbia, where they recruited for laborers.[64] They scoured ethnic neighborhoods and enclaves, inquiring with immigrant organizations and societies, as well as mining and railroad camps. In British Columbia, the Oriental Trading Co. established boardinghouses and storefronts in Victoria and Vancouver, where they advertised and recruited laborers for the Great Northern. As a result, U.S. immigration authorities came to know Takahashi as "one of the numerous persons, who are the cause of the great influx of Japanese."[65]

Oral history accounts and immigration records tell similar stories of cross-border labor recruiting. Nisei Fumiko Noji shared how her father was smuggled from British Columbia to a lumber mill in the border town of Sumas, Washington in 1901. "He was brought here by a general contractor; labor contractor with a lot, quite a few young folks from Japan," she recalled. "And not being able to come directly to the U.S., he went to Canada [first]," coming "across through Sumas" shortly thereafter.[66] Around the same time, U.S. immigrant inspectors suspected the Furuya Company, a Seattle-based Japanese merchant firm and one of Takahashi's main rivals, of importing Japanese contract laborers from Victoria, British Columbia, to put to "work on railways in the state of Washington."[67] Immigration officials also closely monitored Shinzaburo Ban's operations, the prolific Portland-based labor contractor, who was also known to augment his labor supply through cross-border trafficking.[68]

However, acquiring workers from other states and provinces was not a panacea for labor shortages as established labor brokerage firms in each of these locales were already competing over a thin pool of Japanese migrants. In Vancouver, for example, the Nippon Supply Company, formed by Saori Gotoh and Frederick Yoshy, was the exclusive supplier of Japanese labor for the C.P.R., furnishing more than 1,200 laborers to the railroad company in 1907. "Mr. Gotoh's labour," as one Dominion official explained, "was supplied entirely from among the number of resident Japanese, together with some who were brought on occasions from the United States," highlighting the fact that migrants were being trafficked across borders in both directions."[69] Gotoh had managed a labor-contracting business in Tacoma supplying Japanese labor to the Oregon Short Line, Southern and Northern

Pacific, and the Union Pacific in the United States before starting his labor-supply firm in Vancouver. His partner Frederick Yoshy was a member of the Japanese consulate in Vancouver and was thus strategically positioned to negotiate and navigate the complex regulations and bureaucracies involved in the importation of Japanese labor. In 1907, the Nippon Supply Company signed a five-year agreement with the C.P.R. to furnish between 500 and 2,000 Japanese laborers each year.[70]

IMPERIAL CIRCUITS OF LABOR

Facing stiff competition and a diminishing labor pool, the Oriental Trading Company looked abroad in search for new sources of migrant labor. Between 1885 and 1894, close to 30,000 Japanese had migrated to what was then the Kingdom of Hawai'i, recruited there as contract laborers to work on the island's sugar plantations. Not subject to the strict rules and regulations of the Meiji government, they drew the interest of the Great Northern and the Oriental Trading Company. The lawyers for the Great Northern had determined that the Japanese on the islands were residents of U.S. territories, and were therefore allowed to travel to the continental United States, without undergoing another round of inspection. "As Honolulu is a port of the United States very probably the immigration laws would not apply to Japanese laborers brought from Honolulu to this country. The laws should have been complied with when they entered Hawaii."[71]

In 1905, the Oriental Trading Company chartered the *Olympia* from the Northwestern Steamship Company to import Japanese laborers directly from Hawai'i. Several weeks prior to the ship's arrival, Takahashi sent labor agents in advance to advertise and recruit workers. They offered wages ranging from $1.10 to $1.30 per day and promised to provision laborers with food and supplies. Their offer was nearly double what Japanese workers were making on the islands. The *Olympia* departed Honolulu with a full ship totaling 600 laborers in the spring of 1905. The ship and its human cargo returned to a chaotic scene in Seattle harbor, where "Remington sent about sixty men of the most desperate characters, lined upon the dock in one or another, in order to create disorder and confusion, and if possible to steal away the men whom we had brought here." Takahashi boasted to Great Northern executives that, "It was only by the most skillful management the we succeeded in preventing any serious difficulties. We were able to keep most of the men by prearrangement with reference to having cars convenient, and got the men aboard and sent them out on the line."[72] In addition to the daily employment fee, the firm charged each of the Japanese twenty-eight dollars for steamship fare and booking fees. By expanding the geography of the company's labor recruitment system, the firm received an infusion of labor at a time when it was servicing the labor needs of not one but two railroad giants.

Buoyed by the previous year's results, Takahashi chartered the *Olympia* again in 1906, but this time with plans to make three round-trips to Hawai'i and with the goal of returning to Seattle with a total of 1,800 Japanese laborers to divide evenly between his two biggest clients. As before, Takahashi sent company emissaries ahead of the steamship to place ads in local newspapers, make contact with immigrant organizations, and make recruiting visits to the sugarcane plantations on the island. This time around, however, Hawaii's sugar growers organized to meet the challenge to their labor supply. "Mr. Takahashi's emissaries in the Hawaiian Island are, however, meeting with many difficulties in securing the men," reported one Great Northern official. Planters used their considerable political clout on the islands to hinder the firm's labor-recruiting operations at every turn. Takahashi's "four representatives in the islands have each been required to pay five hundred dollars for an employment license and have been several times arrested and imprisoned for alleged offenses, the prosecution simply being for the purpose of preventing the Oriental Trading Company from securing the Japanese."[73] Hampered by these obstructions, Takahashi was only able to secure 600 laborers. Yet, despite the setback, the Oriental Trading Company continued to view Hawai'i as a promising field for labor recruitment.

The intense competition for migrant labor in the Pacific generated new links that would incorporate disparate colonial subjects into an intra-imperial labor system. Almost exactly the same time the Hawaiian Sugar Planters' Association (HSPA) was ruthlessly defending their labor pool from the poaching of the Oriental Trading Company; it was simultaneously scouring the U.S. empire for an alternative labor source. Faced with growing unrest among Japanese laborers, which threatened to shut down sugar production on the islands, the powerful federation of sugar planters dispatched labor recruiters to the Philippines and Puerto Rico in search for a more docile labor force.[74] With permission from U.S. colonial authorities, labor agents for the HSPA, for example, established a recruiting office in Manila. Under their auspices, the first fifteen Filipino recruits came to Hawai'i in 1906,

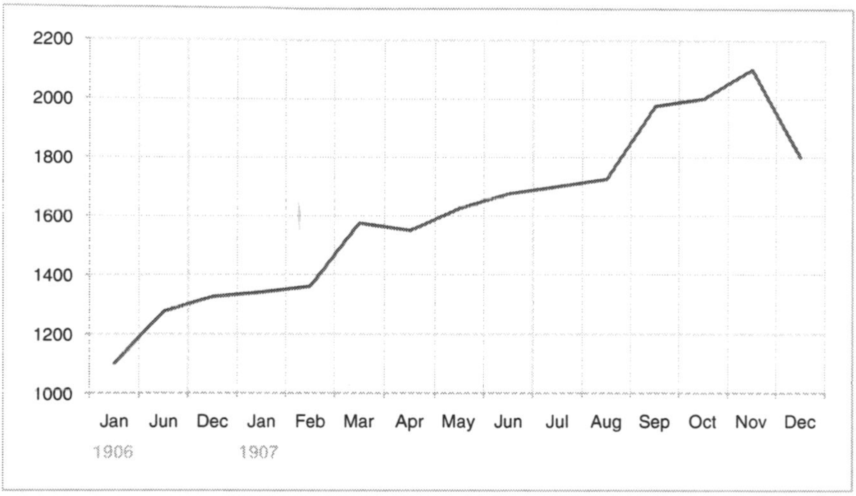

TABLE 2.1. Japanese Laborers Furnished to the Great Northern by the Oriental Trading Company, 1906–1907.

followed by 150 workers in 1907; by 1910, about 3,000 were arriving annually to work on the island's sugar plantations.[75] Thus, as Japanese laborers were departing Hawai'i for the mainland, U.S. colonial subjects from other parts of the empire were being recruited to take their place.

Labor importation of this kind in almost every other instance would have been considered unlawful under U.S. contract labor laws, but Filipino and Puerto Rican migrants, as U.S. nationals (a newly invented legal category), were conveniently exempt from the Foran Act, showing precisely how the production of "excepted populations" and "ad hoc exemptions of the law" were exercises in imperial rule.[76] Decades later, when Filipino laborers began leaving the island as part of the "third wave" of Asian immigrants to the mainland, they were replaced by Samoan immigrants. In this way, the colonial territories of the United States—Hawai'i, Samoa, Puerto Rico, and the Philippines—were integrated into a series of interlocking imperial labor markets, tapped to fill crucial labor needs in the hinterlands of the North American West and across the U.S. empire. Like all modern empires, the U.S. imperial project in the Pacific depended on its ability to shift people and resources from one part of the empire to the other as needs arose. Asian-ethnic middlemen, smugglers, and entrepreneurs played critical roles in putting the networks in place that allowed for these crucial intra-imperial transfers and exchanges.

But shortly after the executives of the Oriental Trading Company had put some of these networks down, President Roosevelt signed an executive order that threatened to cut off their labor supply from Hawai'i. In California, racial tensions were running high since the San Francisco School Board's decision to segregate Japanese students in October 1906. Concerned that Japan would retaliate against the mistreatment of its subjects by obstructing U.S. trade interests in East Asia, President Theodore Roosevelt sought desperately for a workable solution. As U.S. diplomat John Hays Hammonds warned, "Japan will not show the same unprotesting submission that China has hitherto."[77] To assuage white segregationists on the west coast without offending Japan, a rising power in the Pacific, Roosevelt issued an executive order barring Japanese (and Korean) migration from Hawai'i to the mainland as a compromise.[78] Signed into law in March 1907, it instructed the immigration bureau to refuse entrance to Japanese laborers whose passports were issued for any destination other than the continental United States. Immigration authorities hoped this would end the practice, among Japanese laborers, of using alternate routes through empire to gain entry into the country.

For the Seattle-based Oriental Trading Company, this meant that the firm could no longer import Japanese directly from Hawai'i. If the firm wanted to continue tapping into the supply of Japanese labor on the island, Takahashi would have to reconfigure the labor network in such a way as to elude the new regulation. He responded with a complex scheme that involved transporting migrants across multiple national and imperial spaces. Takahashi had migrant laborers from Hawai'i first shipped to British Columbia, where they were processed for admission into Canada, and kept in boardinghouses in Victoria and Vancouver until runners hired by the company were ready to guide them over the border. This multistep process enabled the firm to circumvent the new national and imperial boundaries that were delineated by the March 1907 executive order.

U.S immigration records indicate that over 4,800 Japanese immigrants came through British Columbia ports between January and September 1907, two-third of them having arrived from Hawai'i.[79] U.S. immigrant inspector P. L. Prentis was advised that, "more Japanese are coming from Hawai'i in the near future and that it is confidently expected entrance into the United States will be accomplished by at least a portion of this number."[80] The *Seattle Times*, reporting on the record influx, alarmingly reported: "[O]ver 4,000 Japanese have come to British Columbia the past summer, practically all contract laborers, it would be hard to find one-fourth of that number there now, and the balance will be found in this country, to which they have sneaked across the line, contrary to immigration laws."[81] In August 1907, Seattle immigration officers apprehended several Japanese arrivals from Hawai'i as they were attempting to cross the border. One of them, going under the alias of Matsumoto, confessed to smuggling Yoshio Nimi and M. Yamamoto from British Columbia. The two immigrants in question told authorities that they had arrived in Vancouver from Hawai'i on July 27, via the S.S. *Kumeric.* Officials later confirmed that Matsumoto was a foreman for the Oriental Trading Company in Bellingham, Washington, and suspected him of being "one of the runners engaged in bringing aliens to this country surreptitiously."[82]

In a slightly more ambition operation, labor agent T. Sengoku, who was also very likely working for the Oriental Trading Company, collaborated with the Great Northern to smuggle 300 Japanese laborers over the border in 1907. He told an informant working for the U.S. Immigration Service that he had provided the Japanese with passports for the United States before boarding them on a train, furnished by the Great Northern, heading south to the border town of Blaine, Washington. In exchange for securing passage and employment for the Great Northern, Sengoku collected fees from the Japanese immigrants. He went on tell the informant that he could, rather easily, smuggle additional Japanese laborers and described the process in some detail: "He stated that at present he had a camp at Douglas (located on the Canadian side, opposite Blaine, Washington) near the beach and that from this camp he could get Japanese into the United States. He stated when at Blaine his stopping was in the "Japanese Homestead Hotel."[83] In this way, the Canadian West, the American Northwest, and Hawai'i were turned into intersecting nodes in an interimperial smuggling ring.

Yet, at the same time, Japanese migrants were not simply pawns pushed and pulled across borders at the dictate of corporations and their labor suppliers. By using flight to resist the regime of contract labor and by leveraging their mobility for higher wages and better opportunities, Japanese labor initiative and agency shaped the outcomes of transnational migration. Executives at the Great Northern, referring to the Japanese being imported from Hawai'i, admitted as much: "Of course, it is probable that between twenty-five and thirty percent, of this number will escape the Oriental Trading Company and engage in other occupations, and consequently not be available for our work."[84] Sure enough, in September 1907, an entire crew of Japanese laborers suddenly deserted the railroad construction camp where they were employed, located in a remote area several miles north of the Washington-British

Columbia boundary. Their foreman, S. Sengoku, believed they had been enticed by higher-paying jobs offered by canneries south of the border. According to Sengoku, most of the laborers were recent arrivals from Hawai'i. In an ironic twist, Sengoku appealed to the U.S. immigration office in Blaine, Washington, for assistance in retrieving his men. He agreed to join the U.S. immigration inspectors in visits to the canneries suspected of hiring his workers, "for the purpose of identifying as many of his deserters as possible and furnishing names for the purpose of obtaining warrants."[85]

The Japanese would deploy their mobility time and time again in these fluid borderlands. For instance, in the summers, Japanese railway workers left their jobs as part of a northern exodus, migrating across the border into British Columbia to fish on the Fraser River. As Ryuichi Yoshida recalled, "in terms of short period of income fishing was the best money."[86] Therefore "when salmon fishing on the Fraser River is good," one U.S. immigration official noted, "as many as seven hundred Japanese laborers come from the United States to Canada to engage in fishing during the season."[87] As this suggests, Japanese migrants took advantage of transborder networks in both directions. Attempts to minimize this exodus of laborers by raising wages during the summer months were unsuccessful. Great Northern executive H. A. Kennedy complained bitterly: "I have theretofore noticed that the increased rates as in effect at the present time during the months of June, July, August which are supposed to cover the fishing season, do appear to have the slightest effect in retaining laborers as against their going fishing."[88]

Even the Japanese sugar workers who chose to stay behind in Hawai'i used the possibility of leaving for the Pacific Northwest to extract concessions from employers. As the Dillingham commission reported, as news spread of the Pacific Northwest "as a place where labour was in demand, wages high and opportunity great," the opportunity to migrate was "brought before the minds of the workers in the plantations." The possibilities of higher-paying jobs and better opportunities across the Pacific gave workers the leverage they needed. "[T]he fact that wages for common labourers on the plantations were anywhere from $18 to $35 per month, whereas on the railways of British Columbia they were from $1.35 to $1.50 per day, gave the best of the argument to those who were seeking to bring about an exodus sufficiently great to make the planters aware of the limited supply of available labour, and secure for it remuneration at an increased rate."[89]

The migration and mobility of Japanese laborers from Hawai'i led to massive upheavals in the Pacific Northwest borderlands in September 1907. As we shall see in the next chapter, riotous working-class politics led the United States and Canada to sign the Gentlemen's Agreements with Japan in 1907 and 1908, respectively. The Canadian version permanently limited the number of passports issued to Japanese coming to Canada to 400, which, in effect, closed off one of the main arteries through which overseas Japanese contract laborers flowed. State intervention did not end cross-border trafficking nor did it signal the complete demise of the firm's labor-contracting business but it did dramatically reduce its capacities. After World War One, Filipino labor, arriving from both Hawai'i and the Philippines, started to succeed the Japanese in the Pacific Northwest, taking their place in the intra-imperial circuitry of labor.[90] The Filipinos had the advantage of being exempt from restrictive immigration laws because of their status as U.S. colonials, which entitled them to free movement within territories under U.S. jurisdiction.[91] Fortunately for Takahashi, labor contracting had opened the way for more lucrative business opportunities both at home and abroad. Opportunistic Japanese merchants like Takahashi leveraged the transnational profits and networks they had developed while labor contracting to ship and trade in other commodities. In doing so, Japanese merchants like Takahashi became protagonists in the opening of East Asian markets.

THE LIMITS OF EMPIRE

Following the near-collapse of his labor-contracting business, Takahashi looked into other business and investment opportunities. He used the proceeds from labor contracting and provisioning to expand into banking, construction, and real estate. He became an investor in the Oriental American Bank in Seattle, capitalized at $50,000, and became the bank president in 1912. He also engaged in real estate speculation, partnering with two Japanese businessmen to start the Cascade Investment Company, funded with an initial investment of $100,000.[92] But Takahashi would place his biggest bet on emerging markets in East Asia. Like labor contracting, this new opportunity required careful coordination, an understanding of bureaucratic workings, and knowledge of markets on both sides of the Pacific. Convinced that his previous overseas connections and experience would seamlessly translate into success in his new endeavor, Takahashi invested heavily in foreign markets in China and Japan, adding shipping and commercial trading into the firm's portfolio.

After 1900, the Pacific Northwest economy had entered a new phase in its development, one that was thoroughly more international in orientation. The pace of transpacific trade, while still pale compared to the Atlantic trade, quickened in the first two decades of the twentieth century. The Puget Sound became a principal node in an intensifying global circulation of goods that accompanied the region's integration into a transpacific economy. In the ten years since Seattle became the Pacific terminus for the Great Northern Railway (1893), exports from the Puget Sound had grown almost sixfold, climbing from a little over five million to over twenty-eight million dollars. Exports doubled in the following decade, eclipsing the fifty million mark by the First World War, as the Puget Sound surpassed San Francisco to become the leading port on the Pacific coast.[93] From the region radiated outward widening circles of commodities: Machinery and lumber were destined for Alaska and British Columbia; coal, lumber, and gold bullion left for ports in San Francisco, Hawai'i, and Australia; and wheat, flour, and salted and canned salmon were shipped to China and Japan. The returning traffic of goods had equally diverse origins: silk from Yokohama, rice and tea from Shanghai and Hong Kong, hemp from Manila, and a variety of mineral ores from the Yukon.[94]

Among this array of goods, the "Oriental trade" figured most prominently in the developing transpacific commerce of the Puget Sound. In 1900, trade with China and Japan constituted more than half of all foreign commerce to and from the region. Of the $15,000,000 in goods exported by Seattle in 1902, two-thirds of it went to Asia, mostly in the form of lumber, wheat, flour, and salmon. Beyond the numbers, the "Oriental trade" was steeped in imperial lore and imagination. Expressed explicitly by America's "Open Door" policy, economic penetration of Asia was seen as a prelude to global dominance, by which a continental power would transform itself into an overseas power. Local boosters and developers imagined Seattle growing into an imperial hub within this emerging capital of empire. "With all of these events of world-wide importance of the Puget Sound country is intimately connected. . . . The acquisition of the Philippines by the United States very considerably increases the interest of the Puget Sound region in the Far East and in the millions of people there, whose productions and requirements will form an important part of the commerce of our country hereafter to be largely carried on through Seattle and the ports of the Puget Sound."[95]

At the forefront of this development in which Seattle becomes a hub for international trade was the ubiquitous empire builder James J. Hill. "The

Puget Sound will be the great seaport of the Pacific," he proclaimed confidently in 1905. "It will be the clearing point for the biggest volume of the tonnage going to the Orient and coming from it."[96] As someone who built his fortunes on frontier expansion, Hill became convinced that access to the Asia markets was crucial to the continued development of the American West. By making this link, Hill would be able to integrate the different facets of his commercial empire, moving Asian immigrants (and imports) in one direction across the Pacific and shipping the commodities that their labor produced in the other as part of an interconnected system of mobility and exchange in which Seattle would become a central node. Just as importantly, the commercial traffic to and from Asia would help keep his railway cars full (and therefore profitable) in both directions, balancing eastbound and westbound cargo traffic. As his biographer noted succinctly: "To Mr. Hill an empty car was a thief."[97]

The ever-vigilant businessman, Hill would do his due diligence before becoming entangled in emerging markets in Asia. As the completion of the Great Northern drew near in 1893, Hill sent his most trusted adviser Henry Rosenthal to survey economic conditions in China, Japan, and Korea.[98] This was followed up by another reconnaissance trip three years later, when Hill dispatched agents to China and Japan to obtain manifests of every ship leaving or entering the major ports of East Asia.[99] Their reports showed that Japan had more potential as a foreign market for American goods, pointing to the country's recent modernizing and industrializing trends. Hill became incredibly bullish on Japan as a result: "Presuming that Japan will come to be a great commercial nation, American trade on the Pacific Ocean should soon rival that of the Atlantic."[100]

To actualize this vision, James J. Hill needed to first develop transportation networks by which to connect the region's commodities with markets in Japan (and to a lesser extent, China). In 1896, Hill came to an agreement with the largest Japanese steamship line, the Nippon Yussen Kaisha, to provide monthly service between Hong Kong, Yokohama, Nagasaki, and Seattle, the first formal maritime link between Japan and the United States. The agreement was made with an eye to siphon Asian trade from Vancouver and Hill's main competitor, the Canadian Pacific Railway. The *Mike Maru* made the steamship's inaugural voyage in August 1896, to great fanfare as city leaders and boosters used the event to promote Seattle as the gateway to the Asia Pacific. Yet, already by 1899, the volume in transpacific trade outpaced the capacity on the Japanese steamship line. As a result, Hill started the Great

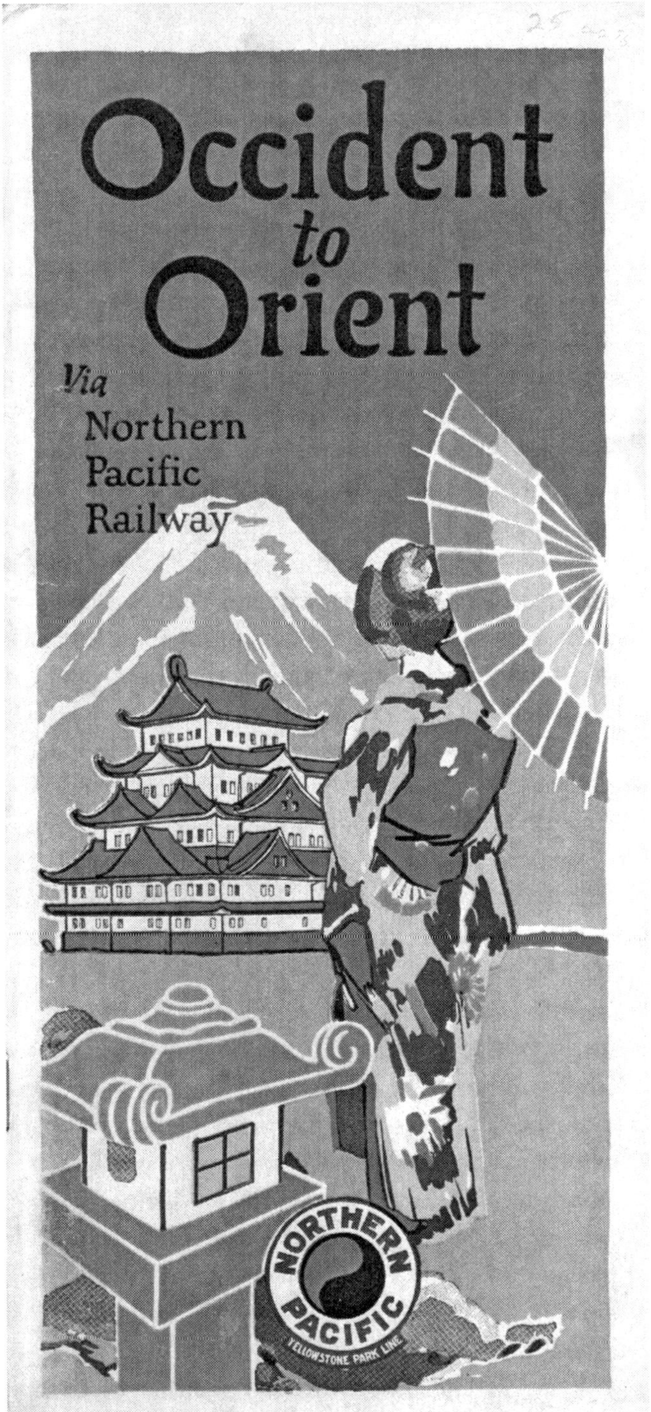

FIGURE 2.3. Occident to Orient. Illustrated brochure promoting travel along the Northern Pacific Railway. Washington State Historical Society, catalog no. 1998.1.51.

Northern Steamship Company the following year, which immediately began construction on three of the largest freight-carrying ships in the world.

To maintain a free and steady flow of laborers and goods between the American West and the Asia-Pacific, Hill also engaged the world of politics, which he was no stranger to given his extensive background in railroad building. So, for example, when the Oriental Trading Company met difficulties recruiting Japanese workers from Hawai'i in the summer of 1906, he contacted the Japanese ambassador in Washington, DC, for assistance.[101] And when he wanted "a national policy to develop and extend our commercial relations with Asia," Hill lobbied the president and leading U.S. senators.[102] He pointed out that other nations involved in the maritime trade subsidized overseas shipping, including competitors like Great Britain and Japan, which put American traders at a distinct disadvantage, he argued. "A nation like the United States must not only have a powerful Navy, but it should also have a large ocean-going mercantile marine."[103]

While developing transportation networks that would integrate disparate sites in the Pacific, Hill also simultaneously worked to drum up demand for American commodities on the Japanese side. He understood that he "could not export very many things to the Orient. A people like the Japanese, who only earn a few cents a day, cannot pay for many luxuries." As it was the case with China, Hill focused on turning the Japanese onto American grain, to consume instead of rice, as well as cotton textile. Adopting a strategy that resembled modern-day predatory pricing, which he deployed earlier to gain a dominant market position in the railway freight business, Hill offered exceedingly low shipping rates as a way to break into each of these markets. His rate on U.S. flour, for example, was less than half of what shippers were charging in San Francisco. Likewise, in making his pitch for American cotton to a delegation of influential Japanese businessmen in 1900, he guaranteed a profit. "Some Japanese were passing through the United States," Hill recalled. "My agents in Japan had reported the amount of cotton spun, there, and the fact that the raw cotton came mainly from India. It made an inferior yarn, and sold at a low price. I got these gentlemen to try a small shipment of American cotton, with the guarantee that, if it did not prove profitable to mix our long staple with their short staple of India. I would pay for the cotton."[104] He made the same bold promise for American steel rail, offering to pay for any losses incurred by Japanese businessman willing to experiment with it.

Hill's aggressive business tactics, along with the improved maritime connections, helped the Puget Sound capture a significant share of the Asia trade by the turn of the twentieth century. Between 1896 to 1903, marking seven years since the maiden voyage of the *Mike Maru*, Seattle's exports had grown from $1,816,577 to almost $12,000,000. By 1903, more than three-quarters of U.S. cotton exports to Japan and China were being shipped through Puget Sound ports.[105] Around this same time, the Puget Sound also became the largest exporter of wheat flour on the Pacific coast, going, again, mostly to overseas markets in Japan and China.

Charles Tetsuo Takahashi vigorously inserted himself into the emerging trade and commerce with Asia. Following the lead of his long-time patron James J. Hill, Takahashi focused on developing the cotton and wheat trade between Asia and the Pacific Northwest. In particular, he went to great lengths to create overseas market for wheat, having become convinced by Hill that it would soon replace rice as the staple of the Asian diet. Seeking to curry favor with officials in Japan, Takahashi couched these efforts in nationalist terms, claiming that he was advancing the cause of his homeland with his new endeavor. "A particularly strong point with the Japanese government would be to have it brought home to them that the natural resources of the Pacific Coast, and especially of this Northwest, are wholly undeveloped, and that it is a great field for those who are willing to get in and do pioneer work in the development of the resource." Extracting overseas resources and making them available for the homeland was congruent with an ideology of mercantilist expansionism in which personal self-interest was mobilized on behalf of the nation.[106]

By the time he entered overseas trading, Takahashi had joined Seattle's elite, joining an exclusive circle of bankers, industrialists, merchants, and real estate speculators. He was able to translate his personal wealth into civic power both in and outside of the Japanese community, becoming both an active member of the Seattle Chamber of Commerce and president of the Japanese Association of North America. He would tap these connections to jump-start the wheat trade between Japan and the Puget Sound. In March 1913, Takahashi hosted a lavish dinner at the exclusive New Washington Hotel in Seattle, in honor of T. Shoda, the Director of the Nisshin Flouring Mill Co., the largest milling company in Japan. The delegation accompanying Shoda included his head miller, I. Azami, R. Yomeda, head miller of the Dairi Mill, the second largest milling company in Japan, and M. Senda, of the Mitsui & Company, the largest importer and buyer of Pacific Northwest wheat and flour. The guest list consisted of the city's political, economic, and social elite: John Edward Chilberg, the president of the Seattle Chamber of

Commerce, the aging banking mogul Jacob Furth, State Supreme Court Justice Thomas Burke, and Richard A. Ballinger, former U.S. Secretary of the Interior, were among the dinner attendees. One local reporter wrote: "These gentlemen represented the great bulk of the purchasing power of the wheat and flour exports from the Pacific Northwest to the Orient, amounting last year to about $3,500,000 and estimated the coming year at about $8,500,000."[107] Takahashi would hold events like this throughout the year, bringing together influential businessmen from Seattle and Japan with a mutual interest in the wheat trade.

Having methodically cultivated relationships with investors, buyers, and shippers on both sides of the Pacific, Takahashi and his Oriental Trading Company made an aggressive bid for the wheat trade between Asia and the Puget Sound in 1913. His firm began shipping large quantities of wheat beginning in September of that year. The firm averaged about one shipment a month for the next year. In January 1914, for example, the Oriental Trading Company chartered the Japanese steamer *Shintsu Maru*, which picked up a cargo of 166,679 bushels of wheat, valued at $143,705.[108] Noting the salutary effects of Japanese trade in a column of the Seattle *Town Crier* in 1913, Takahashi boasted: "This year the exports through Puget Sound [from Japan] will reach a total of $9,000,000, a large proportion of it is being handled by my own firm." He insisted that, "the Oriental business from Seattle is just beginning."[109]

Yet, for all his bullishness on trade with China, Japan, and Asia more generally, Charles Takahashi found himself nearly bankrupt from wheat speculation by the end of 1914. By then, the firm had completely stopped grain shipments to Asia. In what was undoubtedly the lowest moment of his professional career, Takahashi went to his former rival, Masajiro Furuya, to plead for financial assistance.[110] While details of his failed venture are sketchy, Japan's entry into First World War undoubtedly played an important role, having disrupted shipping lines across the Pacific. It was also quite possible, however, that he was encumbered by the same impediments that had bedeviled American traders for years seeking to gain a foothold in the fabled Asia market. Despite all the promise imputed to them, the Asia markets had failed to "mature" to the extent necessary for robust trade, frustrating a long list of foreign traders and businessmen. Indeed, by this time, even the most ardent believer of the Asia markets had lost faith. Having been burned repeatedly by the "Oriental trade" in the 1900s, and with his transpacific steamship liners out of service as a result, James J. Hill reversed course in

1910, calling the "Oriental trade" an "illusion," a "conception still lingering grotesquely in many [American] minds. . . ."[111]

• • •

The follies of James J. Hill, Charles Tetsuo Takahashi, and the scores of other foreign investors who were deluded by the myth of boundless Asian markets reminds us of what historian Tony Ballantyne has said about empires, that they "functioned not in the idealist world of Borgesian fictions, but in a real world limited by capital flows, labour supply, and strict timetables."[112] The networks and systems of exchange that animated an empire of capital were fragile and therefore vulnerable to being destabilized by contradictory state policies, competing capitalists, intransigent immigrant laborers, and any number of international crises. Indeed, the imperial circuits through which people, goods, and capital flowed—the lifeblood of the system—could be chocked off at any point from any one of these occurrences. Thus, despite the enormous financial outlay and careful planning and coordination to build new trade routes and speculate on new commodities, the Asia markets never fully lived up to its promise. Practical realities on the ground thwarted the global ambitions of its most avid adherents and imploded the myth of a hegemonic Western capital seamlessly penetrating foreign markets.

THREE

Circulating Race and Empire

WHITE LABOR ACTIVISM AND THE TRANSNATIONAL POLITICS OF ANTI-ASIAN AGITATION

ON A CLEAR SATURDAY AFTERNOON in September 1907, J. E. Wilton, the secretary of the Vancouver Trades and Labour Council, was on the steps of City Hall rehearsing remarks for the day's event when he started to notice the crowd gathering around him. While the multitude would eventually include politicians, merchants, and clergymen, it was comprised mostly of laborers who had converged on Vancouver from all parts of the region for a rally billed as the "great demonstration" against the attempt "to degrade working people."[1] The recent surge in Japanese immigration from Hawai'i, orchestrated largely by the Seattle-based Oriental Trading Co., had caused widespread alarm in the Pacific Northwest. Indeed, it raised the very specter of the "yellow peril." The *Seattle Times* wrote: "Although over 4,000 Japanese have come to British Columbia the past summer, practically all contract laborers, it would be hard to find one-fourth of that number there now, and the balance will be found in this country to which they have sneaked across the line contrary to immigration laws."[2] Across the border, the *Vancouver World* raised similar alarms calling the "Japanese invasion of Canada possibly the most serious Asiatic attack on this continent" threatening "Republic and Dominion alike."[3] The revelation of an illegal traffic in Japanese migrants galvanized support for cross-border white labor organizing and reinforced the notion that white Euro-American and Canadian workers were bound together in a common cause.

The vociferous opposition to Japanese migration reminds us of the extent to which anti-Asian racism defined working-class politics and culture in the Pacific Northwest. The racialization of Asian migrants as degraded foreign labor mobilized a diverse array of Euro-American and Canadian workers into a transnational white working class. White labor leaders and workers crisscrossed the western U.S.-Canadian frontiers to engage in race riots, lobby for immigration restriction, and establish anti-Asiatic organizations, forging racial and class bonds across national boundaries. But if white working-class formation took shape through these border crossings, it was also animated by a world beyond the Americas. As the genealogy of J. E. Wilton's labor politics reveals, this pattern of racialization drew on larger circuits of movements that linked the proletariat xenophobia in the Pacific Northwest to a wider Anglophone settler world. A recent arrival to British Columbia, Wilton's conviction that "Oriental coolie" labor posed a threat to white workingmen everywhere had been forged during his sojourns across the British Empire, including stops in Australia, New Zealand, and South Africa. As a traveling labor activist, he had circulated the empire carrying his accumulated racial knowledge of "coolie" labor and the "yellow peril" with him. Under his auspices, the Vancouver Trades and Labour Council established the Canadian branch of the Asiatic Exclusion League, the main sponsor of the September 1907 anti-Asian rally.[4] That event, then, was the culmination of years of dedicated service to the cause of Asiatic exclusion spanning the empire.

This chapter traces the emergence of the white working class within a broad transnational context by examining the circulation of key people, discourses, and ideas among white settler societies in the Anglophone colonial settler world. Drawing on recent insights of postcolonial studies that emphasize the importance of interimperial connections in configuring empires, it analyzes white working-class formation in the Pacific Northwest as part of multiple and overlapping imperial contexts in which global systems of racial knowledge were forged.[5] Whereas the California story of Asians as the "indispensable enemy" was rooted in U.S. politics and culture and grew out of the seemingly inexorable east-west push of Manifest Destiny, in the Pacific Northwest, the nexus of white supremacy and Asiatic exclusion was born out of U.S. and British imperialism and a larger struggle to demarcate the boundaries of a "white Pacific."[6] This imagined racial geography naturalized the presence of white colonists in the Pacific world—transforming their empire building into "settlements," which justified Anglo-American imperial projections into Asia and the South Pacific. As this chapter makes clear, the racialized figures of the Asian "sojourner" and "coolie" served as the other against whom white Anglo-Americans could imagine themselves as "settlers"—the two racial identities being mutually articulated. White settler colonialism, then, was realized through not only a series of material processes, but also through a conglomeration of ideas and discourses that constituted the discursive strategy of empire. As Arif Dirlik has observed, "the Pacific was invented by Euro-Americans . . . who gave meaning to the area in terms of European (later Euro-American) concepts, visions, and fantasies."[7]

In this process, race making and empire building came to be inextricably intertwined. Racial ideas and identities were spawned and then circulated through imperial networks that crossed and collapsed geographical spaces in the Pacific, revealing the shifting transnational terrain on which these processes took shape.[8] The paradox of this imperial politics of race was that the transnational motion of white working people and their ideas were ultimately incorporated and materialized in and through national anti-Asian movements and campaigns, through a process in which the global and the national were dialectically defined. Generally, the national and the global have been perceived as being in opposition to each other, always in tension and locked in a zero-sum game.[9] In contrast, my analysis of white working-class formation in the northern Pacific reveals that the global and the national were at times mutually constitutive. In doing so, it shows how a racialized borderland proletariat emerged from the complex interplay between the local, the national, and the global.

MAKING A WHITE SETTLER SOCIETY

By the late nineteenth century, the twin imperatives of capitalist development and imperial expansion brought the Pacific Northwest into the world economy. With the rush of foreign capital and labor came new systems of transportation and communication that accelerated the process of turning nature into commodities. As such, these frontier settlements became outposts of empire, imperial peripheries that extracted raw materials for the metropole. The colonial mode of development there reflected the unique contours of the region, making the Pacific Northwest distinct from the Atlantic South and its plantations, the Southwest and its ranching and commercial agriculture, and the West and its developing industrialization. As historians have demonstrated, each regional political economy had its own racialized class structures and modes of domination, which were often starkly different than those in other regions.[10] If race, then, was, as Stuart Hall reminds us, "the modality in which class was lived" (and thus embedded within historically specific relations of production), how did the colonial pattern of capitalist development in the Pacific Northwest mediate and determine the outcome of social relations in the region?[11] And how did it compare to other places in North America?

To understand the regional dynamics that generated the Pacific Northwest's social structures and class and racial alignments, we first need to examine the migration flows and socioeconomic transformations in Washington and British Columbia at the turn of the twentieth century. After the 1880s, a majority of the region's settlers were immigrants and other newcomers, arriving from the British Isles, continental Europe, the eastern seaboard of North America, and across the Pacific Ocean from Asia as well as other Anglophone settler societies. Between 1900 and 1910, fueled mainly by the infusion of people from outside the state, the population of Washington doubled, a growth rate six times the national average. Likewise, across the border in British Columbia, about four out of five residents were new arrivals.[12] With this rapid population growth came the establishment of a variety of extractive industries, drawing diverse people and cultures into contact through new systems of mobility and exchange. As part of the British Empire, the American West, the Dominion of Canada, and an emerging Pacific Rim, the Pacific Northwest became embedded in multiple, overlapping worlds.

What emerged, then, was a diverse and dynamic society comprised largely of immigrants in which transplanted peoples came into contact as part of an emerging settler society. In that context, social reproduction of a single immigrant culture was impossible as each culture lacked a critical mass; instead, something new had to be built from fragments of the many.[13] According to the historical geographer Cole Harris, the polyglot assemblage of Euro-Americans, Canadians, and Anglos, united by a shared sense of dislocation and uncertainty regarding their new environment, responded to the dizzying heterogeneity and flux by "reconceptualizing themselves; fixing on their whiteness, intensifying their racism," and "abstracting their ethnicity." "Whiteness," Harris argues, "became the first and most essential marker of social responsibility. From this idea of race followed a number of boundary operations intent on affixing spaces for insiders and outsiders."[14] This project of creating a monolithic white racial identity was part of an effort to impose stable categories of difference, bringing ethnoracial order to culturally plural societies.[15]

The process of delineating strict racial boundaries involved transforming Europeans of different national origins into "whites." The Asiatic Exclusion

League, for one, defied the dominant racial ideology of Anglo-Saxonism invented largely by social theorists, intellectuals, and scientists in the eastern United States. The league expunged the word *Anglo-Saxon* from all of its organizational records to underscore the common identity shared by all white people. In response to an editorial in the *New York Times,* which insisted that the nation was fundamentally Anglo-Saxon in character, the league fired back this harsh rebuke in December 1910:

> *The Times* writers, like all the editors of New York daily papers, is ignorant of the ethnology of the American people. Because he and they speak English ergo this is an Anglo-Saxon country and people. There are millions of "Celts, Teutons, Scandinavians, and Latins" in this country, but the representatives of those races are not so ignorant or so egotistical as to assert that it is a Celtic, Teutonic, Slavic, or Latin country. *The New York Times* writer should take a course in American history. To begin with, let him read the latest and most scientific works like Hart's, and Chancellor and Hewes' and John Fiske's, and then devote some time to study of immigration statistics. After that he will be better informed on the composition of the American people.[16]

"The Republic," the League added, "owed nothing to the Anglo-Saxon stock, but much to the men of brawn and brains who are descendants of the races enumerated above." In Washington State, the *Everett Labor Journal* also gave credence to the cultural fiction of a "white race" when it described western Canada in 1910 as a "coming nation including the Yanks and Europeans meeting in the free soil to reunite the ties of race."[17]

This unified white racial identity was also reproduced in daily regional newspapers such as Vancouver's *B.C. Saturday Sunset,* which opined in 1911 that "the White Man even the riffraff of the white race that Europe sends, can be boiled down into a decent Canadian citizen in a couple of generations at least, but an Oriental does not change." Using almost identical language and logic, the Reverend Neville Lascelles Ward of the Anglican Church and the superintendent of the Chinese and Japanese missions in British Columbia explained that "When Frenchmen, Italians, and even Germans come to British Columbia it is only a question of time before they are absorbed into the Canadian commonwealth. Not so with the Japanese and Chinese, who are Mongolian, Yellow, Asiatic, and non-Christian people."[18] Whiteness was thus defined primarily in opposition to the overseas labor and migration of Chinese, Japanese, and South Asian groups.

Racial politics against indigenous peoples also contributed to this process; however, the prevailing belief among white settlers was that native peoples were doomed to extinction and thus posed little threat to white hegemony. Scholars have thoroughly debunked this notion by showing the myriad ways that indigenous peoples engaged, negotiated, and resisted settler encroachment even as these encounters were constrained by unequal relations of power.[19] Nonetheless, nativist groups such as the Asiatic Exclusion League continued to propagate the myth of the vanishing Indian, insisting the following in 1908: "The red natives of America, incapable alike of being assimilated or of becoming beasts of burden, are soon to be numbered, among the peoples of the past."[20]

In contrast, the Exclusion League described the flow of Asian migrants as a "threatening stream of aliens poured in upon us from the inexhaustible fountain of human life now confined beyond the Asiatic shores of the Pacific." They imagined the Asian "coolie" as a foreign menace who threatened to usurp the egalitarian promise of a "white man's country," an ideology that served as the basis of white republicanism from North America to South Africa to Australia. Ernest Crawford, writing for the *American Federationist,* explained that "men on both sides of the international line feel that the continent of North America is intended to afford the largest democratic development to the white men of the earth" and that the West "is the region that the common man finds his last chance; it is the land of the monogramic homestead, high wages, men at work on the soil, women toiling in the home, the scene of the square deal for every square fellow."[21]

This notion of white racial entitlement fueled the labor politics of anti-Asian agitation on both sides of the divide in the Pacific Northwest. In 1912, the labor newspaper *B.C. Federationist* (Vancouver) insisted that the "great question whether this country of ours is to be the heritage of our children or the heritage of the yellow and black races, must be decided now, once and for all," and thus "it behooves us, as workers and citizens, to decide, while yet there is time, whether the future of Canada is to belong to the yellow and black races or the white race."[22] As far as white unionists were concerned, Asian immigrants, due to their status as nonwhites, remained firmly outside the boundaries of both working-class organization and the nation. Across the border, the Western Central Labor Union in Seattle echoed similar sentiments. Calling themselves "true American citizens," white unionists in 1900 urged "those in authority to employ men to desist from using this class of labor: and be it further, resolved, that we petition the Congress of the United States to frame laws for the correction of this crying evil."[23] Constituting a threat to the ideals of free labor and working-class manhood, both being coterminous with whiteness, Asian immigrant labor posed a foreign problem that required state intervention and control. "Against these Mongolian hordes the American laborer must be protected," the *Seattle Union Record* argued in 1902. "It is not a question of race prejudice, but one of conservatism of American homes and American life."[24]

For white workers, identifying with the nation and a white workingman's internationalism were not mutually exclusive. To the contrary, in the Pacific Northwest, the two were contingent upon each other.[25] As C. O. Young, the chief organizer for the American Federation of Labor (AFL) in the Pacific Northwest, declared in 1907: "there is nothing un-American" about "stand[ing] up in defense of this country as a white man's country." The capacious vision of whiteness was, of course, predicated on a united opposition to Asians. He continued, "I want to say that we cannot assimilate those nations and their people; we cannot intermarry with them, nor can we adopt their conditions of life; we do not want anything to do with them as far as their conditions and religions are concerned; and as far as their foreign trade is concerned."[26]

This is not to deny the significance of national differences among white workers, nor is it to suggest that linguistic and cultural barriers were easily swept aside. White racial identity was fractured along the multiple axes of class, gender, and sexuality, among other socially constructed differences, and was therefore rarely, if ever, a stable identity in the North American West.[27] Fissures in white racial formation were evident in the Pacific Northwest borderlands as well, where the process unfolded haltingly and unevenly. Non-English-speaking European immigrant workers, for example, were not always accorded equal status with English-speaking Euro-Americans, Canadians, and Anglos in the Pacific Northwest labor movement, although, significantly, they were never explicitly excluded from the movement either.[28] Additionally, white racial solidarity did little to stop Irish and Cornish miners from clashing repeatedly with one another, culminating in some of the most brutal episodes of interethnic warfare in the North American West and elsewhere in the Anglophone settler world. Nor did it stop native-born white workers in Seattle from invoking American nationalism or Anglophiles in Vancouver from making claims based on "Britishness," both of which infused labor politics with national distinctions even in a region with porous boundaries. White workers therefore drew on parallel as well as overlapping political and cultural sources to animate their labor movements.[29]

Nevertheless, cultural differences were frequently mitigated by appeals to white supremacy, which served as the basis for a supranational working-class identity in the western U.S.-Canadian borderlands. In a speech delivered at the annual convention of the Washington Federation of Labor held in Tacoma in 1907, Canadian delegate M. A. Beach, representing the Vancouver Trades and Labour Council, asserted a unified white working class against an "Asian other." Beach opened his remarks by telling the audience that he felt "quite at home here, in your beautiful city, in fact have spent a number of years on this side of the imaginary boundary line. I say, imaginary boundary line, because I suppose from a national standpoint we are divided, but from a wage-earners' standpoint we are not divided." He claimed that American and Canadian laborers were "brothers working for a common cause . . . bettering conditions for the wage-earner," and insisted to the largely American audience that "what is good for you is good for me, and what is good for me is good for you."

This imagining of a transnational working-class community was, however, predicated on white racial solidarity. "We in British Columbia have existing conditions which are very dangerous to the welfare of the white wage-earners of the country, namely the Japanese, Chinese, and Hindoo," Beach declared. "They are a people totally unfit for the conditions of this country." "The Oriental Problem," he contended, "are just as important to you as they are to us on the other side of the border," and in this struggle "there is a bond of friendship, a fraternity, existing between us that no imaginary line can sever."[30] Beach, along with other labor leaders and activists, exploited anti-Asian sentiments to build racialized class ties across borders in the Pacific Northwest. A racialized borderland proletariat therefore emerged from the mass and concerted politics of anti-Asian agitation. This process was not, however, rooted solely in the local imperatives of the Pacific Northwest. Indeed, its origins could be traced to far-flung sources in the Anglophone settler world where initiatives and concerns over Asian migration intersected and were mutually reinforcing.

IMPERIAL CROSSINGS AND EXCLUSIONS

These white labor mobilizations drew extensively from imperial circuits of knowledge production that spanned the Pacific world and beyond. They were, to borrow Tony Ballantyne's insightful metaphor, embedded in "webs of empire" that bound together in an imperial working-class community of white labor leaders and activists who lived in disparate, widely dispersed settler colonies.[31] The imperial crossings of white labor activists and the networks they generated and sustained facilitated the circulation of practices, identities, and knowledge that became the foundation for anti-Asian movements across the empire. These interimperial links, embodied in the flow of white labor activists and leaders and in the proliferation of labor newspapers and journals, fueled a pattern of anti-Asian riots, petitions, and discriminatory legislation that was almost identical across the Anglophone settler world.[32] The western U.S.-Canadian borderlands emerged as a key node on the imperial circuits of white working people and their ideas.

For the most part, historians have captured these movements under national narratives of immigration and assimilation rather than as part of global histories of race and empire. The terms *sojourner* and the *coolie,* on the other hand, have been applied almost exclusively to describe nonwhite migrants, suggesting that scholars have been complicit in defining "immigrants" as European and white.[33] Yet, in the late nineteenth and early twentieth centuries, skilled white workers, along with colonial administrators, merchants, and farmers, traversed the multicolonial spaces created by Anglo-American imperial expansion. Indeed, the very logic of the colonial enterprise, which presumed that colonies were sites for the extraction of raw materials for the metropole, inducted white migrant workers into an intercolonial system of mobility and exchange. Skilled Anglo miners—English, Scotch, Cornish, and Irish—were the most frequent travelers along these circuits of labor, following the discoveries of gold from one white settler colony to the next.[34] These global flows proved indispensable to colonial development and the functioning of the empire as a whole. As historian Eric J. Hobsbawm has observed, "mines were the major pioneers in opening up the world to imperialism."[35] Thus, Anglo miners were at the forefront of the colonial project in the age of empire, extending British imperialism into Asia, the South Pacific, and the Indian Ocean.

In South Africa, for example, the discovery of gold transformed Johannesburg from a hinterland populated by a few prospectors to an imperial center with close to 100,000 people by the turn of the century, its immigrants coming mostly from England, Scotland, and Australia.[36] The colony eventually became the leading gold producer in the world, yet many of the Anglo miners who came to South Africa during the boom stayed for only a short period, departing as soon as higher wages and better opportunities presented themselves elsewhere in the empire. Their relentless transience prompted one South African mining executive to lament: "the aim of nine miners out of ten is to accumulate sufficient money to leave the country."[37] This complaint about miners' itinerant ways was a refrain repeated over and over again by imperial capitalists throughout the Anglophone settler world. In British Columbia, Francis Dean Little, the general manager of the Willington Colliery Company, shared his frustrations with Canadian officials: "We brought out two hundred Scotch miners, and they were no good. We have twenty left." "Many of them went to Seattle at once," Little complained. "They never came here at all. Dunsmuir spent $15,000 on them. I do not think he got $3,000 back."[38] Because the imperial economies on the British Pacific Rim were based largely on the extraction of precious metals, Anglo miners found it relatively easy to transfer their skills from one colonial society to the next.

The globe-trotting of the lifelong miner Edward Terry exemplifies the far-flung geography of labor mobility in the age of empire. Terry began on the British Isles, migrating to South Africa, British Columbia, and eventually California, before settling permanently back in British Columbia where he became acting secretary of Alexandra's Miners' Union. David Moffat, a miner for 45 years, likewise captures the transient experience of Anglo miners. "Mined in Scotland from the time I was eight years old till I was thirty. Came to the United States and mined in Pennsylvania, Illinois, Wyoming, Utah, and Washington," before finally settling in the mining community of Nanaimo, British Columbia. These labor circuits however, proved to be more than routes to higher wages or better opportunities; they also became conduits for racial knowledge, which facilitated the transmission of racial ideas and identities, spawning anti-Asian racism that reached across national and imperial boundaries. The aforementioned Edward Terry was invited by Canadian officials to appear before the 1902 Royal Commission on Chinese and Japanese Immigration precisely because of his knowledge of the "Oriental question" in different colonial settings.[39] The imperial sojourns of the Scotch miner William McAllan, having worked in New Zealand and Australia before coming to British Columbia, also made him an expert witness in the eyes of the commission. The stints of these two miners in multiple colonial contexts served to reinforce their commitment to white supremacy and its corollary, Asiatic exclusion. McAllan, for instance, became an ardent advocate of stricter immigration policies, citing measures he came across in the Australasian colonies as models. Claiming "no cheap labor is employed in Australia in the mines or surface," he insisted that Canada should follow Australia's lead in legislating against Asian immigration.[40]

The transnational movements and imaginings of imperial white working-class subjects enabled the emergence of a shared pattern of anti-Asian riots, petitions, and discriminatory legislation in Australia, New Zealand, South Africa, and the North American West. For a time, America's 1882 Chinese Exclusion Act and Australia's 1901 Immigration Restriction Act; anti-Asian riots in Brisbane, Vancouver, and Seattle; and the discourse of a "white man's country" in Canada, South Africa, New Zealand, and Australia, formed, in the words of the historian Daniel Rodgers, "a world of common referents."[41] Therefore, when James Riley, the president of the Witwatersrand Trade and Labor Council, called on the legislature to exclude Chinese and Indian "coolies" from South Africa in 1907, arguing that the colony should be maintained as "a white man's country and a home in a British colony for white people," he was drawing on a shared, time-tested racial discourse from multiple, overlapping imperial contexts.[42]

There were, of course, differences in race and class relations between white settler societies. In the South African colonies, for example, the presence of indigenous Africans complicated the white-yellow binary that defined race relations in most of the Anglophone colonial settler world. In the Transvaal, race relations hinged on multiple axes, with black Africans and Asian immigrants occupying overlapping positions in the racial politics of the white working class.[43] Moreover, there were also differences in the labor movements in the various white settler societies. In the dominions of the British Empire, the white working class was largely Anglophone, with white British subjects—English, Scots, Welsh, and Cornish—as its core constituency. In the American West, the white labor movement, due to its significant non-Anglo white population, tended to have greater white ethnic diversity. British Columbia occupied a middle ground; it was home to a white labor movement with strong Anglo overtones, but it was inclusive enough to absorb non-Anglo whites.[44] The experience of A. W. Von Rhein, a German-Canadian unionist and one of the principal organizers of the 1907 anti-Asian rally, was a good example of the movement's capaciousness. Yet for all their differences, these disparate white working-class movements were bound by their mutual commitment to white supremacy, which coalesced primarily around the Asian other as the transnational "indispensable enemy."

The circuitry of anti-Asian politics and ideas was, then, a multidirectional system constantly being remade through the imperial flow of working people and their ideas. The British-born William Lane, a prominent figure in the Australian labor movement, developed his vision of trade unionism during his earlier sojourns to Canada and the United States in the 1870s and 1880s.[45] Lane played a leading role in the anti-Asian movement in Australia, applying the lessons of white supremacy he learned in his global travels. In his speeches on Chinese labor, Lane contended that "the racial phase overshadows us and overpowers all others. Between the white and the yellow there is no possibility of assimilation." "The coolie is a cur, a poltroon, a miserable tinker of a sailor," who imperils "the life of white Australia," he declared. "Unless Australia is to be white, what does it matter to us what becomes of it?"[46] Under his influence, the Brisbane Trade and Labor Council established anti-Chinese leagues in Australia and New Zealand throughout the mid-1880s and 1890s. Together they mobilized political support for a series of anti-Chinese legislation in the Australasian colonies, a combination of poll taxes and tonnage restrictions that imitated policies enacted by Canada several years earlier. News from the United States gave the fledgling anti-Chinese movement in Australia its initial boost. As Joseph Lee explained in an 1889 article: "The report received last spring of a treaty concluded between the United States and China by which the Chinese were to be kept out increased the anti-Chinese feeling in Australasia."[47] In these formative years, white Australians looked across the Pacific to California and the precedents established there for inspiration and ideas.[48] At the same time, these connections generated a friendly rivalry among the disparate white settlements to see which colony could pass the most stringent anti-Asiatic law.

A prolific and flamboyant writer, Lane feverishly engaged print culture, penning several novels and editing two important labor newspapers.[49] His writings became a key venue for disseminating his racial and class politics to a wider public. The international reportage in Lane's newspapers, no doubt influenced by his worldly experiences, informed the Australian working class of developments and events in distant parts of the empire and beyond. The *Worker,* a labor newspaper published by Queensland's trade unions, for instance, regularly carried news on "coolie" labor in South Africa, New Zealand, and western Canada and the United States. A 1907 article reported on the plight of white labor in California: "Economically, the Jap influx has had a disastrous effect. White labor has been completely driven out of the orchards, and now the orchards are beginning to pass into their hands. In the cities they have [also] driven white servants right out of the homes." The article continued: "Americans are not hysterical at all but they have thoroughly awakened to the fact that the Jap invasion is as disastrous as war. It is driving the white population away, it is securing the land and the industry, and if that isn't worse than armed conquest, what is the difference?"[50] The printed word, in this case, facilitated an imagined community exceeding the nation-state.[51]

In a later issue, exemplifying the many working-class ties that had been forged in the crucible of empire, the paper published an interview with South African Independent Labor party member William Bowden, a close confidant of Lane's. In fact, Charles Buxton, a recent arrival from Australia, had started the political party with which Bowden was affiliated in the Transvaal. Bowden was touring Australia when the editors of the *Worker* interviewed him in 1907. He hailed the "white Australia" policy as a historic achievement that served as a much-needed policy paradigm for white settler societies in the English-speaking colonial world. He discussed the recent importation of Chinese labor to South Africa, speaking of them as if they were livestock. "Chow" labor "proved to be a larger and stronger type than that seen in Australia," due to the fact that they were placed in "palatial compounds," "pampered with superior foods," and "allowed to go in and out as they liked and wander anywhere." He was, however, happy to report that, "all the Australians in the country were bitterly opposed to the employment of Chows."[52]

These imperial transplants carried with them the vision of "white Australia," championed by Lane and others, to the English colonies of South Africa. Between 1904 and 1906, South African mine owners brought more than fifty thousand Chinese workers to the Transvaal, sparking massive white working-class resistance. Anglo miners from Australia were at the forefront of the agitation. "The vigour of labor opposition to Chinese workers has a particular relationship to the Australian presence in the Rand [a South African mining district] unions," the scholar Jonathan Hyslop explains. "Australian labour activists on the Rand could thus view the Chinese labour question as a reprise of their own domestic experience and could offer their comrades an already well-formulated model of racially bound Social Democracy as a political ideal."[53] These activists demanded the same sovereign right to a "white man's country" that they enjoyed in Australia, which they insisted was the rightful prerogative of a self-governing society.

The Cornish diaspora was disproportionately represented among the recent immigrants from Australia. Highly sought after for their mining skills and prompted by the discoveries of gold, transient Cornish miners started to arrive in South Africa in the late nineteenth century. From Australia, where they had been deeply immersed in the labor movement, they brought with them the lessons they had learned and the strategies and ideas they had implemented in their protracted campaign for a "white Australia" policy, which was passed in 1901. Therefore, when Cornishman Thomas Mathews, the general secretary of the Transvaal Miners' Union, explained the reason for the segregationist policy of his union, he invoked the "Australian example." Yet, while his Australian connection was crucial, it was not the only site that had shaped his labor politics. Indeed, before finally settling in the Transvaal, Mathews tested his ideas of race and class in the mining district of Butte, Montana, in the 1880s and early 1890s.[54] Thus, Mathews could have just as easily appealed to an "American example." Mathew's imperial sojourns shaped a militant, racialized class consciousness that fused racist xenophobia with radical trade unionism.[55]

These interimperial movements and exchanges profoundly shaped the labor politics of anti-Asian agitation in the Pacific Northwest borderlands. J. E. Wilton's extensive experience with the "coolie" problem based on his sojourns through the empire made him a leading authority on issues of Asian immigration and exclusion within the region's working-class community. In fact, a local Vancouver newspaper invited him to share his knowledge in an editorial, in which he was introduced as a "British gentleman of world-wide travel and a gentleman who has had exceptional opportunities of studying the Asiatic and cheap labor problems at first hand in Africa, Australia, New Zealand, and British Columbia." Penned only a few months before the mass anti-Asian rally in Vancouver, Wilton's piece argued that Canada was at a crucial juncture in its history: The nation would have to decide soon whether it wanted to go the way of the Crown's colony in Natal in southern Africa—where he had witnessed "honest working white men who fought for the country walking the streets by days, sleeping in the parks by nights," a consequence of capitulating to capitalist demands for "cheap Asiatic labor"—or the way of Australia and New Zealand—where "there is prosperity and contentment" and in "none of the cities of these countries will you have to jostle in the streets with Chinese, Japanese, and Hindus," owing to the governments' "stringent Asiatic laws and a determination to keep their country pure." In Australia and New Zealand, Wilton argued, "the capitalists obeyed the law and employed white men at a white wage," thereby preserving the colonies of Australasia as a "veritable white man's paradise."[56]

Joining other imperial transplants, Wilton lobbied Canadian officials to adopt stricter immigration policies against Asian groups, expressing a preference for literacy tests, like those instituted when he was in Australia and

New Zealand. He argued, "What is needed here is the same stringent law as Australasia has. A mere poll tax is not sufficient because any importer of foreign labor will advance a few dollars to land his cheap labor, even if it takes several months work to get the payment. In Australia an Asiatic cannot land unless he can write 50 words of English from dictation. Whilst in New Zealand an Asiatic must write an application in English." He cited statistical evidence to prove the effectiveness of those policies: "In 1881, there were 5,000 Chinese in New Zealand; today there about 2,800," emphasizing that "Canada should welcome institutions adapted to democratic institutions and twentieth-century civilization."[57] Only by doing so, Wilton claimed, could Canada avoid the fate of becoming another Natal, the preeminent symbol of "the white man under siege" in the Anglophone colonial settler world.[58]

Serving as a persistent example of white declension, the South African colony of Natal evoked images of Asian hordes overwhelming the white settler world, and it became part of a racial vernacular that helped perpetuate a "yellow peril" discourse. Between 1860 and 1911, 152,000 South Asians arrived in Natal, mostly as indentured laborers for the colony's sugar plantations. A majority remained and settled in Natal after their contracts had expired, becoming shopkeepers, street peddlers, artisans, and farmers. By the turn of the century, South Asians outnumbered white settlers, a demographic trend that—combined with the South Asian community's growing success in farming—provoked a fierce backlash from white settlers, who resorted to restrictive immigration policies to assuage racial anxieties over the viability of white supremacy. They enacted legislation requiring that all potential immigrants read a European language to be considered for admission, which dramatically curtailed the number of South Asians coming into Natal.[59]

Nevertheless, white labor activists in British Columbia continued to invoke the Natal example as a warning of the inevitable Asian invasion that would take place if Chinese, Japanese, and South Asian immigration continued to go unchecked. One prominent Canadian unionist, using his "personal observation extending over several years," explained how the "Hindoo has slowly but surely displaced the white man in the Garden Colony," and "like the camel in the fable, the Hindoo has turned the trick on the white man, and now has practically the whole tent to himself." "The Hindoo," according to this well-traveled activist, "has carried into Natal his native customs and religions, his indecent and filthy modes of living, his child marriages, his wife slavery, and all the degrading customs he practiced in India" and, in doing so, "has made the fair Garden Colony a new Hindustan, and this is the price Natal paid for her supply of cheap labor." "Is Canada to be committed to a similar fate?" he asked.[60] Indeed, at stake was nothing less than the survival of the white race. "The fate of Canada, as a white man's country, is in the balance," he insisted. "The great question whether this country of ours is to be the heritage of our children or the heritage of the yellow and black races, must be decided now." He admonished that white supremacy was not a given, as Natal vividly illustrated. Thus, preserving the history of Anglo-Saxon expansion, progress, and triumph for white children would require the mass and concerted action of the white working class, which carried within itself the burden of empire. "But Canada, most progressive of all the British Dominions in most respects, purposes, in spite of the lesson to be learned from Natal, in spite of the example set by Australia, New Zealand, and others, to allow the Hindoo to do in Canada exactly what he has done in Natal," he complained vociferously.[61]

The cautionary tale of Natal was told and retold by white labor leaders in every dominion of the empire. In June 1907, William Bowden, the world-traveling labor activist and politician from South Africa, narrated the Natal example to white workers in Australia: "A shocking example of what the continued presence of Chinese in freedom would mean is afforded by Natal, one of the fairest countries ever seen." Calling it an "alien curse," Bowden reported regretfully that "Natal is simply owned and run by Hindoos, who were brought out under a three-year agreement to work the sugar plantations, and were afterwards allowed to remain as free men." But not all the news was bad, he continued, citing the important lessons that his own Transvaal government drew from the Natal example: "There was cause for gratification, however, in the fact that the Boer Government means to expel the Chow from the country." "For the benefit of posterity," the *Worker* asserted, "it is to be hoped that the anti-Asiatic ordinance respecting the Transvaal will not be thrown out by the British government."[62] In this way, the Natal discourse in the Anglophone settler world played a symbolic role that was analogous to the one played by Haiti in the Atlantic world, raising the specter of race war and savagery.[63]

White labor activists in British Columbia raised the threat of another Natal and exploited the imagery of "yellow" domination that accompanied it to justify increasingly restrictive regimes of exclusion. "We have succeeded in a measure in getting the ears of a capitalistic government to listen to our cries when we got the head tax on the Chinese increased from $50 to $500, but we shall not rest until we get total prohibition of the yellow peril," one activist declared.[64] Moreover, the telling and retelling of stories of white decline defined the struggle against Asian immigration as an imperial one that wrote Canada into solidarity with other white settler societies. The *Vancouver World* editorialized that unless whites dealt with the "Asiatic problem" decisively, the region would devolve into a cauldron of racial strife as seen elsewhere in the Anglophone world. "No elaboration of ethics or expressions of sentiment will solve the difficulties of the southern states of America or the newer troubles of the South African Dominions, and if Canada is not to become worse 'mired' than either of these countries there is a need for a much more businesslike and drastic handling of the Asiatic problem [that] has yet occurred."[65]

These dire predictions of a future racial dystopia inspired white labor activists on both sides of the boundary line to mount a significant, if disjointed, campaign against Chinese, Japanese, and South Asian immigrants. In addition to excluding Asian laborers from their unions, white workers stood at the forefront of political efforts to curtail and regulate Asian immigration to Canada and the United States. By engaging in racist practices across borders, ranging from exclusionary politics to organized racial uprisings, white labor leaders and activists instilled substance and reality into the rhetoric of white unity, facilitating the development of a racialized borderland proletariat.

BORDERLAND RIOTS AND VIOLENCE

At the center of the new anti-Asian movement in the Pacific Northwest was A. E. Fowler, the secretary of the Seattle Asiatic Exclusion League. Fowler was hailed as the second coming of Dennis Kearney, the former leader of the California Workingman's party who had organized the "Chinese must go" movement in the 1870s. This is how one contemporary described him:

> Fowler has all of Kearney's fire, earnestness, and honesty, and is way above him in ability and education. Kearney, with all his ignorance, did more for this country by his anti-Chinese agitation of a decade ago than any other one man has ever done on this coast. The anti-Japanese crusade presents more intricacies, but it has at its head a man capable and determined to unravel them. Fowler is the brains of this movement, and although like Kearney he is certain of denunciation as a "demagogue" the time will come when his name will be put upon the roll of patriots.[66]

Fowler was affiliated with the Asiatic Exclusion League, which was first established in San Francisco in 1905, under the rubric of the Japanese and

Korean Exclusion League and with the endorsement of local union officials. The migration of South Asians, in addition to the lingering problem of Chinese immigration, compelled members to modify the group's name in December 1907, to reflect more accurately the organization's vision and goals.[67]

The founders of the league had transnational aspirations, establishing branches up and down the Pacific coast of North America, including in Victoria, Vancouver, and Nanaimo in British Columbia, and in Port Townsend, Seattle, Bellingham, Spokane, Everett, and Tacoma in Washington.[68] In doing so, the league was building on a long tradition of cross-border labor organizing started by the Knights of Labor back in the mid-1880s. They promoted the ideal of a "white man's country" throughout the Americas, and as a symbol of this effort, Fowler partnered with A. W. Von Rhein, the president of the Exclusion League in Vancouver, to organize a mass demonstration to be held on September 7, 1907, in Vancouver. The scheduled anti-Asiatic rally emblematized the effort to build white labor solidarity across borders. The organizers advertised the event in labor newspapers and journals and sent invitations to working-class groups and organizations throughout the North American West. In August, the *Vancouver World* reported that "a movement is on foot to have a meeting held in Vancouver of delegates from the various anti-Asiatic leagues from all points on the Pacific coast."[69]

But just as organizers were making final preparations for the September 1907 protest, news of expulsions of South Asians in Bellingham, Washington, spread throughout the region. The first wave of South Asians had migrated to the Pacific Northwest in 1903, when over four hundred Sikhs from the Punjab region arrived at the port of Vancouver. Many of the early Sikh immigrants served in the British colonial military prior to making the long journey from Calcutta to Hong Kong and finally to British Columbia. The number of Punjabi Sikhs, Indian Hindus, and other South Asian immigrants grew steadily after this first wave, and peaked to over five thousand in 1907.[70] The host society received them much in the way they received earlier Chinese and Japanese immigrants. As the U.S. superintendent of immigration in Seattle explained, "The people of British Columbia, for the most part, have taken a strong objection to the Hindus and have protested against any further immigration of this class." The Hindus, in fact, were "regarded by many people there as less desirable than either Chinese or Japanese."[71] Not surprisingly, South Asians would go on to experience the same pattern of treatment as previous generations of Asian immigrants: first as victims of white racial violence and later as targets of exclusionary policies and procedures.

Bellingham had become a popular destination for South Asian migrants from Vancouver who were attracted by the promise of higher wages offered by lumber mills across the border. White residents accused the new arrivals of usurping their jobs and lowering their wages, calling it a "Hindu invasion." The *American Reveille*, published in Bellingham, Washington, reported on the rising racial tensions and warned that "unless drastic measures are soon taken to suppress the Hindu colony of South Bellingham there is danger that the indignant citizens of that portion of the city will rise up and deal with the brown intruders in their own way. The Hindu colony has assumed proportions as to become a menace, and the people are anxious that something be done to bring about change."[72] These dire predictions started to come to fruition on Labor Day, September 2, 1907. In the midst of the day's festivities, white workers spontaneously attacked South Asians, nearly instigating a riot. Two nights later, in an undertaking that was a bit more organized, a mob of between "400 and 500 white men of every age" marched into the "different colonies of Hindus," committing random acts of racial violence.

By making little effort to preserve law and order or to provide protection for the South Asians, Bellingham's elected officials and leading citizens gave white rioters almost free reign in their racist campaign to forcibly remove the "Hindu menace" from the community. One South Asian lamented that, "Bellingham was no good place for Hindus, and that none of them would ever return to the city again." According to this exile, they were "convinced that they would certainly be murdered if they presumed to remain after the warning given to them by the rioters." While some residents of the city took exception to the method, almost all of them were in agreement that the riots, in the end, served the public good. "What was once their Mecca, and the first stopping place of the invasion into the Sound country will now be free of them. Reports of their chilly reception here and of their spectacular expulsion will be spread among the British Columbia immigrants from Hindustan by the Bellingham exiles and none of them will be bold enough to visit the city of which the ex-locals give such a bad account."[73] The Bellingham riots and the expulsion of South Asians were signs of things to come. The following day, the Seattle Exclusion League sent an ominous letter to President Roosevelt, urging him, "in view of the Bellingham anti-Hindu riots, to take immediate action in checking the Oriental immigration into the Northwest." Written in a tone of prophetic utterance, the communication

FIGURE 3.1. Displaced South Asians huddle in the basement of the Bellingham, Washington, City Hall after being attacked by white workers during 1907 Labor Day celebrations. Reprinted from *Collier's Magazine,* Sept. 28, 1907.

further declared that "if something were not done soon the agitation started in Bellingham would spread all over the Sound country and massacres of the Eastern aliens were likely."[74]

With the "Oriental problem" fresh on the minds of white laborers, league organizers from Seattle and Vancouver moved forward with the anti-Asiatic parade as planned. The September 7 Vancouver demonstration attracted more than twenty-five thousand participants from across the region, including officials from fifty-eight labor organizations. The U.S. labor movement was well represented with the attendance of Frank Cotterill, the president of the Washington State Federation of Labor, George Lishman and J. W. Blaine of the Seattle Central Labor Council, C. O. Young, the chief AFL Pacific Northwest organizer, John Campbell, the international secretary of the Shingle Weavers' Union, and, of course, A. E. Fowler of the Seattle Asiatic Exclusion League.[75] Thousands of marchers, carrying anti-Asian placards and flags, paraded through the streets of Vancouver, affirming white supremacy. On the steps of city hall, invited speakers took turns expounding on the evils of Asian immigration. The orators included white labor activists from across the Pacific world.[76] They made demands for stricter immigration policies, citing those in South Africa and the Australasia settler colonies as models. The white working-class crowd roundly cheered the calls for stricter immigration enforcement and the scathing criticisms of the Dominion government. The inflammatory rhetoric roused the audience to a fever pitch, setting the stage for the racial violence that followed.[77]

During the procession, a group of white participants went into the Chinese and Japanese districts in downtown Vancouver, instigating a small clash with

FIGURE 3.2. The 1907 riots in Vancouver, British Columbia, caused extensive damage to Chinese and Japanese businesses. Facing pressure from the ravaged communities, the Canadian government ordered an investigation to determine compensation. The Japanese proprietor of the storefront shown in this photograph was awarded $139 in damages. University of British Columbia Library, Rare Books and Special Collections.

Asian residents. For a time, it appeared that the minor disturbances would lead to wider social disorder and chaos. However, the militancy of Asian residents forestalled further violence and turmoil. When the white mob returned to the scene the next night, looking to stir further trouble, they found that the Japanese and Chinese had barricaded their quarters and were fully prepared to defend themselves. Armed with guns, Asian residents successfully repelled further attacks, thus squashing white rioters' hopes of expelling them from the city. Furthermore, Chinese and Japanese community leaders called on Asian workers to go on strike to underscore the importance of their labor to the local economy. The *Ottawa Free Press* reported that "Chinese and Japanese labor was completely suspended throughout the city yesterday. Brown and yellow laborers in mills, restaurants, and west end residences were ordered by their own leaders to abstain from work. The evident intention is to demonstrate that Oriental labor is a necessity in the existing situation."[78] Likewise, the *American Reveille* described how Japanese migrant workers "from all parts of the district, from logging camps and from canneries, from vessels, restaurants, and hotels" were leaving their jobs and converging on

FIGURE 3.3. L. Fongoun and Company after the 1907 riots in Vancouver, British Columbia. This store was one of over a hundred Chinatown businesses that filed claims for damages, which totaled about $26,000. University of British Columbia Library, Rare Books and Special Collections.

Vancouver in a show of solidarity for their besieged countrymen.[79] The show of force by Vancouver's Chinese and Japanese communities rapidly brought the violence to a halt but not before the rioters caused tens of thousands of dollars in damages and inflicted injuries on dozens of Asian residents.[80]

Labor leaders insisted that the "selfish policy" of "Messers. Capitalists" were to blame for the riots as the mob violence was merely "expressions of an exasperated people."[81] South Asian writer Girindra Mukerji offered a similar analysis but refused to exonerate the white working class for their riotous actions: "Their presence here has been due to the organized American or Canadian capitalist, demanding labor for the upbuilding of railroads and other industries." Yet, as he pointed out, "the mob vented their unthinking revenge on the Hindus, but little did they think for had they stopped for thought they would not have failed to see that it is their own people at home who were responsible for the presence of Asiatic labor. The Canadian Pacific Company for years packed the Asiatic in their steerage places and gave them ready employment in their railroads. Nobody in Canada would think to say a condemning word to the strongly established company, nor could the emigration laws touch a single hair of high officials of the company."[82]

In an attempt to quell social unrest on the west coast, both the United States and Canada adopted new measures restricting Asian immigration, following a familiar colonial pattern in which racial riots almost always resulted in the implementation of exclusionary policies. Regulations against Asian immigrants, however, were not identical across the Anglophone colonial world. The policies had to conform to local political realities and were inflected by national differences; some white settler societies resorted to taxes and literacy tests whereas others relied on executive agreements and legal quotas.[83] In this particular instance, Canada and the United States consummated agreements with Japan, known as the "Gentlemen's Agreements," which set numerical limits on Japanese immigration to North America. The Japanese government agreed to limit passports to certain categories of people including diplomats, merchants, students, and tourists. The U.S. Gentlemen's Agreement became official policy in 1907 while the Canadian version, also known as the Hayashi-Lemieux Agreement, went into effect several months earlier.[84] For the United States, this agreement came on the heels of a presidential executive order that barred Japanese migration from Hawai'i.

On the ground, the riots intensified and sharpened the racialization of Chinese, Japanese, and South Asian immigrants, with the real and imagined characteristics of Asian workers serving for white workers as disparaging markers of difference. Indeed, anti-Asiatic rioting became rituals of racial and community solidarity through which a diverse array of European immigrants and transplanted Americans and Canadians imagined and performed a white working-class identity. As scholars have shown, traditions of mob violence, crowd rioting, and effigy burnings were not merely acts of political and social protest; they were also constitutive of group consciousness, which was, in the words of historian Phil Deloria, "materialized through one's body and through the witness and recognition of others."[85] In much the same manner, the race riots in the borderland cities of Bellingham and Vancouver facilitated working-class acculturation and racial assimilation for European immigrants.

Several days after the racial upheavals, Dan Riley, a recent Irish immigrant and laborer for the Great Northern Railway in British Columbia, quit his job, and the reason he gave showed just how rapidly he had imbibed the logic of white supremacy: "When it comes to working under a Japanese foreman in a white man's country it is going too far. . . . Before I would do that I'd square my mainsail and run before the wind."[86] One British Columbia newspaper advanced its notion of whiteness when it asked the following rhetorically: "Are we to have this great big province—a land virtually flowing in milk and honey—conserved for the best interests of the white British subject—English, Scott, Irish, Welsh, etc.—or must it be given over entirely to the yellow and brown hordes of China and Japan?"[87]

Anti-Asian rioting helped clarify the whiteness of Scandinavian workers as well. As non-English-speaking people, early Norwegian and Swedish immigrants were often marginalized by native-born white Euro-Americans and Canadians in the Pacific Northwest.[88] However, the riotous opposition to Asian immigrants smoothed over some of the linguistic, and in some cases, ethnic, religious, and national differences among these groups. A small band of Swedish longshoremen, for instance, precipitated a small riot against "fantastically turbaned Hindus" in Seattle only days after the Vancouver riots. The incident started with the Swedes "taunting and jeering" South Asians who were part of the exodus from Bellingham. In this particular case, however, the South Asian refugees refused to be victimized. The "men from India" made a "rush for their tormenters," and "when the Swedes took refuge in a vacant building and barred the doors, even this did not stop the Hindus, several of whom mysteriously came forth with axes and were hammering down the barrier."[89]

By this time, Fowler had made his way back to Washington to continue his anti-Asian agitation. In Bellingham he began planning another mass demonstration. Despite the earlier expulsion of South Asians from the city, Chinese and Japanese continued to work in Bellingham's restaurants, commercial fisheries, and salmon canneries, and thus race relations remained strained there. Seeking to build on momentum of recent events, Fowler—with the support of the Bellingham Central Labor Council—scheduled a rally for September 22.[90] Fearing that another riot might develop out of the mass meeting of white workers, Japanese residents armed themselves and formed a committee to organize a defense of their community. They also received cross-border assistance from their brethren in British Columbia. The *Vancouver World* reported that "the Japanese began buying arms and cartridges early this morning and 300 are now fully armed. It was later learned that the Orientals held a mass meeting last night, attended by delegates from Vancouver."[91]

Hopes of averting another racial conflict came in the form of a letter from K. Sasaki, the general secretary of the Japanese Union in Seattle, addressed to the Bellingham Central Labor Council, in which he requested a meeting with labor officials to discuss the possibility of affiliating with their union. Sasaki organized the Japanese Union in February 1907, and had close to seven hundred members on his rolls by the time the letter went out, with about a hundred of them working in Bellingham's salmon canneries. Ed Hofercamp, secretary of the Central Labor Council, agreed to meet with Sasaki and his interpreter in Bellingham. According to published reports, Sasaki claimed that "the Japanese in nearly all of the coast cities were forming organizations, and it is the intention of extending the influence throughout the United States. The object of the organization is to establish closer relations with the labor unions, to raise the standard of wages among the Japanese and to prevent the importation of Japanese contract labor." In making his case for an interracial alliance, Sasaki emphasized their common class interests. "They claim to be working for the same principles which dominate the American labor unions, and they desire to affiliate with the American workmen," the *Seattle Union Record* reported. "Sasaki asserts that the importation of large numbers of Japanese laborers would injure the Japanese union man as well as the American unionist." Sasaki did acknowledge the disparity between Japanese and white workers' wages, but he contended that unionization would "elevate the wage scale of his countrymen near to that of the Americans."[92]

Those members involved in the conference agreed to allow him to make a similar presentation to a larger audience at the next Central Labor Council gathering. At that meeting, however, before Sasaki was given a chance to speak, A. E. Fowler preempted his proposal by shouting a constant stream of racial insults and taunts at him, prompting Sasaki to storm out of the meeting. "Sasaki went to the meeting with the intention of speaking, should Fowler give him an opportunity to speak. Yamato, speaking for him, says he left the hall because Fowler did not talk like a gentleman." The Japanese were "keenly disappointed over the reception they received from Fowler, who addressed several of his remarks in their direction." A reporter for the local paper commented that the "Japanese as a people never received from a public platform in Bellingham a more severe arraignment as to their morals than that delivered by Fowler."[93]

Fowler was not alone in his disdain and mistrust of Sasaki and his proposal to join the union movement. Indeed, union officials were deeply suspicious of him: "This wily Seattle Jap appeared before the Trades Council of Bellingham recently with a proposition to amalgamate American and

Japanese labor unions on the Sound. The fact that the Japs have organized among themselves is in itself not a sufficient reason for entertaining the proposition." Denying that racial prejudice had anything to do with the union's rejection of Sasaki's offer, they insisted that "trade-unionism knows no race distinction" and that "any man, no matter what his nationality, will be admitted to an American labor union if he possesses the right principle." Sasaki's interest in joining their unions, they claimed, had little to do with empowering Japanese and American workers, but was instead about "carry[ing] out their spying tactics" with his main objective being, "to serve the Mikado."[94]

Unable to secure a hearing with white unionists, Sasaki spent the rest of his time in Bellingham enrolling new members into his union and speaking with local authorities about protecting his countrymen in case of another white uprising. Fowler's mass demonstration, however, never materialized as the labor activist became embroiled in a fund-raising scandal, which discredited his work for the Asiatic Exclusion League in Bellingham. A couple of weeks later, his promising career as a leading anti-Asian activist ended suddenly when he was committed to an "insane" asylum. The same white unionists who had lauded his achievements only weeks before now described him as a "raving manic" who "kept up a wild harangue on the imaginary Japanese invasion," diagnosing his condition facetiously as "Oriental on the brain."[95]

Sasaski's efforts to achieve interracial unionism were almost destined to fail from the beginning. The riots in Bellingham and Vancouver had polarized race relations to new extremes, and any dreams of working-class interracial unity had died in the disorder and the violence of those September days. The fraught environment was due, in no small part, to the growing militancy of Asian workers in the aftermath of the riots. For example, in the logging town of Mukilteo, Washington, Japanese lumber workers grew increasingly defiant upon hearing the news of the racial violence committed against their countrymen in Vancouver. It was reported that, "the Japs for several days, since the outbreak against them in Vancouver have loafed at their work in the Mukilteo mill, becoming insolent and cursing their white bosses when told to exert themselves."[96] Even more alarming to white residents, the Japanese armed themselves with revolvers, raising the possibility of a "race war" in Mukilteo.

At a different lumber mill in Aberdeen, Washington, local police arrested two South Asian immigrants for assaulting a Finnish foreman. Occurring several days after the riots, the altercation started when the South Asian workers refused to perform a task for the foreman. Following a heated

FIGURE 3.4. This cartoon depicts A. E. Fowler, a key figure in the Asiatic Exclusion League and one of the organizers of the 1907 Vancouver, British Columbia, labor demonstration that resulted in a violent race riot. Fowler was committed to an insane asylum only two weeks after the riots, haunted by the specter of the "yellow peril," according to a labor newspaper that had previously been a supporter of Fowler. Reprinted from *American Reveille,* Sept. 28, 1907.

exchange, one of the South Asians struck the Finnish foreman with a piece of lumber, sending him to the local hospital. The mill owner, A. J. West, while issuing bail for his two workers, told the chief of police that "the white men had been aggravating the Hindus for some time and that there had been bad blood between them."[97] In a similar incident, several weeks later in October, Japanese laborers M. Terada and J. Shindo attacked Sam Cole with a pickax at the Great Northern roundhouse near Bellingham.[98] Radicalized by the riots, Japanese and South Asian laborers became much more militant in the face of white provocation. These everyday acts of resistance signaled to white workers that they would not easily bend to the will of white supremacy.

CONCLUSION

The shared experiences of labor mobility, border crossings, and organizing against Asian immigrants gave rise to a transnational white working-class movement in the Pacific Northwest borderlands. White labor activism and rioting emerged from the mass and concerted politics of anti-Asian agitation. By participating in race riots, calling for immigration restriction, and establishing nativist organizations such as the Asiatic Exclusion League on both sides of the imaginary line, white workers developed a racialized class consciousness that cut across national boundaries. This cross-border working-class community was animated by intercolonial movements and exchanges that brought transient Anglo laborers into contact with anti-Asian movements and ideologies in Australia, New Zealand, and South Africa. Paradoxically, however, the imperial circulation of working people and their ideas was ultimately actualized through national movements and campaigns for Asiatic exclusion and its concomitant white supremacy, which, in turn, gave birth to distinct "white men's countries"—a "White Canada," a "White Australia," and so forth. Thus, even as the Pacific Northwest became part of a global pattern of anti-Asian racism and riotous working-class politics, local dynamics shaped nationally specific results. Working-class whiteness was, then, constituted in multiple places and varying scales, from the local and national to the imperial and global.

FOUR

Pacific Insurgencies

REVOLUTION, RESISTANCE, AND THE RECUPERATION OF ASIAN MANHOOD

IN 1908, THE *VANCOUVER WORLD* reported that South Asian anticolonial activists were "subscribing money for seditious purposes" in British Columbia, turning the province into a veritable "centre for revolutionary agitation." Elaborating on this new foreign menace, the paper claimed that, "there is a certain school there, ostensibly for the instruction of Indians in English which is actually being managed by agitators for the purpose of imbuing Sikhs with revolutionary ideas."[1] The Colonial Office in London, similarly, maintained that a clandestine revolutionary cabal was operating out of the Pacific Northwest. "I have been informed that it is likely bombs are manufactured in Vancouver and also probably in Victoria," as one colonial official testified. "Men have been taught there on the Coast how to make bombs, and are capable of readily assembling the parts when same have been successfully smuggled across the Pacific."[2] With this, the problem of transpacific Asian migration was recast, from one concerned with the invasion of inferior and inassimilable aliens to one about foreign insurgency and revolutionary violence.

The threat of foreign subversion, both real and imagined, grew more dire when U.S. officials in the Immigration Bureau passed on intelligence that South Asian nationalists were joining forces with other radical groups in the region. In 1914, U.S. immigrant inspector Charles Riley reported that, "as evidence of their proficiency in the art of "blowing people up," I was assured that most of the members of the Hindu nationalist party were also "IWWs."[3] He was, of course, referring to the Industrial Workers of the World, who had recently made waves by mobilizing workers to take direct action against some of the most powerful corporations in the North American West, leading to a series of violent confrontations with the ruling elite that roiled the region.[4] Accustomed to using race as a wedge issue to divide workers, the region's capitalists were also concerned to hear that the IWW was organizing around the principle of interracial unionism with the aim of broadening the labor movement. The organization's opposition to the color bar, moreover, opened the possibilities to new political alliances and mixing of white and Asian radicals. The merger of "militants and migrants" would therefore pose a profound threat not only to capitalist relations but also to national security.

The revolutionary bonds between the Industrial Workers of the World and diasporic South Asian anticolonialists coalesced around emancipatory visions that transcended the nation-state. For white labor radicals in the Pacific Northwest, the independence struggle in India provided a way to imagine a worldwide revolution against global capitalism. Indeed, the militant anticolonialism of the South Asian revolutionaries that called for the immediate overthrow of British rule on the subcontinent resonated deeply with IWW leaders and activists, for it spoke to their own hopes for a revolutionary workers' internationalism. South Asian revolutionaries, in turn, adopted strands of the class-based internationalism of the IWW, among other ideas, to generate a diasporic nationalist consciousness among colonial subjects in exile. This was, then, a case of a workers' internationalism finding expression in a global liberation movement, and vice versa.

These mutually constituted internationalisms were also bound together by a shared imagining of insurgency as a gendered cause, by the vision of a coalition of virile white and Asian men rising up to overthrow the ruling elite. In the Pacific Northwest, the transnational cultural politics of South Asian revolutionaries to recuperate South Asian manhood—so as to stake their claim to self-determination—intersected with white labor radicals' efforts to redeem Asian manhood as part of a strategy to transform Asian migrants into manly unionists worthy of class inclusion. This imagined gendered insurgency—in which the promise of liberation would be realized through virile subaltern men acting out their "manhood"—produced moments of interracial unity and interradical cooperation in the Pacific Northwest that was not tethered to the nation. But if the figure of the masculine revolutionary hero brought white and Asian radicals together in solidarity, it also, paradoxically, served to limit the possibilities of a lasting political alliance, forestalled, ultimately, by its own racial and gendered underpinnings. Being closely bound up with the ascendant ideas of manhood at the turn of the twentieth century, these gendered revolutionary discourses reproduced the historical pairing of whiteness and manliness.[5]

This contradiction aggravated, and was aggravated by, other cleavages between the two groups, fraying the alliance on multiple fronts. Of these, perhaps the most splintering was that the two political movements could never fully reconcile their respective visions: one a class struggle, the other, an anti-colonial struggle. There were, to be sure, instances when the programmatic aims and political commitments of white and South Asian radicals came into alignment, when IWW activists, for example, identified the racial character of colonial exploitation in India, which was a recognition that Western imperialism could not simply be reduced to a materialist dialectic, or when South Asian anti-colonial intellectuals attributed a capitalist logic to British imperialism, to its ever expanding drive for resources and markets that subordinated other classes and groups of people around the world. But these synergies were neither cultivated consistently nor deep enough to bridge the gulf between anti-capitalist and anti-imperialist forces in the region, resulting in a short lived interracial coalition.

This chapter, then, explores the convergent and divergent radicalisms of the South Asian diasporic revolutionary movement and the Industrial Workers of the World in the Pacific Northwest, showing how they were animated by, and helped to animate, larger struggles that were being staged across the Pacific and across the globe. The imperial networks that held together and perpetuated the empire simultaneously traced pathways through which a global politics of resistance circulated and proliferated. Refashioning the networks that knit together the empire into global circuits of resistance, South Asian anticolonial revolutionaries, white labor radicals, and Chinese nationalists all contested the terms of their incorporation into a world defined by Euro-American imperialism. But because their challenge adopted as much as they transcended the logic of a colonial modernity, they produced cross-cutting social movements that were as fragmented as they were united in the face of tightening imperial control. This was the condition of a subaltern politics born out of a Euro-American colonial modernity.

REVOLUTIONARIES IN THE DIASPORA

In the late nineteenth century, colonial India experienced a massive groundswell of nationalist sentiment and activities. Nationalist organizations, revolutionary clubs, and political newspapers and journals sprouted across India. While most of these expressions of nationalism were peaceful—which is why

British authorities gave sanction to their formation in the first place, believing they could channel anti-imperial sentiments into controllable native organizations and institutions—a small segment called for violent retribution resulting in several high-profile assassination attempts on British Crown officials on the subcontinent. The colonial state used the attacks as a pretext for a full-scale government crackdown on political dissent, as imperial authorities proceeded to round up and imprison "extremists," censor nationalist literature, and shut down nationalist organizations.[6] This heavy state repression led to the mass exodus of nationalist activists and intellectuals, who fled to North America, Asia, Europe, and Africa to continue the struggle for independence away from the immediate gaze of the colonial state.

Inspired by rising discontent over British imperial rule, South Asian nationalists mobilized a worldwide movement in the first two decades of the twentieth century. This transnational nationalist community was far from homogenous, fracturing along political, religious, and ethnic lines.[7] Yet, despite these cleavages, diasporic nationalists of various political persuasions were connected across space and time through the aspiration of a free India. The revolutionary paper *Ghadar* spoke to this imagined transnational nationalist community when it declared the following: "In London, Paris, Geneva, New York, San Francisco, Vancouver, Fiji, and Natal, in all these places patriots are working with a singleness of purpose for their country."[8]

The borderlands of the North American West emerged as a critical node within this larger network of political mobilization, becoming a site for perhaps the most radical brand of nationalist politics and resistance in the South Asian diaspora.[9] The director of criminal intelligence in India, C. J. Stevenson-Moore, called the area the "chief school for revolutionary Indians." "Many revolutionary activities in India," he explained, "were believed to be plotted in Pacific Coast cities." Citing a specific example, Stevenson-Moore noted that, "when Lord Hardinge's party was made object to a bomb attack in New Delhi, it was suspected that the bomb had been produced in Seattle."[10] South Asian revolutionaries would eventually connect these Pacific coast cities in North America to other points in the Pacific to form a loosely organized revolutionary network in which Vancouver, Victoria, Seattle, Portland, San Francisco, Manila, and Tokyo became links in a transnational revolutionary chain that anticolonial supporters hoped would end in an insurrection against British rule in India.

The siting of anticolonial diasporic politics was determined, in part, by South Asian radicals' imaginings of the United States and Japan as emblematic anticolonial projects. South Asian revolutionaries drew eclectically from a number of different intellectual traditions and sources but iconic American revolutionary figures—George Washington, Thomas Jefferson, Patrick Henry, and Thomas Paine—were especially prominent in their revolutionary writings and thoughts. In the United States, revolutionaries found inspiration in a nation born of rebellion against an empire—in fact, the very same empire they were squaring off against. In the case of Japan, South Asian radicals saw the country's stunning 1905 military victory over Russia as proof that Asian nations and peoples could match and perhaps in time eclipse the West; as such, Japan was a valuable model to study for South Asian revolutionaries.

In contrast to more moderate nationalists and reformers, such as those associated with the Indian National Congress and Mohandas Gandhi's passive-resistance movement in South Africa, anticolonial activists in British Columbia, Washington, and California called for the immediate overthrow of British rule in India and considered revolutionary violence a legitimate response to colonial power. Among the most active members of this revolutionary exile community in North America was Bengali nationalist Taraknath Das, who worked tirelessly to bring the group's anticolonial message to South Asian communities straddling the Pacific Northwest borderlands. British colonial agents had very early on identified him as a key player in the diasporic revolutionary movement. "The person whose movements he thought should receive special attention, is one Taraknath Das, the editor of a paper published in Vancouver, called *The Free Hindusthan*. This man makes his headquarters at Vancouver, and then for a time at Seattle, going to and fro considerably between these places."[11] Prior to his exile, Das had been an active member of the Bengali nationalist society known as the Anushilan Samiti.[12] The group was known for its militant tactics, having plotted a number of high-profile assassination attempts and bombings in India.[13] British colonial authorities were very close to apprehending Das in 1905 when he narrowly escaped to Japan.

Japan's military victory over Russia in 1905 had stirred new hopes of liberation on the subcontinent and across Asia and the Middle East.[14] Feted as a champion of Asian peoples, Japan became a gathering place for a small cadre of South Asian revolutionary activists, including Taraknath Das, who settled in Japan shortly following the war. Revolutionaries would however become quickly disillusioned with their host country, as authorities there showed little sympathy for their cause and, at times, were outright hostile to their liberationist agenda.[15] Having recently renewed the Anglo-Japanese alliance, the Meiji government came under pressure to not provide a safe haven for people considered enemies of the Crown. As a result, Das and other South Asian anticolonialists were now forced to continue the independence struggle elsewhere.

Following his expulsion from Japan, Das moved to the United States, arriving in San Francisco in 1906. A year later, he secured a position as an interpreter for the U.S. Immigration Bureau in Vancouver. In his capacity as Bureau translator, Das learned firsthand of the myriad ways Canadian and U.S. immigration laws discriminated against his countrymen. During his tenure, he clashed repeatedly with U.S. immigration officials over inspection procedures and administrative rulings involving South Asian immigrants, protesting their arbitrary enforcement. Immigration bureaucrats focused on several key statutes within U.S. immigration law to deny admissions to his countrymen. Das took particular exception to the way officials indiscriminately applied the LPC clause ("liable to become a public charge at time of entry") to South Asian immigrants. In 1908, for example, three hundred South Asians were excluded on this ground. Immigration authorities justified mass statutory exclusion by insisting that it was a humane response that saved South Asian immigrants from being victimized by aggrieved white laborers. "There is more than one way to become a public charge," U.S. Immigration Inspector Ellis de Bruler wrote, "and one of the ways in which these men would all finally become public charges would be the fact that American laborers would drive them from the fields and camps and then they would force us to feed and not only feed, but to protect [them] from violence which would ultimately ensue." The riots in Bellingham, Vancouver, and elsewhere had given authorities a convenient excuse "to refuse to open the gate," as one official put it.[16]

The U.S. Immigration Service also interpreted clauses on physical and mental defect, disease, contract labor, and moral turpitude as broadly as possible as part of its larger effort to exclude South Asian immigrants. The U.S. Bureau in Vancouver, for example, rejected more than 20 percent of South Asian applicants because of their polygamous beliefs, even though it was widely acknowledged among immigration officials that Sikhs, who represented the largest South Asian group in the Pacific Northwest, did not subscribe to the practice. As Dominion Immigration Officer Malcolm Reid reported, "polygamy is believed in and practiced by Mohammedans and Brahmins but not by Sikhs." He explained "the majority of East Indians in

FIGURE 4.1. Recent Sikh immigrant with two bags in Vancouver between 1900 and 1910. University of Washington Libraries, Special Collection, UW15673.

Canada are Sikhs, among whom there is no caste system and no polygamy." Yet in conversations with "U.S. Immigration Officers at Vancouver, I gather that they reject a considerable number of East Indian applicants for admission to the United States on the ground of belief in or practice of polygamy."[17] A departmental memorandum written for the U.S. Secretary of State in 1913 showed precisely why this was the case. "Since at least 1909 it has been the general policy of the Immigration Service to exclude Hindus. If such aliens

FIGURE 4.2. Sikh immigrants arriving in Vancouver between 1900 and 1910. University of Washington Libraries, Special Collection, UW18744.

were not found to belong to some of the definitely fixed and excluded classes such as paupers, criminals, or contagiously diseased, ground for exclusion was found either in the fact that they were person of poor physique (afflicted with physical defects affecting ability to earn a living) or that they were likely to become public charges."[18] As this clearly shows, U.S. immigrant inspectors were given the widest latitude possible to read and enact South Asian exclusion from existing statutes. Taraknath Das tried to combat the Bureau's exclusionary agenda by clandestinely coaching South Asian immigrants prior to their inspection.

Thoroughly transnational in his approach and politics, Das also went on to challenge the discriminatory features of Canadian immigration law and policy, establishing the Hindustani Association in Vancouver for the express purpose of supporting the immigration rights of South Asians in British Columbia. While still in the employ of the U.S. Immigration Service in Vancouver, Das organized a mass demonstration bringing together Canadian Sikhs, Hindus, and Muslims to protest the Continuous Journey Order (1908), which barred immigrants not coming directly from their country of origin. The technical language obscured its racist intent, as there was not a single steamship line providing direct service from India to Canada at this time. It was a duplicitous way of achieving South Asian exclusion without explicitly discriminating against them. In this regard, the Continuous Journey Order shared much in common with the 1907 executive order signed by President Roosevelt that banned Japanese migration from Hawai'i to the U.S. mainland. Das challenged the order-in-council, arguing that it violated the rights of British subjects. He maintained that South Asians were entitled to free movement within territories under British jurisdiction by virtue of their status as Crown subjects.

Das and the other South Asian revolutionaries fought so mightily against immigration restriction, not only for the fact that it made for good anti-imperial politics, but because they understood that the right of migration was not simply about freedom of movement but that it was bound up with the freedom to organize and resist from abroad. They realized what Hannah Arendt would recognize a half century later: "Freedom of movement . . . is the indispensable precondition for action."[19] This was the specific lesson Das drew from his earlier expulsion from Japan.[20] He and other revolutionaries recognized efforts to exclude South Asians from the United States, Canada, Australia, South Africa, and New Zealand as an imperial strategy to box in the diasporic nationalist movement. Not surprisingly, Das's immigrant advocacy eventually led to his dismissal from the Bureau, after which time he assumed a more active role in anticolonial politics and organizing.

Fellow activists Teja Singh and Hussain Rahim joined Taraknath Das in turning the immigration issue into a referendum on British imperial rule. The Sikh community in Vancouver had invited Teja Singh to be their religious leader just as the Dominion government was offering to "relocate" Canadian Sikhs to British Honduras, where "there was good demand for labour and ample land available for settlement." This scheme was proposed in the immediate aftermath of the Bellingham and Vancouver riots, as a solution to the "Hindu Problem." British colonial officials endorsed the plan and suggested that Canada "pay the expenses of a delegation of East Indians to British Honduras in order that the East Indians see for themselves whether Honduras would be a good place for them." Although the offer was ostensibly voluntary and subject to the approval of the Sikh community, the Dominion attached a thinly veiled threat to the proposal. "If Hindus are without work and without money this winter, and thus become public charges, they cannot be allowed to remain a charge on Vancouver, and will have to be deported."[21]

As the newly appointed leader of the Sikh community, Teja Singh rejected the government proposal, believing it to be an expulsion campaign in disguise. He accused Dominion officials of attempting to bribe the Sikh delegates who visited British Honduras, to elicit a favorable account of their trip. The U.S.

Immigration Bureau in Seattle was of the opinion that he was intentionally keeping "the issue alive by adroitly manipulating the proposal by the Canadian government to send indigent South Asians to British Honduras to make it appear to be a devious plot to deport all South Asians."[22] In place of the emigration plan, Teja Singh offered a vision of cooperative living where Canadian Sikhs would pool their resources to engage in business ventures that could support independent agricultural communities. To this end, Teja Singh formed the Guru Nanak Mining and Trust Company in Vancouver, which Dominion authorities alleged was nothing more than a cover for his revolutionary conspiracy. In 1908, U.S. immigration inspector P. L. Prentis reported to his superiors in Washington, DC that "This mining and trust company has been organized and is being used for the sole purpose for furthering the seditious plans of East Indians and that members of this company are being sent to the United States and elsewhere for the ostensible purpose of promoting the interests of the company, but in reality for the purpose of collecting funds to be used in the manufacture of bombs and other explosives."[23]

Revolutionary nationalists were venerated for openly and brazenly defying colonial authority on the immigration question, facilitating their rise as community leaders, which made their anticolonial message more credible in turn. A prime example of this strategy at work involved the enlistment of the generally "apolitical" Sikh immigrant community into the nationalist cause. The first wave of South Asian migrants to the Pacific Northwest came from the Punjab region. Prior to their emigration, these Punjabi Sikh migrants had served in the imperial military and colonial police force. As such, they seemed hardly the ideal group for fermenting revolutionary radicalism. In describing their political attitudes, historian Harish Puri has argued that, "these people had little political consciousness and nationalist interest when they arrived in North America. They had come from closed village communities and their aspirations related mainly to earning of money."[24] However, by highlighting immigration restriction as an egregious abuse of colonial power, revolutionary nationalists managed to persuade members of the Sikh immigrant community to their anticolonial cause. British intelligence pointed to this alarming trend in Vancouver, where revolutionaries "had worked up the Sikh labourers there to such an extent that those of them who had been soldiers in the Indian army and had war medals and army discharge certificates in their possession, burnt them on a bonfire at a public meeting; at the same time denouncing the British in violent terms."[25] The real danger behind this kind of political agitation, according to J. C. Kerr, assistant to the director criminal intelligence, "lies in the fact that the Indians concerned are Sikhs, many of whom have formerly served in the Indian army, and that on their return to India they are likely to sow the seeds of disaffection amongst the classes from which the Sikh regiments are recruited."[26]

THE GENDERED INSURGENCY

The issues surrounding South Asian immigration came to a head in the fall of 1912, when seventy-three South Asians from the Philippines were summarily rejected at the port of Seattle under the LPC statute. This was, of course, standard procedure by now, at least when it came to South Asian immigrants. But this particular case was not as open and shut as it first appeared. The South Asian immigrants from Manila should have been admitted without further examination under existing immigration protocol. The Philippines was, after all, a territory of the United States and so the administrative ruling to admit them in Manila should have been the final word on their admissibility. But in a logic hewing very closely to the ruling in the Insular Cases, immigration officials maintained that there was a distinction between the mainland of the United States and its insular possessions in matters of immigration, which justified the reexamination that led to the second administrative ruling.

For revolutionary activist Hussain Rahim, who was based in Vancouver, the ruling was a travesty of justice. He himself having been subject to the arbitrariness of immigration bureaucracy at the time of his entry; when Dominion officials, concerned with Rahim's radical ties, tried to deport him back to India, Rahim was especially invested in gaining justice for his detained brethren in Seattle.[27] Rahim had prior success using the legal system, having his own deportation ruling overturned by the courts, which allowed him to remain in British Columba, where he was instrumental in building a revolutionary network. Going back and forth between Vancouver and Seattle, Rahim mobilized support from South Asian communities on both sides of the border in the Pacific Northwest. For example, he hired counsel for the seventy-three South Asians awaiting hearing with funds provided by the United India League and the Hindustani Associations of Canada and the United States.

During a mass community gathering he organized in Vancouver, Rahim made an impassioned plea by appealing to the audience's affective ties to a wider imagined community that transcended territorial boundaries. "Tonight we have come here for the purpose of first of all out of great love for your country," he declared. "Now I ask you tonight why are you reaching out your hands to them" because "looking across the line there, we see your brothers" and "you love them and thus you try to help them as you stand between them and this deportation." Employing nationalist language to great effect, Rahim encouraged a shared sense of predicament stemming from their common colonial subjugation, emphasizing that South Asians everywhere—whether Hindus, Muslims, or Sikhs—were victims of white colonial oppression. "When these Canadians, Australians, and New Zealanders do not allow us to enter their country, why should we not drive them from India? We should take those steps and we could start a struggle and exclude those people from India."[28] This fiery proclamation recalled the defiant language that Rahim voiced at his own deportation hearing when he declared, "You drive us Hindus out of Canada and we will drive out every white man out of India."[29] The night ended with Rahim and fellow organizers collecting funds toward a bond to be posted on behalf of the Seattle South Asians. The bond was to be offered to the U.S. Immigration Service as insurance that the men would not become public charges.

This highly militant and capacious sense of national belonging constituting a radical transnational nationalist consciousness was largely imparted through the language of revolutionary manhood and as such, South Asian anticolonial resistance was, at least in part, lived through gender. Revolutionary activists very consciously represented the South Asian as a martial type full of virility, militancy, and physical prowess. Gendered tropes and metaphors were therefore a staple of revolutionary publicity. The masthead of the *Ghadar,* for example, read, "O People of India Arise and Take your Sword." The elements of this gendered revolutionary discourse could also be readily identifiable in a poem the revolutionary paper published in 1913:

> O people of India take this ship to shore
> Drive away the storm of troubles from you.
> All the world has risen up and we are left behind.
> You also build up your home and independence with your life-blood.
> Throw away your heavy feeling.
> O heroes get up and take the lead.
> All your gardens up and take the lead.
> Start to water them again and build them up.
> There is still life left among us to rise again.

But we must not leave it too late.
All over the world they call us useless.
Get up heroes and bring forward the name of your country.
Wake up the sleeping and the lover your countrymen far away.
Bring to light the land of India.
Bring her forward before the eyes of all the world.

This anticolonial vision of masculine South Asian brothers locked in arms in which a self-sacrificing manhood would emancipate the nation (signified by a woman) helped smooth over, however ephemerally, the myriad divisions fracturing the nationalist movement.

Beginning with the last quarter of the nineteenth century, British colonial authorities worked concertedly and deliberately to deracinate the manhood of South Asian nationalists as part of an imperial strategy to undermine the nationalist movement on the subcontinent and beyond. Portrayed as effeminate and childlike, South Asian nationalists were rendered unfit for self-rule, justifying an independence denied. Historian Mrinalini Sinha argues that this discursive move was an imperial state adapting itself to new challenges to colonial rule: "It was the shift in British colonial attitudes towards Western-educated Indians, from mediators between the colonial administration and the rest of the Indian population to an unrepresentative and artificial minority representing nothing but the anomalies of their own situation, that was signaled by the late nineteenth-century concept of the 'effeminate babu.'"[30] The figure of the effeminate babu stood for the degenerate Bengali male, and, more broadly, the Indian middle class—the personification of a pretentious and superficially refined group who, in reality, lacked internalized controls for manly, independent conduct. Leading revolutionaries Taraknath Das and Hussain Rahim, both Bengali intellectuals and Western-educated, embodied this imperial representation. The myth of the effeminate babu created a crisis of masculinity among the Bengali nationalist elite in India. They responded to the national problem of the emasculated Indian male subject by introducing a middle-class, reformist agenda that included building gymnasiums and promoting physical activity.[31]

South Asian revolutionaries in the North American West (and elsewhere), on the other hand, called for the redemption of national manhood through armed struggle, by literally taking up the sword. For revolutionaries, the anticolonial struggle was *the* test of South Asian manhood and, as such, revolutionary violence was simultaneously an act of masculine regeneration. "We have a right to create revolution in India," Das declared. "The only question is whether we have the desire and power to carry it out." Contending that their "national life is at stake" with the "British government in India [having] already adopted all possible repressive measures to crush our national aspirations," he implored his "dear brothers of Hindusthan" to "be united together and exert our best energies to get Swaraj—absolute self-government."[32] In his article, "Hindu Fitness for Self-Rule," Das harkened back to revolutionary men of the past: "Luther, Mazzini, Patrick Henry, Thomas Paine, and other workers for the cause of humanity . . . were invariably in the minority at the beginning and came out victorious in the end."[33] In this imagining of anticolonial resistance, the comity of brotherhood, manly honor, and the prerogative of self-rule were inextricably bound up.

The gendered analogies and metaphors revolutionary intellectuals employed should then be seen as a carefully scripted response to the colonial politics of masculinity that rendered them unmanly and therefore incapable of self-rule. This discursive strategy may have also been designed to reach their target constituency in the Pacific Northwest: The martial language of revolutionary manhood would have surely resonated with many South Asian Sikh immigrants, for it hewed closely to their virile self-image.[34] Yet, as postcolonial and feminist historians have convincingly argued, this counterdiscourse to resist imperial domination through the language of a virile manhood reproduced the hegemonic logic of colonial masculinity, which was deployed precisely to delegitimize nationalists' claim to self-determination.[35] In fact, South Asian revolutionaries could be found, at times, taunting their more moderate, reformist-minded countrymen in a gendered and sexualized language that was almost identical to the one articulated by their imperial overlords.

FORGING A TRANSNATIONAL REVOLUTIONARY PUBLIC

South Asian revolutionary activists understood very well that the fight against British imperialism was, by necessity, an ideological struggle. Therefore, they combined their advocacy work with sustained efforts to publish and disseminate their anticolonial message through newspapers, pamphlets, books, and public speeches. In April 1908, Das launched a revolutionary paper known as the *Free Hindusthan.* He used the paper as a platform to offer a withering critique of British colonial rule. "We are treated worse than cats and dogs of

Englishmen in the British colonies. Today the door of Hindusthan is open to the hungry Britishers and other colonists who are wrongfully robbing our nation while millions are yearly starving to death."[36] He printed the paper for worldwide distribution, mailing the *Free Hindusthan* to readers in India, England, Japan, South Africa, Germany, Southeast Asia, and the Philippines. Dominion authorities, responding to its sharply worded criticism of British colonial rule, moved swiftly to halt its publication and distribution.

Following his departure to Seattle, revolutionary activists Guran Ditt Kumar and Hussain Rahim continued the publicity campaign in British Columbia by starting their own papers. Kumar was a college instructor in Calcutta before migrating to Victoria in 1907. His contacts at the National College in Calcutta put him in touch with the revolutionary movement in Vancouver that included Taraknath Das, Surendra Mohan Bose, and Bhawat and Harnam Singh.[37] With financial assistance from Das, Kumar opened a storefront in Victoria, which he stocked with nationalist reading materials including copies of the *Free Hindusthan* and the anti-British paper *Indian Sociologist,* published in London. In 1909, Kumar relocated to Vancouver to become secretary of the Hindustani Association, and began circulating the *Swadesh Sewak* shortly after his arrival. British intelligence maintained that "[t]he paper was undoubtedly intended to reach the Sikh sepoys and ex-sepoys of the Indian army. It was written in their language by one of their countrymen, and dwelt on the unjust treatment suffered in Canada by ex-sepoys, and the copies were sent out to India to men in the regiments."[38] Concerned with the possible negative impact that the nationalist writings might have on some of their most loyal native troops, colonial officials prohibited the importation of the *Swadesh Sewak* under the Sea Customs Act of March 1911. Despite writing numerous letters to the Indian government protesting the order, Kumar was unable to remove his publication from the list of censored material and, as a result, he was forced to shut down the paper.

Hussain Rahim began publishing the *Sansar* in 1913 to oppose Canadian parliament member H. H. Stevens's plan to deny admission to immediate family members of South Asian residents. In his writings, Rahim contended that colonial authorities were behind every discriminatory measure taken against South Asians throughout the empire. "Bastards like Stevens the member of parliament for Vancouver, in the British Government, are using thousands of abusive epithets against our race. These people are cowards. The treatment of Hindus in Canada and South Africa is prompted by the British Government to ill-treat the Hindus as much as possible."[39] Dominion

Immigration Officer Malcolm Reid reported that, "over a thousand copies" of the revolutionary paper were addressed abroad "to the members of the International Congress of India . . . the organization which is pressing for self-government in India."[40] As part of a diasporic nationalist community, the scope of these publications reached well beyond the North American activist community, including activists and intellectuals in India, Japan, Hawai'i, Germany, South Africa, and the Philippines.

South Asian liberationist writings often referred to the Irish independence movement as a model for their revolutionary cause. "Twenty-five years ago Ireland was oppressed," the *Ghadar* explained, but as the Irish "took up arms and made use of bombs and dynamite and formed secret societies," they were ultimately successful in winning their country's freedom. And just as "Ireland has managed to free herself we should also believe that we can free ourselves and make India a republic in which her people have a whole say."[41] As Arun Coomer Bose has argued, allusions to Ireland were not merely for rhetorical effect. South Asian independence activists regularly accessed and consulted journals, newspapers, pamphlets, and other resources within the Irish American community, hoping for insights into their strategies of resistance.[42] And while the two groups on the west coast had little contact, South Asian revolutionaries expressed solidarity with the Irish based on their shared oppression under British colonial rule. "The Indian people should sympathize with the Irish in their loss, as they have the same enemy among them, and there should be a permanent friendship," declared the *Ghadar*.[43]

However, the question remains whether these revolutionary periodicals influenced South Asian immigrants in the Pacific Northwest. Was there an audience open to persuasion by these radical nationalist writings? Harish Puri contends, citing the English-written *Free Hindusthan* specifically, that the publications were not directed at South Asian migrant communities, but rather at reading publics in North America and around the world, for the purposes of influencing the educated classes within the diaspora, and gaining international support for the independence movement. His argument is based on the fact that South Asian laborers who comprised the bulk of the community were not literate.[44] Other scholars have disputed this assertion, insisting that many Canadian Sikhs were literate because of their previous assignments in the British military and police force.[45] Arguments on both sides of the debate presume that literacy is a necessary precondition for engaging and acquiring nationalist thought and consciousness. However, recent scholarship has shown that subaltern classes around the world participated in the public sphere of nationalist writings and ideas without being able to read or write. Nonliterate subjects from the sugar fields of Cuba to the colonial prisons in French Indochina actively discussed and debated the merits of the various publicities that the nationalist press generated.[46] And this was also true of South Asian migrant workers in the Pacific Northwest borderlands.

Revolutionary nationalists traveled up and down the Pacific coast, delivering pro-independence lectures in immigrant temples, societies, and reading rooms. The prominent Ghadar revolutionary Har Dayal, who led the radical movement from San Francisco, toured the Pacific Northwest in 1913, as part of an effort to raise revolutionary consciousness among South Asian residents in the U.S.-Canadian borderlands.[47] The U.S. Immigration Bureau described him as "a very violent Anglophone of frankly anarchist views" who was "delivering a course of lectures in Oregon and Washington, advocating anarchism."[48] In 1909, Taraknath Das and Guran Kumar established the United India House in Seattle, "where lectures were given every Saturday by [Das] and other Bengali students to the Sikh laborers." The mass meetings where such lectures were delivered also furnished opportunities for revolutionaries to inform nonreading compatriots of recently published newspaper articles and books. In one of the rallies protesting Canadian immigration restriction, independence activist Sohan Lal read anti-British poems and essays from various revolutionary periodicals to the audience.[49] Revolutionary activists also coordinated grassroots campaigns in the immigrant enclaves of Victoria and Vancouver, "preaching sedition from house to house," according to one British informant.[50]

The immigrant communities in these cities supplied the base from which to coordinate outreach to migrant workers. Anticolonial activists followed South Asian migrants workers into the hinterlands, bringing the gospel of Indian freedom to their work camps and bunkhouses. Because of their direct engagement, revolutionary leaders believed that they were making significant progress among this transient constituency. Das, for one, insisted that these Sikh laborers, once "the backbone of the British Empire in India," were now coming "in contact with free people and institutions of free nations" and were now assimilating "the idea of liberty." This political awakening was crucial in winning "over the native Indian army to the nationalist side." As Das explained, "We all know that the national uprising of 1857 would have been successful in throwing off the foreign yoke if our own people had not engaged in helping the tyrants. . . . [N]ow the problem before us is to see whether the native troops of the British government which number over 200,000 will again join hands with the tyrants or not. We believe not, if work could be carried on in giving the idea of the benefits of independence among the native troops."[51] British colonial officials also seemed aware of the potential impact that nationalist agitation in the North American West could have on the Indian countryside. They noted that "Sikh laborers on the Pacific Coast might come in time to assume a greater importance particularly in view of the indirect effects likely to be produced in the Punjab and elsewhere in India by a prolonged and carefully planned campaign of misrepresentation conducted by men like Taraknath Das and Guran Ditt Kumar among the Sikh immigrants in British Columbia."[52]

Their growing political consciousness was not, however, solely the work of the revolutionary literati; it was also the product of everyday conversations and interactions that took place in workers' bunks and cookhouses. In these spaces of migrant sociality, South Asian workers engaged one another in the political debates of the day. A literate member of the group informed others about news coming from India or read out loud nationalist writing, which then served as the basis for discussion among the entire group. Ranjit Hall, for example, described how, as one of the few literate members in company housing, he translated political literature on Sunday afternoons for South Asian workers in the Fraser Mills.[53] Similarly, another migrant laborer recalled the following: "In the cookhouse they'd have speeches about politics and all that, what's happening in India and who's right and what the Congress Party and the British are doing."

By the eve of the First World War, a loosely organized revolutionary structure had emerged with the movement's leadership organized around the cities on the Pacific coast. In 1914, British agents intercepted a communication between Guran Kumar and Taraknath Das that revealed the division of labor within the revolutionary movement. Writing from his new base in Manila, Kumar wrote to Das: "You should be pleased as I had left Seattle for you and Vancouver for him (Harnam Singh) and Victoria for Dr. Sundar Singh and California for Lala Har Dayal. In Portland, one Ramchand is coming. You fellows must do something co-operatively."[54] In late 1914 and early 1915, anticolonial leaders and activists mobilized their supporters on the west coast and across the Pacific to join the pending revolution on the Indian subcontinent.[55] Several Canadian Sikhs awaiting deportation in Seattle wrote to a fellow insurgent: "Even if they send us to India it will be alright. We will go and work in the revolution. Let us know about the revolution, also send us a copy of the Ghadar, and write all the news as to whether the revolution is started in India or not, and if the revolution is started we will not go straight home but will go and join the revolution."[56] Hundreds of South Asian Sikhs took up the call and departed the west coast for India, the Philippines, and Southeast Asia with the belief that they were about to join a coordinated uprising against British rule.

REDEEMING ASIAN MANHOOD

The militant anticolonial politics of the South Asian revolutionaries intersected and overlapped with the cultural campaign of the Industrial Workers of the World to redeem Asian manhood in a collaboration of white and Asian radicals, who were brought together around visions of a gendered insurgency in the Pacific Northwest. Unlike other labor organizations in the region, the IWW looked to organize Asian workers and was committed to the ideal of interracial unionism. Written in 1911, one activist editorialized that "[U]nion[s] could pass resolutions galore or try to kill the Orientals there, like some fools did about four years ago at Vancouver, but so long as labor is brought and sold upon the market, so long will the master class bring these people in to compete with us as sellers of labor power." The IWW therefore called on white workers to "do away with racial prejudice and imaginary boundary lines, recognize that all workers belong to the international nation of wealth producers, and clearly see that our only enemy is the capitalist class and the only boundary line is between exploiter and exploited."[57]

IWW activists took this vision of an interracial working-class internationalism directly into the logging, mining, and railway construction camps straddling the U.S.-Canadian boundary, organizing white and Asian workers on both sides of the imaginary line.[58] In doing so, they challenged at once the boundaries of race, class, and nation extant in the Pacific Northwest borderlands. These were, as one prominent activist insisted, nothing more than artifices of the ruling classes to keep workers divided and powerless. "The financier recognizes no boundary lines, no colors or creeds or races when it comes to profitable investments," as one IWW activist declared, "But he makes use of all ancient superstitions and prejudice in the form of patriotism, religion and race hatreds to protect his investments."[59] Actualizing these aspirations and ideas, IWW leaders "Big" Bill Haywood, Elizabeth Gurley Flynn, and John Riordan frequently traveled back and forth across the northern boundary to give speeches, organize workers, and to participate in strikes and protests. As a result of such intentional cross-border outreach, the IWW was able to establish nine locals across British Columbia by 1909, combining for a Canadian membership of close to 4,000.[60]

In their appeals for an interracial working-class internationalism, the IWW transformed Asian migrants into manly unionists deserving of class inclusion. IWW leaders and activists understood that their fight had to be waged on cultural as well as political grounds, and that their success in building an interracial and international labor movement would depend on their ability to chip away at the dominant representation of the Asian worker as "coolie" labor—perhaps the most preeminent figure of degraded manhood during this time. His was a manhood tainted by a fusion of race and class failing. Unskilled and footloose, his "sojourning," among other things, was a mark of his degradation. As the Seattle *Union Record* noted rather scornfully, "Deprive a Jap of work in one place and he will hustle until he gets another."[61]

White labor leaders across the political spectrum denied Asian migrants entry to their unions precisely on these grounds, insisting they lacked the accoutrements of manhood for working-class membership. The Socialist paper *Western Clarion,* for example, made the case explicitly when it editorialized the following: "The desire of the capitalist for cheap and servile labor, here is, no doubt, just as strong as elsewhere. . . . Industries have been prostituted by Asiatic corruption to such a low level that white workmen are debarred from honorable competition."[62] Merging the two most potent symbols of degradation in the late nineteenth century—the prostitute and "coolie" labor—Chinese, Japanese, and South Asian laborers were represented as thoroughly unmanly and therefore beyond the redemption of working-class organization and acculturation.[63] The servility to their corporate masters, the willingness to subject themselves to grinding poverty and a condition of dependence and insecurity, and their constant engagement in "women's work" all served as proof of their unmanliness, justifying their exclusion from the revolutionary vanguard of radical working-class organizations as well as the conservative craft unionism of the AFL.[64]

Hoping to facilitate their acceptance into the region's working class, IWW leaders and activists produced an alternative discourse of Asian manhood. Elizabeth Gurley Flynn projected an image of the Asian laborer as a highly class-conscious workingman who challenged the prerogatives of the capitalist boss at every turn. "He will go to work in a fruit country and he will wait until the fruit is ripe and then if it isn't picked at once it will spoil, out walks the Jap and he doesn't savvy anything but more wages; and he usually gets than more wages."[65] In the same vein, the *Industrial Worker* called the

Japanese the "most merciless" of any seasonal laborer while discussing how employers "bewail the mistake . . . in getting Japanese who will exact everything possible, if they have but a half a chance." Taking on the often-made charge that the Japanese were chronic strikebreakers, the leader of IWW local in Spokane, J. H. Walsh, insisted that "[t]he average Japanese simply will not scab. He knows too much, and is too much of a man."[66] Flynn concurred, insisting that the Japanese "once a union man, always a union man."[67]

IWW writers and activists also used these occasions to offer an incisive critique of the color consciousness of conservative craft unionism. In an article titled "Silly Race Prejudice," Walsh denounced the AFL porters' union for their efforts to expel Japanese labor from industrial competition. He asked, "Will any man explain just why, as long as the Japanese are here, it would not be better to unite with them to fight the common enemy, the master, than to waste time, energy and strength in fighting another group of workers simply on account of their color—to the huge delight of the employer?" Walsh opined that, "If the porters' union were but half as class conscious as the average Japanese worker, there would be better wages and better conditions for the porter than the wretched ones they are now forced to submit to."[68] "The American Federation of Labor, [remains] true to its sacred principles of dividing the working people either on craft line or those of race and religion."[69] Turning the tables on conservative white unionists, the IWW called the manliness of the AFL into question, insisting that it was they who failed to measure up to the standard of manhood. "The American Federation of Labor," they claimed, "is run in the interest of the employing class, and the bosses, big and little, are there to keep down the spirit and fighting blood of the workers." Thus, "any man who has the nerve and the backbone to stand up for what's right should leave this aggregation who have long since become merely a cat's paw for the bosses."[70]

Reversing traditional stereotypes, the IWW portrayed Asian workers as labor radicals who were willing to challenge the capitalist system while depicting white laborers as corporate lackeys devoid of manly courage. Using labor relations at the Port Blakely Mills as an example, IWW activists argued that the Japanese possessed the quality of "stick" that was essential to becoming a manly unionist. "The Japanese decided to ask for a raise of 20 cents per day. One morning they all rolled up their blankets ready to leave camp if their demands were not granted. The 20 cent raise was granted." In contrast, they contended that at the very same mill, white men were treated and driven like "Mexican peons" and earned fewer wages than the Japanese. They asked,

"How long will it be before the body of 5,000 American laborers will have the energy and manhood to strike in a body? Many of those patriotic Americans in Washington and in the Northwest, for instance, who will follow the harvest, eat rotten food, and sleep in their masters' straw stacks, will be among the fools who cry out against the 'foreigner's and the Japanese!" And this was why a "yellow skin" was to be preferred "thousand times" to a "yellow heart."[71]

This cultural campaign to redeem Asian manhood was carried out in a variety of venues including published literature, public meetings, and soapbox oratories. At a town hall gathering of the IWW in Vancouver, a Scottish migrant worker confessed to being disabused of this notion of Asian male unmanliness when "he was picking grapes in Sacramento, California, in 1911, and had to get to work at 6:30 in the morning while the Japs rolled out of bed and got to work at eight." He added that, "The Japs also quit at five o'clock, while the whites worked on. In the one case, it was $1.75 for an 11-hour day, in the other $5.00 for an 8 hour day." Another IWW speaker recounted a similar incident where Japanese section hands walked off the job because the Great Northern Railway failed to give them a raise in a timely fashion: "The men were assured that the company was no doubt going to give them this raise and that the matter should come up in three or four weeks." This timetable was apparently unacceptable to the Japanese railway workers as they had their spokesperson tell the foreman the following: "Boss, we are going to give you a little rest and we are going take a little rest ourselves. We stop work this afternoon." As the speaker recalled, the foreman "wired the company who wired back the same night saying that the raise had been granted and that the men should go back to work the next morning."[72]

The most productive sources for their reclamation project were found in revolutionary and radical movements being staged across the Pacific. For example, in Hawai'i, thousands of Japanese plantation laborers had walked off their jobs in 1909, after their demands for a wage increase went unmet, leading to a standoff that lasted several months. The Japanese couched their demands in the slogan of "equal pay for equal work," insisting that they be paid the same as the Portuguese and Puerto Rican laborers who performed similar work on the plantation. Sugar planters responded with force, mobilizing state power against the "intransigent" Japanese workers.[73] Labor leaders were arrested and imprisoned and the rank and file were beat back by police violence and surveillance. The repression eventually took its toll on the strikers, as the workers agreed to go back to work three months later. However, their efforts were not entirely in vain. Several months following the end of the strike, the planters agreed to bring up their wages and to abolish the system of wage differentiation based on nationality.[74]

The dramatic uprising of Japanese sugar workers on the Hawaiian Islands gained the attention and admiration of IWW activists in the Pacific Northwest. For them, it served as proof that Japanese workers were capable of direct action—the telltale sign of a virile working-class manhood. "The Japanese workers in the sugar plantations, and the agricultural laborers generally, in the islands, have formed a union called the 'Higher Wages Association.' They have been conducting a strike, many features of which show the discipline and fighting spirit of our Japanese fellow workers." In particular, the IWW emphasized the manly virtues of Yasutaro Soga and Fred Makino, the leaders of the movement, praising their willingness to suffer persecution and abuse for the cause of class liberation. According to the *Industrial Worker,* "Their foremost fighters may suffer imprisonment," however, "such persecution will only be one more shake to rouse the sleeping giant of Labor." Moreover, by highlighting details of the Japanese strike of 1909, the IWW once again destabilized the racial logic that made manly unionism indistinguishable from whiteness. "An attempt is being made by the employers to break the strike by means of 'white' scabs!" On the other hand, the Japanese "who are supposed to be slavish for revolt," the IWW argued, "are rapidly showing the world that they are the most merciless in their demands of the employer."[75] Furthering the case for workers' internationalism, white labor radicals pointed to the fact that the "Japanese government [has] vied with the American employers" in persecuting the strikers to show that "the struggle is on class lines between the workers and the employers without regard to nation or race."[76]

Throughout the duration of the strike, T. Takahashi, a Japanese labor activist from Chicago, wrote updates for the *Industrial Worker,* narrating the epic struggle between the island's sugar planters and Japanese workers for the paper's working-class readership. Describing the situation in Hawaii as a "war between working-class and capitalist class," Takahashi reported that the "brutal police force" was unable to "crush the vigor of the awakening giant, the Japanese strikers." In his accounts, Takahashi used martial language and imagery to great effect, reinvigorating Japanese manhood by tying it to class warfare and militancy. "The capitalists of the island with the aid of governmental force succeeded at first battle, but our boys, whose spirit is expressed in their song, 'We rather die and scatter like cherry blossoms than to be a coward of shame,' existing like mere brick and stone, will never rest till they shall win."[77]

In search for additional expressions of Asian radicalism and militancy, the IWW took stock of Asian labor radicalism on both sides of the Pacific. In 1911, for example, a Chinese crew working on one of Great Northern's transpacific steamships went on strike on their stop in Yokohama, Japan, demanding higher wages and improved work conditions. The impasse lasted ten days before the company finally capitulated and met their demands. In covering the story, the *Industrial Worker* noted that, "it is significant in view of the fact that even though they be members of the 'yellow peril' race, they were powerful enough when acting together to force more wages from the boss."[78] In what was perhaps the most dramatic mobilization of Chinese laborers on the Pacific Rim, thousands of Chinese maritime transport workers in Hong Kong walked off their jobs in January 1922. Formed in 1921, the Chinese Seamen's Union had made repeated demands for wage increases, better working conditions, and an end to the extortionist practices of company foremen. When the steamship companies refused to meet their demands, the union ordered a strike that brought Hong Kong to an almost complete standstill.[79] As one Wobbly leader marveled, "[the] walkout of the workers was the most uniform action ever taken by the Chinese. The strike extended to lightermen and dock workers and to laundry employees, sampan navigators, and any form of labor that would hold up the movement of vessels." Another IWW writer, contributing to the *Industrial Worker,* emphasized that by their show of force and solidarity the Chinese maritime workers "have won every demand they advanced." Moreover, he used the Chinese Seamen's Union strike to discipline American workers who he chastised for failing to evidence the boldness and savvy necessary for labor mobilizing and collective class action: "When the American worker will act as did the Chinese in the late strike the question of decent working conditions will soon be settled. Our yellow-skinned fellow workers have shown us the way to win a strike."[80] The writings and images IWW activists and propagandists put forth attested to the symbolic importance of the Pacific in their imagining of a virile Asian manhood in an age of exclusion.

CONVERGING ON REVOLUTIONARY MANHOOD

Within IWW circles, no figure was held in higher esteem than the South Asian revolutionary. Venerated for his militant radicalism that called for immediate revolution and aggressively confronting the ruling elite, the South Asian revolutionary was held up as a paragon of virile manhood. "There may not be as much sedition among the Hindus of British Columbia as among Canadian-born Socialists who rant of the flag as 'a bloody rag'; but our Socialistic seditionists have never yet been accused of collecting two million dollars to send home to India to buy rifles for the revolution."[81] The emphasis on militancy, confrontation, and direct action—that is, the vision of a gendered insurgency—brought virile white and Asian radicals together in moments of interracial and interradical solidarity. As a spokesperson for the IWW boasted, "Our workers—revolutionists, you would call them—are at work among the Hindu in India."[82]

The rendering of the South Asian as a heroic insurgent helped to distance him from and complicate his racial identification as an "Asiatic" and facilitated an interracial alliance that brought South Asian revolutionaries in contact with white labor radicals and their aspirations and ideas, and vice versa. Leading revolutionaries Hussain Rahim and Taraknath Das cultivated close ties with intellectuals, unionists, and activists associated with the IWW and the Sociality Party in Canada and the United States. Das began publishing his anticolonial newspaper, the *Free Hindusthan,* with financial assistance from the Socialist Party in Canada (SPC), and when he needed to relocate to avoid government censors in 1908, the *Western Clarion* offered the use of its offices in Seattle. The editors of the socialist paper also furnished Taraknath Das with space in its newspaper to air his anticolonial views. In the case of Hussain Rahim, you will remember that it was his radical ties that so worried Dominion officials at the time of his entry and had them working so hard to keep him out of Canada. Confirming their worst fears, Rahim went on to engage in free speech fights, raise funds, translate organizing literature, and recruit members for the IWW and the SPC in British Columbia. His efforts earned him a seat on the SPC's Executive Committee, which made him the first nonwhite person to be elected into the party's leadership.[83] In this capacity, Rahim was believed to be the key figure in the spread of subversive ideas among the South Asian immigrant population: "The Hindus have up to the present never identified themselves with any particular political party and the introduction by Rahim of the socialist propaganda into this community is, I consider a very serious matter, as the majority of these people are uneducated and ignorant and easily led like sheep by a man like Rahim."[84]

Indeed, Rahim and other revolutionary leaders served as a bridge between white labor radicals and South Asian migrant workers. In 1913, Agnes Laut, reporting for the *Saturday Night,* wrote that she saw "long lists of subscriptions from Hindu workmen to the IWW strike funds" during her investigations into Wobbly activities in British Columbia.[85] The two groups met and interacted at meetings and demonstrations jointly held by the IWW, the SPC, and South Asian revolutionaries. At these venues, white and Asian radicals tried to rally their respective constituencies around a common purpose, insisting that the struggles against capitalism and imperialism were one and the same. This mixing raised concerns that the disparate radicals in the region were merging into a single movement—a nightmare scenario for Dominion and British colonial authorities. As one official reported alarmingly: "It is stated on good authority that the Hindus are preparing to take an active part in strikes and other anti-war demonstrations fomented by the IWW, Bolshevik and kindred groups in this country."[86]

White labor radicals of the IWW did little to temper these fears of amalgamation, touting their alliances with South Asian and other Asian insurgents. "The Chinese are awakening to freedom," one IWW activist declared. "They recently celebrated the first anniversary of the overthrow of the Manchu. Saturday night is the night arranged for them to meet in the IWW hall and take up the matter of uniting their forces with their fellow workers of this city."[87] This newfound revolutionary consciousness was exemplified by Chinese nationalists like Arthur Wann who was recognized for his exceptional courage in the IWW free speech fights in Vancouver. As one observer recalled: "He fearlessly took the box in the vast sea of humanity on the Powell Street grounds and defiantly delivered a most revolutionary address in the teeth of the police." The socialist *B.C. Federationist* also echoed these sentiments, asserting that, "China will not be long in awakening with revolutionaries like this. Comrade Wann is quite hopeful of being enrolled on the exchange with all Socialists and revolutionary papers in the States and Canada, and already has the encouragement of a few."[88]

As it was the case with South Asian radicals, revolutionary Chinese nationalists helped to bridge the racial gap between white and Chinese workers, bringing the latter into the union. In testimonials given by veteran IWW members in Vancouver, they recalled that in some years the IWW had as many Chinese members as white ones. In 1919 specifically, they remembered "[t]he Chinese and whites went thru one very successful strike in the lumber mills together . . . at which time they got a very satisfactory increase in wages."[89] The IWW did its part by translating organizing literature into Chinese (as well as Japanese and Punjabi). Some IWW locals also hired Chinese (as well as other Asian) organizers to recruit directly among their countrymen. The discursive strategy to redeem Asian manhood was accompanied by a genuine effort to organize Chinese, Japanese, and South Asian workers in the Pacific Northwest.

THE LIMITS OF REVOLUTIONARY MANHOOD

Yet despite these moments of interracial and interradical solidarity, uniting white and Asian radicals behind a single movement proved difficult. To start with, organizers faced the logistical challenges posed by cultural and linguistic differences, though they were certainly not insurmountable. Beyond that, there was the problem of convincing their respective constituencies of their shared purpose, which meant, among other things, getting white workers to care about an independence struggle that was a half a world away. These difficulties were exacerbated by tensions and contradictions within and between their movements. In the case of the IWW, however much the organization preached the gospel of racial equality and workers' internationalism, its leaders and members could not entirely transcend the dominant culture of white male supremacy. In a borderland society that was defined, to a very large extent, by an intense and at times a fanatical anti-Asian racism, signaled in the oft-repeated calls for a "white man's country," this was no doubt a tall order. But the fact was, for all their eloquent pronouncements for interracial unionism and solidarity, IWW activists found themselves denigrating Asian labor much in the same manner as their white labor counterparts in the AFL.

The *Industrial Worker*, for example, reproduced some of the most common racial tropes of Chinese labor in an article, "Chinese Displace American Sailors: Ships Are Manned by Orientals while American Seamen Starve on Shore," which told the story of how Chinese sailors were displacing American sailors on transpacific steamship liners by underselling their labor. "Chinese sailors receive about $20 a month," according to the report. "That is sufficient to keep their fit for the day's toll." On the other hand, "American sailors, on the Pacific, have a scale calling for $72.50 a month," in addition to demands for "good, wholesome food." With the white workers, there was also the "danger of them organizing into unions that sometimes made it disagreeable for the bosses." Compared to white workers, "Chinese workers are more docile when dealing with the bosses," the article explained.[90]

The failure of interradical unity, however, was not simply a problem of race; it also proved to be a problem of gender. For even as white labor radicals could imagine building alliances with virile Asian radicals, the gendered discourse they employed inescapably reproduced the historical links between whiteness and manliness. And as such, the discursive strategy to promote class unity through a redeemed Asian manhood was limited by its own racial and gendered logic. Being closely aligned with the ascendant ideas of manhood at the turn of the twentieth century in which manhood and whiteness were coterminous, the radical manhood of the IWW was also, by extension, a racialized manhood. By appealing to a virile manhood in their efforts to overcome race, white labor radicals employed notions of race and gender that rehearsed the ruling logic of white male supremacy, which made the assertion of Asian manhood hardly feasible.[91]

Take for example the case of Seattle labor activist K. Sasaki who in many ways epitomized virile working-class manhood. He worked tirelessly to organize Japanese railway workers, challenged unfair employment practices, and reached out to white labor leaders in the hopes of building a cross-racial labor movement in the Pacific Northwest. Yet his manhood continued to be in question. Indeed, despite Sasaki's long list of accomplishments and working-class credentials, white laborers continued to demand proof of his manhood, insisting that "If the Jap [Sasaki] wants to become a unionist he has only to prove himself a man."[92] Against the standard of a racialized manhood, Asian laborers would always fail to measure up. Invigorating anticapitalist resistance and challenging the color line through gender had the paradoxical effect of reinscribing racial divisions within the labor movement, and ultimately dimmed the possibilities of a lasting political alliance.

Thus, even in cases where Asian workers were shown to be acting out their manhood, they were invariably racialized. In 1909, a Chinese crew working on the steamship S.S. *Lillie* traveling between the Gulf of Mexico and the eastern seaboard of the United States threatened to strike unless their demands for higher wages were met. The *Industrial Worker* reported that the "captain was forced to pay the increase asked," thereby making the Chinese sailors the "highest paid crew," more than all the other white crews on the Gulf. Nevertheless, as the article title ("Whites Cheaper than Chinks") suggests, by expecting higher standards from white sailors, white labor radicals used the Chinese as a benchmark of degradation and unmanliness.[93] Indeed, the IWW continued to reify the Chinese as "coolies" in their writings and speeches. Referring to white contract laborers in Alaska, IWW activists were incredulous to learn that they accepted "the same identical contracts that were printed to enslaved Chinese coolies." They noted that while the "Wa Chong Co. of Seattle prefer to have yellow cannery workers," the terms were so appalling that even "the Orientals refuse to labor for them." To further shame and discipline this particular group of white workers, they made invidious racial comparisons, seeking to capture the full extent of their degradation. As the *Industrial Worker* reported, "White workers in cannery live on Chinese food and contract to obey orders of the Chinese boss."[94]

The racial and gendered persistence of revolutionary manhood severely undermined the IWW's internationalist vision for emancipation. Indeed, despite the organization's inclusive proclamations, the boundaries of race and gender continued to hamper white labor radicals from accepting Asians as social equals. This helps explain why at one of their regular meetings at the IWW meeting hall in Vancouver, "not a man in the hall and there must have been at least 150 men present" could recall "ever gotten acquainted with an Oriental while on the job."[95] It was reminiscent of the dilemma that the socialist editor of the *B.C. Federationist,* R. P. Pettipiece, found himself in when investigative reporter Agnes Laut probed about his commitment to racial egalitarianism in 1913. She asked Pettipiece, "Have you no objection to these Asiatic people coming in and cutting your wages?" His response was a forceful and unambiguous case for interracial unionism. "Not a bit," he answered, "[t]hat day of narrow outlook has gone past in the labor world. We aim to unite the laborers of all nations in one solid army against capital." He stated emphatically, "Let them come in, we say! They will make so many more votes to overthrow capital! It isn't labor that opposes the Oriental. No—you bet! Let 'em come in! We'll take care of them! We'll take 'em right in our ranks!"

His response to the reporter's second question, however, betrayed his earlier antiracist sentiments. "Would you like your little daughter to sit in the same class at school as a Hindu or Jap?" the reporter queried. "No, I would not," he answered soberly. To make certain that his calls for interracial unionism would not be mistaken as an appeal for social equality, he clarified, "As a father, I don't want the Hindu in here any more than you do as a woman. Let the Asiatics have separate schools. As a citizen, I do not want the Asiatic." Attempting to reconcile this statement with his earlier antiracist pronouncements, he elaborated, "You can't assimilate him to our civilization; but this labor movement is no longer provincial. It is a world movement; and labor has found that we might better have the cheap Asiatics come in here and organized into our fighting ranks, than have the cheap products of Asiatic labor come in here and undersell our labor products." His ambivalence toward Asian migrants was perhaps best reflected in his final response to the question when he said, "Hindus are not dangerous as laborers, only as neighbors."[96] In other words, it was one thing to be part of the same union as the Asian male worker, but quite another to break bread with him.

The lack of social acceptance undoubtedly impeded the IWW movement for interracial class unity in the Pacific Northwest. What is more, it appears that the line between social rejection and racial hate proved to be extremely thin. Nisei Shigeru Osawa remembered white union men frequently gathering in front of his parent's restaurant in Seattle to give and listen to anti-Asiatic speeches. According to Osawa, white labor activists took to the streets during the evening hours to give soapbox oratories on the evils of Japanese labor and the threat they posed to the white workingman. He explicitly recalled rank-and-file members of the IWW joining these impromptu anti-Asiatic demonstrations.[97]

. . .

These divergences hindered cooperation and dimmed the possibilities for a grand political alliance between white and Asian radicals in the Pacific Northwest borderlands. The problems of racial, cultural, and linguistic differences undercut efforts to bring disparate insurgents together. These fissures were exacerbated by political outlooks and ideological commitments that did not neatly align. For white labor and South Asian radicals alike, it was not always transparent what their causes—one anti-capitalist, the other anti-colonial—held in common. Yet, these divisions notwithstanding, this revolutionary project to join white and Asians radicals in a transnational movement that was both explicitly antiracist and anti-imperialist was still remarkable by any standard. White and Asian radicals found common ground in their emancipatory (albeit gendered) internationalisms to produce and sustain meaningful ties—an alliance deemed dangerous enough to warrant brutal state repression. The converging radicalism of the IWW and South Asian revolutionaries caused widespread alarm and would justify an enormous expansion in state surveillance around the time of the First World War. As we shall see in the next chapter, white and Asian radicals would come under the relentless persecution and surveillance of an emerging national security state that arose to pacify their respective insurgent movements in the Pacific Northwest and beyond.

FIVE

Policing Migrants and Militants

IN DEFENSE OF NATION AND EMPIRE IN THE BORDERLANDS

IN JULY 1914, THREE CANADIAN Sikhs, Bhag Singh, Balwant Singh, and Mew Singh, crossed the boundary into the sleepy border town of Sumas, Washington. They were trailed closely by U.S. immigration inspectors who had been tipped off to a possible meeting of South Asian radicals there. While the exact purpose of the gathering was unknown, authorities suspected it was part of an ongoing plot to exploit the controversy surrounding the *Komagata Maru*. The *Komagata Maru* incident, as it was called, involved the standoff between Dominion immigration authorities and 376 South Asian passengers on board a Japanese steamship liner that had sailed directly from India to Vancouver in the summer of 1914 in an explicit challenge to the Continuous Journey Order.[1] Canadian officials attempted to force the ship back to Asia but were met with stiff resistance from the South Asian passengers on board who took control of the ship. The standoff lasted for several months, with the ship remaining undocked in Vancouver harbor for most of the summer, as South Asian immigrant leaders and Dominion officials tried to negotiate an end to the stalemate. As the impasse dragged on, British colonial officials worried that South Asian radicals, with aid from white labor militants, were using the incident to foment sedition among South Asian immigrants in the Pacific Northwest.[2]

In Sumas, Washington, the American inspectors observed the three Canadian Sikhs along with known revolutionary agitator Taraknath Das going into a store where they eventually purchased revolvers and ammunition. As one of the Sikhs later confessed, "I took my revolver and hid the same in my pants, and also took the three boxes of ammunition and put one box in the sock of my right foot and one in the left foot, and one in the inner vest pocket and left for Canadian territory." Their intention, according to

Canadian immigration officer Malcolm Reid, was to "convey these weapons to the *Komagata Maru*."[3] But when they attempted to reenter British Columbia, Dominion officers were at the border waiting for them. The U.S. immigration inspectors who had been closely monitoring the men had passed on the information they had gathered to their Canadian counterparts. Such exchanges were conducted routinely under a working agreement between the Canadian and U.S. Immigration Service. This particular exchange happened to lead to the arrest of three alleged South Asian radicals, who were immediately taken under the custody of Dominion and British colonial agents for interrogation.

The problem of policing the U.S.-Canadian boundary, initiated under Chinese Exclusion, evolved into a multifaceted, multiracial challenge by the first two decades of the twentieth century. The threat constituted by illegal Asian aliens now overlapped and, at times, was superseded by the challenge of radical nationalism and labor militancy. The multiple challenges posed by Chinese and Japanese migrants and smugglers and white and South Asian radicals brought the United States, Canada, and Britain together in defense of national and imperial borders. Together, officials from these self-proclaimed white men's countries developed a surveillance network to police illegal migrants, monitor and track radical nationalists, and to suppress labor militancy and revolt across the U.S.-Canadian boundary and across the Pacific. In responding to these perceived political and social threats collectively, Anglophone powers worked collaboratively to establish control over their respective imperial frontiers. The border was, then, a product of intercolonial cooperation and exchange, as Anglophone empires supported each other's prerogative to imperial rule in Asia and the Pacific.[4] In this regard, Asiatic exclusion (and the migration and border controls it spawned in the white settler colonial world) was as much about defending and preserving the empire as it was about keeping out undesirable foreigners.[5]

This multinational campaign to enforce the border against illegal Asian aliens and foreign radicals, involving agencies and departments from Canada, Britain, and the United States, concretized the U.S.-Canadian boundary and justified nation-states' claims to territorial sovereignty on both sides of the border. The patchwork system of customs officers and local deputies improvised under Chinese exclusion gave way to new forms of governmentality including border patrol, immigrant detention and deportation, checkpoints, and intelligence gathering, transforming a once fluid borderland society in the process. In this way, the border became the locus for new disciplinary power through which an emerging surveillance state collected information, distributed regulations, and imposed spatial order, which in turn established the border as an objective spatial reality that the nation-state had a "natural" right to delimit and control. The U.S.-Canadian boundary, in short, was rendered "legible" through the application of new state technologies and practices and became a laboratory for social control.[6]

POLICING ILLEGAL ASIAN ALIENS

The renewed emphasis on border control and surveillance was initially in response to the growing public hysteria over transpacific Asian migration. In 1907, the region experienced a record influx of Japanese and South Asian immigrants (though still considerably smaller than immigration from Europe) with close to 10,000 Asian immigrants landing at the British Columbia ports of Vancouver and Victoria. U.S. officials worried that the new wave of Asian immigrants were using British Columbia as a "side gate" to gain surreptitious entry into the United States. As U.S. Secretary of Commerce and Labor Oscar S. Straus explained to Secretary of State Elihu Root in 1907, "The result has been that these aliens, in pursuance of their original intention, have immediately applied to the officers of the United States Immigration Service for certificates of admission entitling them to enter American territory. Such as were found inadmissible remained in Canada and often resorted to means of securing unlawful entry to this country across the landed boundary."[7]

Reports of unauthorized Asian aliens coming across the border unimpeded roused public opinion in the Pacific Northwest. In July 1907, the *Port Townsend Leader* raised the alarm in an article title, "Japanese Hordes Still Pouring In," reporting that, "Hundreds of Japanese coolies are crossing the international boundary into this country from Canada, despite the vigilance of the immigration force which has been doubled with the past sixty days."[8] The growing public hysteria worried U.S. officials from the standpoint of maintaining social order. U.S. immigration inspector John Sargent warned that "the number of Japanese and other aliens who are now in British Columbia and the state of public feelings on both sides of the border in this vicinity against these aliens is such that an emergency has arisen, whereby it is absolutely necessary to have additional men appointed, if the border is to be properly guarded."[9] The bureau responded to these concerns by hiring watchmen to form a border detail under immigrant inspector C. A. Turner. This newly created unit patrolled the border between Steveston, British Columbia, and Point Roberts, Washington, on a full-time basis for the first time.[10]

Government civil servants legitimized and reinforced the popular image of a leaky U.S.-Canadian boundary being deluged by sneaky Orientals. Prompted by public clamoring, the U.S. Immigration Service commissioned Inspector-at-Large Marcus Braun to investigate conditions along the northern boundary in 1907. Braun had emerged as a leading proponent of border management within policy circles, believing it to be a vital operational feature of the modern state. Not surprisingly, his findings confirmed public sentiments. In his final report, Braun depicted the border in the Pacific Northwest as a porous line that Asian migrants and smugglers could easily circumvent: "There is undoubtedly a large number of Japanese, Hindus and other aliens now in British Columbia, many of them near the boundary line who are awaiting opportunities and the proper time to effect surreptitious entries into the United States." He thought that it would take at least sixty officers guarding the border "to effect proper control of the territory . . . in view of the fact that so many Japanese and other Orientals are now landing in British Columbia with the object of entering the United States."[11] In making his recommendation, Braun was requesting to have as many officers posted along the Washington–British Columbia border as there were patrolling the entire length of the 1,900-mile-long U.S.-Mexican boundary at this time.[12] His colleague, John Sargent, concurred with the proposed numbers, explaining that, "[t]he character of the immigration to the Pacific coast . . . is much more difficult and requires vastly more labor to handle Oriental than European immigrants."[13]

In pressing for increased border security, Braun and other officials portrayed Asian immigrants as unscrupulous people, who had little regard for the rule of law. "The smuggling of Chinamen and Japanese is a regular profession," he insisted. "If we really want to keep out Chinese and Japanese," Braun explained, "we will have to change our laws . . . we need an alien registration law, it should be required that aliens keep on their person their passport which should be stamped at the time of their arrival, and that until they become citizens of the United States, they should be required to register either with local police or with a special bureau."[14] Being made ineligible to citizenship by a provision of the 1882 Chinese Exclusion Act, which kept Chinese immigrants in a permanent state of alienage, Braun's recommendation would have placed the Chinese and their communities under perpetual surveillance.[15] Their cultural penchant for deceit warranted and justified extreme measures, he contended.

Braun's clarion call may well have fallen on deaf ears if it were not for the September riots. Indeed, perhaps no single event or development did more for the cause of border security than the anti-Asian upheavals in Vancouver and Bellingham. A *Seattle Times* editorial written two weeks after the riots demanded swift state intervention: "The troubles of local immigration officials with Mongolians who insist upon entering this country either lawfully or unlawfully were never more numerous than at the present time, and it is apparent that the present force of inspectors and watchmen is totally inadequate, even with the unusual zeal with which is shown, to cope with the horde of Japanese and Chinese who are making their way across the border."[16] The *Vancouver World,* noting their "common cause against the yellow peril," declared illegal Asian immigration a threat to "white men's countries" on both sides of the boundary line: "Owing to the rush of Japanese to this province and particularly to this port, a point has been reached where the population of the coast south of the boundary line is attaching the highest importance to the Japanese invasion of Canada as representing the most serious Asiatic attack on this continent, threatening republic and Dominion alike."[17] These racial anxieties helped to spawn a new system of border surveillance and control that would make a once invisible boundary in the Pacific Northwest visible.

The cross-border transience of Asian migrants was, of course, not unique: Other groups also went back and forth across the international line. Euro-American and Canadian workers traveling by way of the northern boundary were regular fixtures on the region's landscape.[18] Coastal aboriginal groups in British Columbia were also known to migrate seasonally to southern hop fields in Washington State to supplement their traditional mode of living.[19] Yet it was the Chinese, Japanese, and South Asians who would ultimately be defined by Anglo-American law and culture as the "aliens," the racialized "other" in the borderland region. Moreover, it was the decisively Asian nature of migrant transborder mobility and labor that drew the attention and opposition of white residents, eventually becoming the object of the state's disciplinary strategies and power.

In a rush to quell social unrest on the west coast, the United States and Canada consummated agreements with the Japanese government, known as the "Gentlemen's Agreements," which set numerical limits on immigrants coming from Japan. The U.S. Gentlemen's Agreement became official policy in the summer of 1908 whereas the Canadian version, also known as the Hayashi-Lemieux Agreement, went into effect several months earlier.[20] The Seattle Immigration Service was also endowed with new powers and resources to significantly upgrade its border enforcement operation. Efforts to control the boundary in a more systematic manner began with increasing the size of the border force and positioning agents strategically along the international line dividing Washington and British Columbia. Immediately following the riots, Commissioner General of Immigration Frank Sargent secured funding for a new team of border inspectors and ordered the Immigration Service in Washington to "utilize their services in guarding the British Columbia boundary, bending every effort towards preventing the illegal entry of Japanese."[21] The upgrade in border personnel, however, failed to appease local residents. The Bellingham *American Reveille* wrote, "If the Japanese so choose to smuggle into this country they can easily do so because it is impossible to watch every foot of the boundary line and it is equally impossible to patrol every part of the sea. Additional watchmen have been placed on duty by the immigration department, but more are needed."[22]

The rugged and varied terrain extending from west of the Cascade Mountains to the Pacific Ocean presented enormous challenges to the officers tasked to defend it. Aside from the problem of sheer size, the natural landscape provided would-be border crossers with a labyrinth of dirt roads and forest trails leading back and forth across the international line. As one immigrant inspector explained, "The road extending East of Blaine and Douglas, known as the Border Road, is heavily wooded on both sides with underbrush and second growth timber with trails every few roads, leading north and south, and brush and woods affording an excellent cover during the day time, while under the leadership of an experienced guide they continue their journey southward at night time."[23] If that was not enough, the natural waterways of the Puget Sound—dotted with tiny islands and teeming with fishing trawlers, sailboats, and oceangoing steamship liners—furnished yet another passageway for Asian immigrants seeking to effect illegal entry. Immigrant inspector John Sargent called the "district one of the most difficult in the United States to guard against the surreptitious entry of unlawful aliens."[24]

U.S. immigrant inspectors in British Columbia and Washington estimated that more than 90 percent of unauthorized border crossings in the Pacific Northwest occurred somewhere between Port Angeles on the west and Sumas on the east. Based on this intelligence, the U.S. Immigration

Service deployed border inspectors and mounted watchmen at Ferndale, Lynden, Everson, and Blaine. All these towns ran along the Nooksack River, which flowed westward from the Cascade Mountains near the U.S.-Canadian boundary into Bellingham Bay, furnishing a myriad of routes, passageways, and bridges for would-be border crossers.[25] In addition to the mounted inspectors on the boundary line, the U.S. Immigration Service also stationed agents at the Great Northern, Northern Pacific, and British Columbia Railway depots in Bellingham, where they daily inspected trains coming in from Canada. Finally, to guard the waterways of the Puget Sound, inspectors patrolled the waters, monitored the countless small islands, and checked ships and boats coming into Seattle. Officials also maintained regular contact with the different transportation lines and were alerted to the arrival times of steamships, boats, and railroads.

According to a 1910 roster, the immigration force in the Washington jurisdiction alone consisted of close to fifty full-time immigrant and Chinese inspectors and border watchmen. This figure did not include border personnel the Seattle Service hired on an ad hoc basis in cases of "border emergencies." In December 1909, for example, immigration authorities in Washington learned of an illegal smuggling ring operating on the Puget Sound. In response, the bureau put in a request for eight temporary watchmen.[26] The Immigration Service, with its close ties to the labor movement, recruited most of their full- and part-time watchmen from among the white working class. William G. Minter was a case in point: He was forty years old and worked twenty years for the Northern Pacific Railroad prior to being hired by the Immigration Service. Fred Pannell was another typical recruit: He was thirty-eight and had worked as a longshoreman for seven years before accepting the position of immigration watchman.[27] To match the increase in the size of the force, the Immigration Service also expanded its facilities to include substations in almost every border town along the boundary. Whereas inspectors in 1900 used the city jail to temporarily house suspects, the Immigration Service by this time had its own detention centers at its disposal.[28]

In addition to the new personnel and infrastructure, the revamped border regime implemented a series of reforms, one of which was to abolish the long-standing policy of allowing lawful Asian residents to move freely across the border. Prior to this, the boundary was fluid, allowing Japanese and South Asians to cross and recross unimpeded, with their migration patterns being determined largely by human agency and local labor markets. As U.S. Immigration Inspector P. L. Prentis told Commissioner General of

Immigration Frank Sargent in 1908, the cross-border migration of the Japanese was "not at all strange, for the reason that the commercial, social, and labor conditions existing in British Columbia and contingent United States territory, are such as have made it convenient to alternate in their residing in Canada or the United States."[29] In addition to seeking seasonal wage labor, Asian migrants also regularly traveled along and across the international boundary to engage in the border economy. Immigration Inspector C. A. Turner confirmed that "it is the custom to allow all of these aliens to cross the boundary at will for trading or other purposes, there being no watch of any kind kept on roads leading into Blaine from Canada and no check obtained of the number who came or returned."[30] Thus, when the reform was first announced, immigrant inspectors were concerned that the new restrictions would elicit protest from local businessmen and shopkeepers, which might in turn impede their "work of carrying out the Immigration Laws."[31] Nevertheless, the Immigration Service moved forward with its plans to bring this informal cross-border movement to a halt. Inspector Charles Babcock explained this shift in policy: "The custom of allowing the Japanese to cross the border . . . was done away with and Inspectors are endeavoring to prevent it as far as possible."[32]

These reforms introduced a new set of geographic exclusions, which had a profound impact on the everyday life of Asian immigrants in the Pacific Northwest. The fluid borderland world they once knew and experienced slowly faded as Asian migrants quickly discovered they could no longer freely cross the boundary as they once did. In the summer of 1909, hundreds of Japanese migrant laborers were caught in this changed geography. Described as "mostly men who have worked on farms, sawmills and other laboring employment in the state of Washington," they had come to the Fraser River in Vancouver, anticipating a prolific salmon run. As they had done in the years past, at the end of the fishing season, they packed up their belongings and headed south to return to the United States. But this time, they were barred from reentry under the new regulations. In their appeals to the Japanese consul in Vancouver, they insisted that they had "lived a number of years in the United States" and had "made such trips before returning to the south without hindrance heretofore."[33] As the travails of these Japanese migrants indicates, the transborder world of cross-border labor opportunities, shopping, and family visits had given way to a more hardened spatial discipline that increasingly confined Asian immigrants to one side of the border.

The disciplining of Asian mobility also involved the construction of a dense intelligence-gathering network. The Seattle Immigration Service established regular contact with numerous state agencies in Washington and British Columbia regarding Chinese, Japanese, and South Asian communities. They also hired mobile informants who toured the borderlands—including Steveston, Vancouver, and Westminster on the Canadian side, and Blaine, Anacortes, Bellingham, and the San Juan Islands on the U.S. side—in order to report on the movements and activities of Asian groups. Finally, the Immigration Service relied on the eyes and ears of the local population to help monitor the border, ushering in a citizen surveillance network. As one U.S. immigration inspector reported, "There are several thousand people living in Whatcom County . . . many of whom are in possession of telephones and most of whom are willing to give our officers any information they may secure regarding aliens passing their residences or places of business."[34] Similarly, in British Columbia, Canadian immigration authorities sought the cooperation of borderland residents by installing telephones along roads and byways thought to be routinely traveled by illegal Asian migrants.[35]

Taken together, this patchwork intelligence network (including citizen spies) enabled state bureaucrats to place Chinese, Japanese, and South Asian immigrants under surveillance. In one instance where intelligence sharing led to successful interdiction, U.S. immigration authorities learned that large numbers of Japanese were traveling south from Vancouver to Cloverdale, a small town about eight miles north of the international line. While this movement was initially thought to be of laborers moving to perform extension work for the Great Northern Railway, information obtained from the Vancouver office made it clear "that these construction camps could not possibly have absorbed the constant stream of Japanese traveling from Vancouver toward the boundary." The Immigration Service thus deduced that these Japanese were proceeding south into the United States unlawfully. Positioning border watchmen in the vicinity, their strategy paid immediate dividends. On the very first night of their deployment, border inspectors captured three Japanese attempting to cross the border.[36]

Authorities on both sides of the border closely monitored economic conditions, labor markets, and employment practices as part of their effort to secure the border. In one case, the Bureau learned that the Canadian Pacific and the Anglo-American Lumber Companies were planning to discharge their entire South Asian workforce so as to be in compliance with a recently passed municipal ordinance prohibiting the City of Vancouver from making contracts with companies employing Asian labor.[37] In anticipation of increased illicit movement across the border, the Seattle Immigration Service deployed extra forces along the northern line that resulted in the arrest of quite a few South Asian immigrants. In Washington, near the border, inspectors detained "three Hindus who had been employed in the vicinity of Vancouver and apparently had gone to that point for the expressed purpose of securing admission."[38]

Maintaining the territorial integrity of the nation-state required regulating the boundaries of America's empire as well. Concerns that Asian migrants would use the colonies as a backdoor into the country were raised even prior to their acquisition, dating back to the late 1890s, when the country was debating whether or not the United States should acquire a formal empire. The anti-imperialist coalition made this a central issue in its campaign. AFL leader Samuel Gompers argued on the eve of America's entry into the Spanish-American War. "If the Philippines are annexed, what is to prevent the Chinese, the Negritos and the Malays coming to our country? How can we prevent the Chinese coolies from going to the Philippines and from there swarming into the United States engulfing our people and our civilization? If these new islands are to become ours, it will be either under the form of Territories or States. Can we hope to close the flood gates of immigration from the hordes of Chinese and the semi-savage races coming from what will then be part of our own country?"[39] The acquisition of a formal empire, Gompers and other anti-imperialists maintained, would only serve to facilitate unwanted Asian immigration, aggravating the "race problem" in the United States.[40]

Just as Samuel Gompers had predicted, U.S. imperial expansion into the Pacific introduced new nodes and spaces through which Asian migrants evaded immigration law and policy, becoming sites of unregulated mobility and movement. The Chinese, Japanese, Koreans, and South Asians would all take their turn in exploiting alternative routes through empire to gain entry into the United States. The first attempt at exerting control over Asian migrants crossing the empire was President Roosevelt's March 1907 executive order, which authorized the Immigration Bureau to refuse entrance to Japanese and Korean laborers whose passports were issued for any destination other than the continental United States. In subsequent years, U.S. immigration officials applied this principle of migration control to South Asian migrants, who were accused of using the Philippines as a stepping-stone into the United States.

In the fall of 1912, U.S. immigration officials in Seattle denied admission to seventy-three South Asian immigrants from Manila on the grounds that they were "liable to become a public charge." This was, of course, standard procedure; however, this particular case posed a dilemma for U.S. immigration officials. Having been previously inspected and cleared for entry into the Philippines, a territory of the United States, they should have been admitted without further examination under existing immigration protocol. As one U.S. official explained, "The Hindoos in question, have been admitted into the United States (Philippine Islands), their status as alien immigrants is discharged.... Unless therefore you find some irregularity amounting to fraud in the matter of the entry of these men into the Philippines, you cannot without doing violation to the law, now take jurisdiction of their case, and hold either that they are at some other place in the United States 'alien immigrants,' or that the Philippine authorities had no right to admit them to this country."[41]

To get around this "technicality," U.S. immigration officials in Seattle extrapolated a general principle from the 1907 executive order, which dealt specifically with Japanese migration from Hawai'i, and applied it indiscriminately to South Asian immigrants coming from the Philippines. Commissioner General of Immigration Daniel J. Keefe argued in 1913 that, "The propriety of distinguishing between the mainland of the United States and its insular possessions, in the matter of immigration, is already recognized in principle, in the matter of the immigration of Japanese laborers."[42] The U.S. Immigration Service invoked this newly invented principle to nullify the earlier ruling in Manila, which had cleared the South Asians for entry, and treated the South Asians as "alien immigrants" who were entering the United States for the very first time. This principle hewed closely to the logic of a series of Supreme Court rulings, known collectively as the Insular Cases, which relegated the colonies to a "liminal space" that fell "both inside and outside of the boundaries of the Constitution, both 'belonging to' but 'not part of' the United States."[43] The crisis of Asian migrant illegality was thus a product of state policies and regulations as well as public hysteria.[44] Indeed, these dynamics were mutually reinforcing, generating a feedback loop of anxiety that served to justify the expansion of state power in the name of national and imperial protection.

ENFORCING WHITE MEN'S COUNTRIES

The problem of illegal Asian immigration ran in both directions across the border in the Pacific Northwest. In 1908, Canada enacted the Continuous Journey Order, barring admission to South Asian immigrants. South

Asian migrants evaded the law by first migrating to the United States and then surreptitiously crossing the border into Canada at some later point. "It is the understanding of the Dominion Agent that many of them who have landed at San Francisco and Seattle are in reality destined to British Columbia points, and ultimately succeed in effecting surreptitious entry into Canada."[45] Similarly, the *Vancouver Ledger* obtained information that smuggled Japanese were part of an underground traffic from south of the border. "Latest reports state that an unusually large number of Japanese are arriving from the Orient at Seattle, and it is expected that many of these will come across the unprotected boundary into British Columbia."[46] As it was the case in Washington State, the force of public opinion pressured the province to invest manpower and resources to border security, which conferred the border with new power and meaning. Like its American counterpart, the Canadian Immigration Bureau assigned personnel to border detail. This involved the stationing of Dominion officers alongside U.S. inspectors in Washington State and the placement of ethnic informants and agents within the different Asian communities.

The seemingly intractable problem of Asian migration had brought together officials from the United States and Canada who were equally intent on preserving a "white man's country." With a mutual interest in policing the boundaries of race and nation, the two countries engaged in collaborative transnational policing and enforcement of Asian immigration. Canadian immigration officer Malcolm Reid boasted that "the utmost harmony prevails between the United States Immigration officers and our own officials, not only in Vancouver but throughout this whole district, especially in Oriental matters; as it seems to be realized that the Oriental question is a menace both to the United States and Canada, hearty cooperation is necessary to deal with this momentous question adequately."[47] A number of U.S. and Canadian bureaucracies, including local law enforcement, customs houses, and immigration departments, coordinated joint efforts to address the problem of illegal Asian immigration across the border. One U.S. official described the working agreement with Canadian officials to the Congressional Committee on Immigration and Naturalization in 1913: "American immigration officers board boats and examine passengers landing in Canadian ports, join in border patrols, and obtain the assistance of Canadian immigration officers in investigating records of immigrants coming from Canada."[48]

The jointly enforced border had the quality of a selective membrane, permeable to certain people and groups but not to others, calibrated by race. Thus, even as the boundary emerged as a barrier to Asian migrants, it remained porous and open to white Euro-Americans and Canadians. As the *Industrial Worker* observed in 1912, "Thousands of migratory workers have gone to Canada in the past year, there to work for American contractors. Thousands of Canadians come here to work for American employers. In either case the lives of the workers were not influenced by the form of government, by tariff laws, by income taxes, by municipal ownership or any other legal enactment."[49] This fluid situation was created, in part, by the arbitrary manner in which state immigration authorities applied and enforced border policies. In determining who possessed the privileges of border crossing, U.S. and Canadian immigration bureaucrats distinguished between "undesirable" and "desirable" groups, and in the process, became entangled with the larger project of defining national belonging.

U.S. and Canadian immigration officials stationed in the Pacific Northwest treated the cross-border flow of white Americans, Canadians, and European immigrants mostly with benign neglect and in some cases outright support. Recent scholarship shows that illegal European immigrants frequently entered the United States across the northern border. Historian Marian Smith notes that unauthorized European migration across the U.S.-Canadian boundary first became an issue in the 1890s and 1900s. U.S. lawmakers responded by instituting formal inspection regimes along the northern boundary, starting on the eastern seaboard. European immigrants, according to Smith, "simply moved further west or to some other unguarded point" to avoid inspection, although by 1908, "a string of entry posts dotted the northern boundary line from east to west."[50] Yet the correspondence of local inspectors and border watchmen in Washington State rarely, if ever, mention any groups other than Asian immigrants crossing the border unlawfully. U.S. border inspectors likely ignored or overlooked European immigrants coming across the northern boundary. Highlighting the interplay between race and spatial belonging, the border, as far as ethnic Europeans were concerned, became softer—as they, concomitantly, grew whiter—the farther west they went.[51]

The struggle over Asian migration also shaped notions of national belonging on the Canadian side. As Minister of Labor William Mackenzie King declared in 1908, "That Canada should desire to restrict immigration from the Orient is regarded as natural, that Canada should remain a white country is believed to be not only desirable for economic and social reasons, but necessary on political and national grounds."[52] Thus, when designing its immigration and border policies, Dominion authorities in British Columbia considered how they could meet the demands of the labor market without compromising the racial integrity of the nation. They endeavored to attract immigrant laborers, who were essential to economic development and growth, while simultaneously maintaining a "white man's country." When the Dominion passed the Continuous Journey Act in 1908, which barred immigrants not traveling directly from their country of origin, Canadian lawmakers unknowingly prohibited Euro-Americans in the United States from entering Canada. Dominion authorities quickly remedied the situation by passing an addendum to the order in council allowing non-Asians to emigrate from places other than their country of origin, and in doing so, reopened the border to Euro-Americans while keeping it closed to Asian immigrants.[53]

Moreover, the Immigration Department in British Columbia implemented explicit policies to promote the migration of "desirable" groups, which was code for white Euro-Americans. In 1914, immigration officials distributed a departmental circular to all boundary inspectors that encouraged them to allow European migrants from the United States to enter Canada. More specifically, it authorized Canadian inspectors stationed in Washington and other bordering states to issue letters of entry to European immigrants interested in settling in western Canada.[54] As historian Bruno Ramirez explains, "Canada had to resort massively to immigration" because workers "were needed in new mining districts and lumber camps, on railroad lines, and in the construction of urban infrastructures."[55] As part of this wider effort, the Canadian government used head taxes collected from Chinese immigrants, which started at $50 in 1885, then progressively increased to $500 by the end of 1903, to subsidize immigration from Europe. Furthermore, in March 1913, the superintendent of immigration temporarily suspended monetary qualifications for prospective immigrants provided "they are natives or citizens of Great Britain, or Ireland, or if natives or citizens of some other European country . . . and that they are not persons of Asiatic origin."[56] By contrast, Canada required that non-Chinese Asian immigrants possess two hundred dollars at the time of entry.

Dominion immigrant inspectors regularly manipulated border policies in the hopes of "whitening" the labor force in British Columbia. "For many years past Japanese fishermen have monopolized the catching of the fish for the salmon-packing industry, and have driven white fishermen of all kinds almost all out of the waters. Some of the canneries however appear to have become tired of the Japanese alleging that they are far from straight, and are attempting to replace them with white men." Considering the cross-border migration and labor of U.S. and European migrants far more desirable than Asian migrants, Canadian boundary inspectors attempted to accommodate the canneries by relaxing their border regulations in regards to American and European migration from the U.S. Northwest. "Of the white men on the coast, both on the Canadian and American sides, Greeks are probably the most numerous class, and many of them, as well as other American and European fishermen, have been yearly frequenting the Fraser River, some of them going back and forth through port of entry and being inspected by our officers, and others traveling in their own boats and thus entering Canada without inspection." Even though the latter were in violation of immigration law, and thus in the country illegally, the Canadian Immigration Bureau was "fairly well at ease" with these particular groups of immigrants and therefore gave sanction to their transborder movements.[57]

The border remained fluid to immigrants from southern and eastern Europe as well, even as their social desirability and inclusion in the nation was being questioned on the eastern seaboard at the same time.[58] In the summer of 1912, Canadian boundary inspectors stationed in Seattle suspected a large number of Greek and Italian immigrants of illegally crossing the border from Bellingham, Washington, to Steveston, British Columbia. Immigration officials dispatched inspector Hopkinson to investigate the situation, who upon reaching the fishing town of Steveston, discovered a group of unauthorized Greek migrants from Seattle working in one of the canneries. He promptly arrested them on the grounds that they had violated immigration laws by entering Canada without inspection. They were later convicted of the charge and levied a fine of $5.00. More interestingly however, Canadian immigration inspectors recommended that the illegal Greek immigrants be allowed to stay in British Columbia: "The men in question, appeared to be fair class of fishermen, and because it was impossible for their employers to secure white men of this type in this Province, I have no hesitancy in recommending that they be permitted to proceed with their season's contract, and so have taken no steps securing their deportation."[59] While still requiring the Greek immigrants Nick Vallas, Angelo Keane, Nick Dupont, and John Maleson to pay the nominal fine, border practices such as this one served to distance ethnic Europeans from the so-called status or category of "illegal aliens," facilitating their national and racial assimilation as "white" Americans and Canadians in the North American West. In these and countless other ways, the boundaries of race and the boundaries of nation became inextricably intertwined on the U.S.-Canadian border.

SUBVERSIVE MOBILITY

The efforts to define and institutionalize the border invariably led to struggles between the state and the Chinese, Japanese, and South Asian migrants who were intent on maintaining control over their mobility. Asian migrants, whether on their own or with the assistance of professional guides, found creative ways to defy the borders and boundaries designed to keep them out. In a passport scheme, Japanese immigrants in Washington State sold their passports to countrymen in British Columbia seeking to enter the United States. Once the immigrant secured entrance, individuals would continue the cycle by selling or circulating it to yet another immigrant across the border:

> Ten Japanese caught at the international boundary line in one week with bogus passports shows the wholesale extent to which coolie laborers of the Mikado's empire are attempting to deceive the United States Immigration department. The favorite system is that of the use of the same passport over and over again. Nine out of the ten men who were detained at the boundary last week and finally refused admittance to the United States confessed that they had been supplied with the passports of Japanese now in the United States. These had been mailed back to Vancouver and were resold at from five to twenty-five dollars each.[60]

In 1913, Dominion officials discovered South Asian immigrants employing a similar method to effect illegal entry into Canada. The lax record keeping in immigration offices encouraged South Asians to apply for multiple papers, which they used to bring family members from India: "A man applied here [Seattle Immigration Office] for an outward permit, and fortunately we noticed on his ticket, purchased in Vancouver, your office stamp. He was endeavoring to obtain another certificate, in order that he could return to Victoria himself, as he admitted he had sent the certificate he obtained from you to his brother in India, so that he too could come to Canada."[61] As one historian has explained, the "extensive records designed to establish 'true' claims and prohibit fraudulent entry actually served to create, systematize, and facilitate fraud."[62]

One of the more imaginative (and humorous) ploys to gain illegal entry involved the complicity of unsuspecting border inspectors. Issei Izo Kojima recounts how Japanese seeking entry from British Columbia deceived

U.S. border inspectors into believing they were residents of the United States. "There were many iron bridges, and those who tried to get into America from Canada thought up many tricks to get across. There was the trick of walking backwards inconspicuously. Sooner or later such a walker would be discovered by the American guards, and when called he would turn around, as if trying to escape from America to Canada."[63] Border inspectors thinking that Japanese immigrants were unlawfully crossing the border to Canada would apprehend the suspects and unknowingly allow them into the United States. There was also the use of racial disguise in attempts to surreptitiously cross the border: "When questioned the Oriental gave his name as R. Abe and said he wanted to go to Seattle to look for work. Before crossing the line near Blaine, he smeared his face with grease and blackening, giving him the appearance of a Negro."[64] In a different case of quasi-racial passing, there were, prior to 1908, instances of Chinese migrants trying to blend in with Japanese fishermen, who were returning to Washington State from the Fraser River at the end of the summer season.[65]

Other undocumented Asian immigrants in British Columbia relied on family and kinship networks to make it across the boundary. Take the case of Sahuro Iguchi, who traveled on the Pacific steamship liner *Athenian* and arrived in Vancouver on May 30, 1907. About a month later, he applied for admission to the United States but was rejected on account of having contracted trachoma, which historian Nayan Shah has aptly termed the "signature disease of medical exclusion."[66] Unable to deport him back to Japan, the bureau returned him to Vancouver where he received treatment for trachoma. He applied for admissions two additional times in October 1907 and March 1908, and each time, U.S. immigration authorities denied him entry based on his medical condition. Desperate to gain entry, Iguchi contacted a friend in Seattle, Nada Tokujiro, "to find some way by which [Iguchi] could enter the United States." Tokujiro sent one Mr. Hashizume to Vancouver with the intention of having him escort Iguchi across the border and into Seattle, Washington. The plan comprised several steps: They took a train from Vancouver to Cloverdale, British Columbia, and from there they walked by foot across the international line to Blaine, Washington, and spent the night at a nearby hotel. In the morning, they left for Bellingham where they were supposed to take a boat to Seattle; unfortunately for them, U.S. border inspectors apprehended the Japanese migrants before they could complete the final leg of their journey.[67]

Precisely because of cases like this, U.S. officials applied pressure on Canada to modify its immigration standards and regulations to conform to those of the United States. U.S. immigration inspectors complained that the less rigorous inspection standards encouraged Chinese, Japanese, and South Asian immigrants to exploit Canada as a backdoor into the United States. In his final report to Congress in 1907, Marcus Braun wrote "[t]hat the medical examination conducted by United States surgeons at Vancouver and Victoria is thorough and rigid, but that any alien so rejected can do as he pleases thereafter, staying in Canada if he desires and later smuggling himself across the line into the United States with little difficulty."[68] Under pressure from U.S. authorities, the Canadian Immigration Bureau in 1909 began to summarily reject Asian arrivals diagnosed with "loathsome disease" and prohibited them from landing at their ports of entry, putting their policy in line with American immigration procedures.[69]

In the Pacific Northwest, professional smugglers helped unauthorized Asian migrants circumvent the border. Prior to the boundary enforcement buildup, Chinese, Japanese, and South Asian immigrants could pay a nominal fee to be guided across the international line. Coastal aboriginals in British Columbia, for example, piloted Chinese and Japanese transients to the United States for as little as three dollars. Fumiko Uyeda Groves shared that her grandfather and his friends in 1900 paid five dollars to have "somebody row them from Vancouver Island to Port Blakely on Bainbridge Island."[70] By 1914, Special Immigrant Inspector Roger O'Donnell testified before the House Committee on Immigration that the Chinese were willing to pay anywhere between one hundred and one thousand dollars to be smuggled into the United States.[71] While inspector O'Donnell may have exaggerated the figures, he was accurate in suggesting that Asian smuggling had become big business in the new era of the border. Noted Asian smuggler George Nelson told authorities that he charged between $125 and $150 per Chinese alien. Working as a fireman for the Great Northern, Nelson concealed his human contraband in the toolbox within the engine tender, and once his train made it safely across the border, Nelson delivered immigrants to a Chinese labor agent in Seattle.[72]

Asian ethnic labor contractors also contributed to the cross-border flow of illegal Asian migrants. In 1907, Japanese labor agent T. Sengoku confided to an informant for the U.S. Immigration Service that he had "taken three hundred Japanese across the Border at Blaine" and "placed [them] at work in the state of Idaho in the building of the Great Northern Railway." In the same conversation, he boasted "he would be able to get Hindoos across the border without examination provided they were first taken down and put to work on the Canadian side for a few days' time."[73] U.S. immigration officials also suspected the Green Investment Company, based in Walla Walla, Washington, of smuggling South Asian laborers across the border. The firm was part of a growing number of South Asian-owned lumber businesses in the region. In 1914, the Bureau intercepted a letter from company executives addressed to Gurdit Singh, encouraging him to recruit South Asian laborers. They assured him that they could find employment for his men in the state of Washington.[74]

In May 1914, Gurdit Singh chartered the Japanese steamship liner *Komagata Maru* to sail directly from India to Vancouver. Dominion immigration officials refused to dock the ship and attempted to force it and the passengers on board back to Asia. When those on board resisted, the Dominion police attempted to take control of the ship by force but the ship's passengers prevented them from boarding. Dominion authorities proceeded to deprive the passengers of food and water, and called in the Royal Canadian Navy.[75] For Gurdit Singh, the standoff was about claiming the full rights of English subjects. "We are British Citizens and we consider we have a right to visit any part of the Empire," he declared defiantly. "We are determined to make this a test case and if we are refused entrance into your country, the matter will not end here." For U.S. immigration officials, however, the *Komagata Maru* incident was nothing more than the ruse of an unscrupulous labor contractor who was landing South Asian immigrants in British Columbia, whom he would eventually sneak into the United States, for personal gain.

THE IMPERIAL COUNTERINSURGENCY

Dominion and British colonial officials, on the other hand, saw the *Komagata Maru* incident as the work of agents-provocateurs, of revolutionary sedition, as part of a worldwide plot to topple British imperial rule on the subcontinent. "The evidence in the case shows how deeply Gurdit Singh and his associates were implicated in the plots of the murderous revolutionary Indians in America. These plots are at present time being pursued with great vigour . . . and we have ample evidence that the extreme party among the Hindus in British Columbia sympathize actively with these 'Ghadar' efforts."[76] The arrests of Bhag Singh, Balwant Singh, and Mew Singh, for attempting to smuggle arms onto the ship, only served to heighten these concerns. The threat of radical nationalism turned the problem of illegal Asian immigration into a matter of national-imperial security. Indeed, unauthorized Asian border crossings now became tightly linked with foreign sedition, sparking widespread fears that foreign agents were circulating their radical agenda and ideas across porous and unprotected national boundaries.

However, as it was the case with illegal Asian aliens, menacing foreign Asian radicals were racialized constructs, elaborated to legitimize imperial rule and repression. "I endeavor to put before the East Indians the folly of disloyalty to the British Crown," British colonial official R. O. Montgomery asserted in 1915. "But once the seeds of disloyalty have taken root in the Oriental Mind it is hard to combat the results. Untrained in European ways (or Western) the mental attitude is different and failure to comprehend our ways and methods of progress and means of settling difficulties leads only to the employment of unlawful agencies."[77] Acts of anticolonial resistance were taken to be signs of racial inferiority and as evidence of their unfitness for self-rule. In 1905, Lord John Morley, the Secretary of State in India, opposed South Asian emigration to Canada precisely because of the "consequent danger" of the "untrained Oriental mind" being imbued with socialist and other radical doctrines abroad.[78]

Revolutionary activities in the South Asian diaspora led British colonial officials to construct an imperial system of surveillance at the turn of the twentieth century. Believing that the growing political unrest on the Indian subcontinent was connected to revolutionary agitation abroad, colonial agents tracked the movements of South Asian radicals to Europe, Asia, Africa, and North America. Judged to be the most subversive site of Indian diasporic nationalism, the borderlands of the North American West drew the highest level of scrutiny. British colonial authorities, working closely with government officials from Canada and the United States, developed a counterinsurgency strategy to dismantle the international revolutionary network. The centerpiece of this strategy was to suppress the migration and mobility of South Asian radicals, across the Pacific and across landed borders in the North American West, through a transnational system of surveillance and control.

The newly created Department of Criminal Intelligence in India selected William Hopkinson to lead these efforts in the Canadian outpost of the empire. The son of a British military officer and a Brahmin mother, Hopkinson was born in Delhi in 1880. In India, Hopkinson was a member of the colonial police and was, at different points in his career, responsible for pacifying the Punjab and Calcutta—known hotbeds for anticolonial insurgency. Familiar with the backgrounds of revolutionary exiles on the west coast of North America and fluent in a number of South Asian languages, he was the ideal candidate for the position.[79] Relocating to Vancouver in 1908, Hopkinson initially split his time between the Canadian Immigration Service and the Dominion police force. There, he methodically assembled a team of loyal ethnic informants to assist him in monitoring the movement and activities of South Asian migrants and their communities on both sides of the U.S.-Canadian boundary. In agreeing to provide translation services for the U.S. Immigration Bureau in Seattle, Hopkinson and his informants obtained the right to freely move across the border, allowing them to expand their area of surveillance to include Washington, Oregon, and Northern California.

Hopkinson used this arrangement to develop a transborder network of surveillance in the North American West. In 1913, financed by the India Office in London and the Canadian government, he was granted a paid leave from the Immigration Department in 1913 to investigate the South Asian radicals associated with the revolutionary Ghadar Party in San Francisco.[80] For months, Hopkinson tracked the "extremist" Har Dayal, the reputed leader of the movement in that city, who was suspected of playing a role in an assassination attempt on Viceroy Lord Hardinge in December 1912, following his movements and those of his followers.[81] By 1913, Hopkinson was on the payrolls of the Dominion government, the British India Office, and the U.S. Immigration Service. His multiple affiliations enabled him to construct and maintain an elaborate intelligence network on the North American continent.[82]

Hopkinson's transnational policing operation consisted of identifying and censoring seditious publications, pursuing suspected political agitators, and infiltrating the revolutionary organizations they were tied to. Hopkinson and his cadre of informants spent much of their time and energy tracking the steps of revolutionary leaders across the North American West. Hopkinson intercepted a letter from G. D. Kumar, addressed to Taraknath Das, that showed the division of labor among the leaders of the agitation, as well as the matrix of sites linking the revolutionary movements in Canada and the United States. Upon learning of the movement's infrastructure and networks, Dominion counterinsurgency strategies focused on harassing key revolutionaries, and maintaining surveillance networks in each of these locales. Hopkinson, on the trail of Taraknath Das for some time, eventually convinced Canadian authorities to shut down two nationalist projects of his: his school for South Asian laborers in New Westminster, and his newspaper, the *Free Hindusthan*, published out of offices in Vancouver. While Das insisted that the school was strictly for language-training purposes, he did later admit that they not only taught Sikh laborers "how to read and write English" but also "about their rights" and making "every Hindusthan understand how he is oppressed at home." Yet even after Das relocated across the border to Seattle, seeking to escape the surveillance of British and Canadian authorities, Hopkinson arranged for his contacts in the Seattle Immigration Bureau to sift through his mail and monitor his whereabouts.[83]

In his role as immigration inspector, Hopkinson used his discretionary powers to hinder the growth of anticolonial resistance by denying admissions to incoming South Asian immigrants suspected of having subversive ties and by deporting those radicals who had already been admitted. The ambiguous citizenship status of South Asians made them vulnerable to the latter state tactic. In the case of Hussain Rahim, Hopkinson's attempts to deport the political agitator were thwarted by the Canadian legal system. In an earlier search of Rahim's place of residence, Dominion police discovered "letters from Taraknath Das, editor of the *Free Hindusthan*, together with a notebook which contained, amongst a miscellaneous collection of memoranda, the addresses of a number of Hindu agitators in different parts of the United States of America, South Africa, Switzerland, Egypt, France, etc., also notes on the manufacture of nitro-glycerin."[84] Rahim's affiliations with white labor militants served to further enhance his image as a dangerous radical. At the time of his arrest, Rahim defiantly declared the following to Hopkinson: "You drive us Hindus out of Canada and we will drive out every white man out of India."[85]

Rahim emerged from the proceedings as a nationalist hero among the various South Asian immigrant communities, for he was viewed as a patriot who was willing to stand against the injustices of imperial rule. Several months earlier, the Hindustani Association in Vancouver had written a letter of protest to the Canadian Immigration Department, charging Hopkinson of malfeasance:

> We the Indian residents of British Columbia beg to bring to your notice a serious grievance that the Interpreter named Mr. W. C. Hopkinson employed by the Immigration Officer at Vancouver, B.C. does not understand Punjabi language of the Punjabis forming 95 per cent of the Indian population. Many instances have occurred in which several of us know that he has intentionally or unintentionally rendered misinterpretation of deposition in Courts and

> Immigration Department and thus justice being miscarried and many of the Hindus, Sikhs, and Mohammedans being victimized.[86]

Rahim's legal victory over Hopkinson and the Canadian Immigration Department had therefore "bolstered up his position in the Hindu community here as to make him a leader and counselor in respect to all matters concerning their community."[87] In the case of Rahim, Hopkinson's attempt to contain radical nationalism through immigration restriction had backfired in a big way.

The most dramatic confrontation between South Asian revolutionaries and Hopkinson occurred in May 1914, when Gurdit Singh challenged Canadian immigration restriction by sailing into the port of Vancouver on the Japanese steamship liner *Komagata Maru* with close to four hundred Punjabi passengers. Denied entry, the South Asian immigrant community vigorously challenged the ruling, demanding that the rights of Crown subjects be recognized. Revolutionary activists collected funds for provisions and legal assistance for the South Asians on board. The stalemate lasted for two months, with the boat remaining undocked in Vancouver harbor, as the Dominion delegation, including Hopkinson, tried to negotiate a settlement with a committee representing the immigrants, chaired by Hussain Rahim. The conflict served to galvanize and unite the disparate members of the South Asian community in British Columbia's lower mainland, and attracted South Asian nationalists and concerned countrymen from all across the North American West.

Following a legal battle, the Canadian courts upheld the Immigration Department's early decision, ruling that only 24 of the ship's 376 passengers would be landed. On July 23, 1914, exactly two months after the ship's arrival, the *Komagata Maru* sailed away from the shores of Canada and started its return voyage to Asia. Hopkinson suspected that Rahim and other revolutionary agitators had orchestrated the entire affair to encourage sedition among South Asians in the Pacific Northwest.[88] And while it was certainly true that the incident exacerbated their grievances against British colonial rule, it did so because it revealed the emptiness of the Crown's promise of equal rights and privileges for its imperial subjects. Hopkinson and his cadre of imperial informants emerged as exemplars of abusive British colonial power and became targets of political violence. Following the departure of the controversial steamship liner, revolutionary nationalists murdered Hopkinson and several of his Sikh informants for being British collaborators.

FIGURE 5.1. Indian immigrants on board the *Komagata Maru* in English Bay, Vancouver, British Columbia. 1914. Library and Archives Canada/Credit: Woodruff/Natural Resources Canada fonds/PA-034015.

The string of assassinations was part of a systematic strategy to dismantle the British surveillance system in the Pacific Northwest—a tactic made popular by nationalist militants in India.[89] South Asian militants threatened U.S. immigration inspectors as well, alleging that they were in alliance with Dominion authorities to oppress the South Asian people. U.S. immigration inspector Charles Reily, for example, told his superiors that he had been "approached by Hindus who have warned me if any effort was made to find either Har Dayal or R. Chandra they would personally see that I was 'blown up,' or 'pushed off the dock at night,' or my family molested. It was explained to me that the work of Har Dayal, and the interests of the Hindu Nationalist Party were of such importance that rather than permit any interference with their plans they would cheerfully dispose of me in some manner."[90]

As tensions between colonial authorities and anticolonial activists intensified in the period leading up to World War I, sites along the border dividing Washington and British Columbia emerged as highly contested spaces. Revolutionary agitators had turned the boundary into an arena for subversive activities. Traveling between the United States and Canada, they

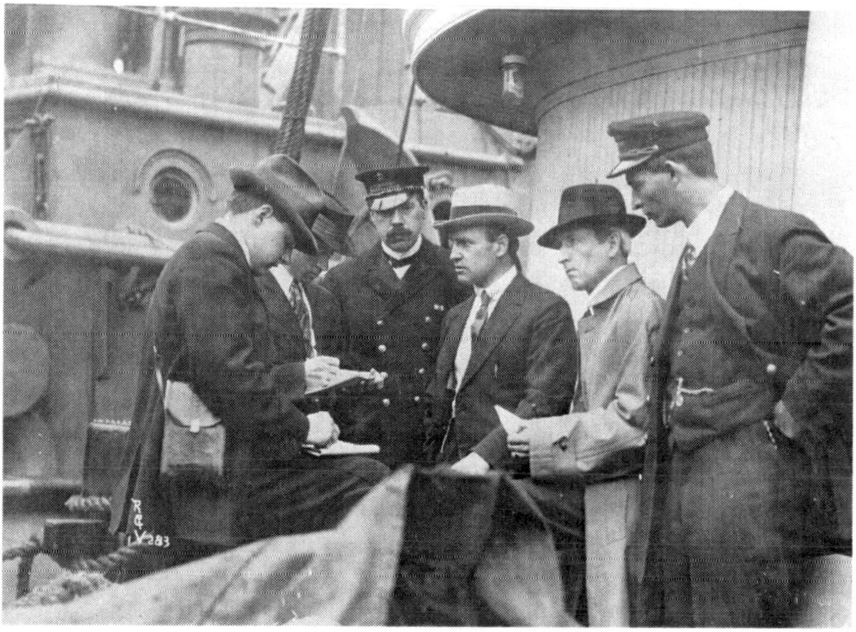

FIGURE 5.2. H. H. Stevens (center) interviewed by reporters, while Inspector Reid (center left) looks on, on board the *Komagata Maru* in English Bay, Vancouver, British Columbia. Vancouver, BC, 1914. Library and Archives Canada/Credit: Woodruff/Natural Resources Canada fonds/PA-034017

persuaded, conspired, and established links between the different immigrant groups and communities on the west coast of North America. In addition to organizing, radicals exploited transborder mobility to clandestinely smuggle arms and revolutionary propaganda. In 1915, the Dominion government passed an order in council that gave Canadian officials the authority to censor materials considered "likely to cause disaffection to her Majesty's forces." Local authorities used the power to intercept and filter mail addressed to South Asian residents in the province. Revolutionary activists evaded state censorship by having members covertly convey nationalist writings like the U.S.-based papers the *Ghadar* and the *Free Hindusthan* across the northern boundary.[91] "Many of the copies which have been intercepted show signs of having passed through many hands," explained one government official. "We may safely assert that there are very few among the 5,000 Indians on the Pacific Coast who do not read or listen to the contents of the *Ghadar* every week," and therefore, "we may hold with tolerable certainty that a considerable proportion of the Indian settlers . . . look upon armed rebellion in India as both desirable and practicable."[92] Canadian immigration officials acknowledged that this cross-border "means of entrance is one hard to overcome."[93] Indeed, even after enacting the ban, the Dominion chief of police received word that the *Ghadar* continued to circulate among South Asian lumber workers. The *Daily Province* reported similarly that South Asian nationalists circumvented government censorship by having "the paper addressed in special wrappers to European residents in the city, who not knowing they were assisting in the distribution of the paper, handed it over to their East Indian acquaintances."[94]

Consequently, Anglo-American powers moved to exert greater control over the U.S.-Canadian boundary, seeking to suppress the movement of South Asian nationalists, the circulation of anticolonial literature, and the smuggling of arms and explosives across the border. In this way, the border was elaborated against the menacing Asian insurgent as well as the illegal Asian alien. The counterinsurgency campaign on the border involved cultivating closer ties with the U.S. Immigration Service. U.S. authorities were first made aware of the problem in December 1907, when an undercover British agent sent an urgent cable to the U.S. Immigration Bureau in Washington DC, stating that South Asian revolutionaries "were proceeding from British Columbia to the United States for the purpose of promoting sedition against the British government, and particularly for the purpose of engaging in the manufacture of bombs and other explosives to be used by their countrymen against the British government." The cable petitioned the Bureau to forward all leads and information concerning South Asian political agitation to Dominion officials in Ottawa, who would in turn transmit the findings to the India Office in London. The India Office in London, in turn, materially assisted the antiradical efforts on the North American continent by providing resources for additional border personnel to monitor and enforce the boundary. There were also rumors that the British consular offices were paying U.S. border inspectors for information concerning the movement of suspected political agitators.[95]

These ties grew as the insurgency gained traction with South Asians in the Pacific Northwest. Prior to his death, W. C. Hopkinson furnished the U.S. Immigration Service in Seattle with "confidential information relative to the movements of Hindus, both in the United States and Canada, and through his efforts were able to identify and return to Canada quite a number of Hindus" who were falsely claiming residence in the United States.[96] This alliance was formalized in the wake of the *Komagata Maru* incident when U.S. Commissioner General of Immigration Anthony Caminetti arranged a conference with Richard McBride, head of the provincial government, to discuss how American and British Columbian authorities could "cooperate to suppress the Hindu immigration movement."[97] Soon after the meeting, Caminetti announced his intentions to secure appropriations for a "fast power boat," establish a more dense "border patrol from the Cascades to the coast," and consult with the British Foreign Office regarding the "serious and menacing aspect" of South Asian nationalism and anticolonial resistance in the Pacific Northwest borderlands.[98] The additional surveillance soon reaped dividends; several months later, the Seattle inspector in charge reported to Caminetti that a "number of Hindus have been apprehended while attempting surreptitious entry into the United States from Blaine, Washington and as far east as Eastport, Idaho."[99] The U.S. Immigration service had successfully leveraged its anti-Asian immigrant policy to the benefit of the Dominion's counterinsurgency strategy. That these revolutionary activities coincided with the onset of the First World War only served to intensify state responses to foreign radicalism on both sides of the border.

SUPPRESSING WHITE LABOR RADICALISM

Part of the reason the United States became so keen on assisting the British and the Dominion in suppressing radical nationalism was because, by World War I, the problems with "foreign sedition" and "subversive" advocacy had become their own. White labor radicals in the Pacific Northwest and across the North American West, in their militant calls for the overthrow of capitalism and the end to the war in Europe, were viewed as a grave threat to national security. Their associations with other "kindred groups"—South Asian and Chinese nationalists and foreign-born Bolsheviks and anarchists—only served to heighten these concerns.[100] In this wartime environment, fraught with fear of sedition from within and without, the United States and Canada deployed policing tactics and strategies that they honed against unauthorized Asian migrants and radicals—surveillance, deportation, covert infiltration, censorship, and intelligence gathering—to put down white labor revolt in the western U.S.-Canadian borderlands. In this way, the suppression of white labor militants contributed to the consolidation of nation-state sovereignty in the Pacific Northwest that complicates the genealogy of the border traced thus far.

The IWW in their effort to build "one big union" took their gospel of workers' internationalism directly into the logging and mining districts straddling the U.S.-Canadian boundary, organizing on both sides of the imaginary line in the Pacific Northwest. This mobile strategy reflected the organization's transnational aspirations, which were recognized in the opening moments of its founding convention when Canadian delegate John Riordan made the case for naming the union the Industrial Workers of the World instead of the narrow, nation-based Industrial Workers of America, which was the other proposed name on the table. Activists in the Pacific Northwest embraced this internationalist vision, insisting there was "no difference between Canada and the United States."[101] Putting this idea into practice, white labor radicals of the IWW frequently crossed the border to engage in labor organizing, general strikes, free speech fights, boycotts, and sabotage. Part of this transborder labor activism also involved the circulation of revolutionary literature and publicity. The *Industrial Worker,* for example, which was published in Spokane, Washington, was distributed on both sides of the border.[102] This intentional cross-border outreach resulted in the establishment of nine local unions in British Columbia in 1909, combining for a Canadian membership of close to 4,000.[103]

Yet, at the same time that IWW activists were traversing the boundary line, unionizing excluded migrant workers and calling for the end of capitalist rule on both sides of the border, the state was looking for ways to contain the "red menace" of the West. Across the region, state authorities confiscated and destroyed revolutionary publications and arrested and deported hundreds of IWW members, all under the pretext of wartime emergency.[104] The wartime panic that saw foreign subversion behind almost every social disturbance gave the state considerable latitude to pursue alien labor agitators.[105] The organization's steadfast work organizing among racially suspect, immigrant laborers—pejoratively labeled "hoboes" and "tramps"—made charges of disloyalty and un-Americanism easier to stick.[106] As it was the case with Asian aliens and activists, white labor radicals were tarred as foreign imports that threatened the fabric of American society. And as it was the case with Asian aliens and radicals, the modest success that IWW members had in using the court system to obtain relief from infringements on their liberties only served to bring down the full array of state powers upon them.

Having already dealt with the various foreign threats posed by Asian migrants, the U.S. Immigration Service in Seattle was at the cutting edge of state antiradicalism. The general strikes, work slowdowns, and sabotage the IWW engaged in on the waterfront and in the forests and mines of the Pacific Northwest proved to be highly disruptive to the war effort. Thus, with the full support of the Commissioner General of Immigration, Anthony Caminetti—who believed that the IWW posed the "same menace in the West" as the Russian Workers' Union in the East (the group that was targeted in the infamous Palmer Raids of 1919)—the Seattle Immigration Service, led by Henry M. White, set an ambitious agenda to rid the region of foreign radicals and agitators.[107] In this effort, deportation would become the weapon of choice. As historian William Preston Jr. has written, "The battle focused on the immigrant and produced new and more effective deportation legislation to destroy the supposed alien foundation of the radical superstructure."[108] Reading the revised Espionage Act as broadly as possibly, Henry White and his team of immigration inspectors, with the support of employers, the military, and racist-nativist organizations like the American Legion and the Klu Klux Klan, aggressively pursued leaders and members of the IWW. Because of their concerted effort, the Pacific Northwest identified more foreign immigrants for deportation than any other region.

The Immigration Service's repressive tactics, which grossly stretched the letter of the law, received considerable pushback from certain members of President Woodrow Wilson's administration, especially from the secretary of labor, who held final authority on matters related to deportation. The legality of the administrative orders that were sending foreign radicals east by the train full was questioned by labor department officials, who argued that "mere membership in that organization [IWW] does not bring aliens within scope of act of October, 1918." Unless he'd "advocated or done anything or conspired with others to do anything bringing him within the scope of said statute . . . warrant will not issue without the usual prima facie proof showing such advocating or acting or conspiracy."[109] The antiradical stalwart Anthony Caminetti, in his capacity as Commissioner General of Immigration, argued unsuccessfully that the members of the IWW should be placed on the same legal footing as the communists of the Russia Workers' Union who were detained and deported en masse under "the anarchistic provisions of the immigration laws."[110] His arch-restrictionist ally in Congress, Albert Johnson, echoed his argument, insisting "that the joining of an organization such as the Industrial Workers of the World by an alien is of itself the overt act sufficient to warrant deportation," but to no avail.[111]

Facing this setback, Henry White and the Seattle Immigration Service worked diligently to conform to the Labor Department's administrative interpretation. Going forward, immigration inspectors were instructed to detain and deport IWW members on the very specific charge that they were "teaching or advocating the destruction of property," which was established "by the nature of the literature which it publishes, sells, or disseminates."[112] In cases where this charge could not be clearly established, the Bureau went back to using tried and true methods of exclusion. For example, a good number of IWW members, who were in the country less than five years, were rounded up and deported on the grounds of being a "public charge."[113] The transience of IWW members, who frequently moved back and forth across the U.S.-Canadian boundary, and their status as migrant workers, left them especially vulnerable to this strategy. The deportation proceedings brought against Bulgarian immigrant Golf S. Marhow were a case in point. Unable to sustain the charge of anarchism, that he was neither calling for the overthrow of the government or advocating for the destruction of property, the Bureau instead claimed that the "petitioner was a person likely to become a public charge at the time of his entry into the United States."[114]

The government's war against foreign radicalism also involved suppressing the transborder mobility of white labor militants. The Immigration Service in Seattle directed U.S. border inspectors and mounted watchmen to guard the boundary against members of the IWW. During the free-speech fights in Spokane, Aberdeen, and Missoula in 1910 and 1912, for example, border inspectors were deployed on the line to turn back a "Wobbly invasion" from Canada.[115] Border controls that were initially designed to restrict Asian mobility were now being deployed against white labor radicals. Like Asian migrants before them, white labor activists, who were used to moving back and forth across a fluid landscape, would, too, begin to feel the effects of a spatial discipline of a more strictly delineated boundary line. "This freedom of passage [across the border] was less restricted in earlier years than now, with the tightening of Immigration and Customs laws," socialist trade unionist Angus MacInnis recalled, when "organizers, both for unions and for radicals groups, were free to come and go." He remembered very specifically the "Russian Revolution" being the moment when all of this had changed.[116]

Joining these efforts to control the transborder mobility of white labor radicals were authorities from Canada, who also viewed the labor politics of the IWW as an existential threat to the existing social order.[117] In 1912, the IWW was involved in several high-profile labor uprisings, including walkouts that stalled the construction of the Canadian Northern and Grand Trunk Pacific Railways and free-speech fights in Vancouver that led to violent clashes between local authorities and labor activists, which brought the IWW to the attention of the state. Referring to the growing agitation and radicalism among laborers on the west coast, Earl Grey, Governor General of Canada, fretted that "the beautiful Province of British Columbia has the clutch of Yankee Unionism upon its lovely throat and it can only gasp, not breathe."[118] Canadian officials came to view Wobbly organizers as dangerous radicals who threatened to import their brand of revolutionary unionism to British Columbia. Thus, in response, Canadian authorities, including the Customs and Immigration Department, Royal Canadian Mounted Police (RCMP), and local police, worked collaboratively to restrict the mobility of foreign radicals, believed to be the main agitators behind the social unrest and disorder engulfing their westernmost province.

Dominion officials modeled their antiradicalism and labor repression after the United States, having adopted many of the same measures. Like the United States, Canada organized a campaign of mass raids, lockups, and deportation of foreign agitators, which was given sanction by a series of orders in council passed as wartime measures.[119] Like their U.S. counterparts, Dominion officials, in their efforts to quell labor radicalism in their westernmost provinces, did violence to the law. As Canadian immigration officer Thomas Gelley admitted, "our legal action in these cases has not rested upon a very solid foundation."[120] Dominion authorities also concluded that breaking up the anarchist-radical network of the IWW would require restraining white labor mobility across the border. In 1913, Canadian officials ordered the deportation of leading IWW activist Joseph Ettor from British Columbia. Before being detained by immigration inspectors at White Rock, British Columbia, Ettor was in Seattle organizing workers for the IWW. He was scheduled "to address two IWW meetings in Victoria, and one in Vancouver," when Canadian immigration officers boarded his train and "showed him deportation orders from the chief of police at Vancouver and Canadian immigration headquarters at Ottawa."[121] He was placed aboard a train returning to Seattle the next morning and was told that if he tried to return to Canada he would be arrested and subject to a penalty of two years in prison and a heavy fine. Canadian immigration inspectors were also instructed by Ottawa to detain and deport IWW leaders William D. Haywood, William E. Troutman, Vincent St. John, and Floyd Lake if they ever tried to enter Canada.[122]

Having previous experience working together policing the boundaries of the nation, much of these antiradical efforts were coordinated jointly by the United States and Canadian governments. For example, blacklists and intelligence reports on individual IWW members and their whereabouts and activities were shared routinely between different individuals and across different departments, between the U.S. and Canadian Immigration Departments, the Royal North West Mounted Police (RNWMP), the Dominion Police, the U.S. military, and private militia and police groups such as the Pinkertons. Under this bilateral arrangement, some IWW members were deported twice, in succession, being deported from Canada to the United States and then from the United States to their country of origin.[123] This bilateral relationship in which Canada and the United States exchanged intelligence and internal security methods, streamlined exclusionary policies, and reinforced each other's border patrol was a shared commitment to a national security state as well as the prerogatives of capital.

CONCLUSION

The struggles waged between the state and illegal Asian aliens and foreign radicals in the Pacific Northwest never took place under equal terms. Unauthorized Asian migrants and political operatives still continued to cross the border, but as the state's intrusions into their world were backed by new systems of surveillance and control, their movements and activities became much less frequent. Their earlier success in crossing the boundary line only served to justify and expand the reach of sovereign power into their lives and their communities. The application of new coercive state powers rendered the border legible and eventually bred compliance.[124] "Some of them do get by without a doubt," wrote Commissioner Weedin of the Seattle Immigration station in 1924, "but we do not think there is a great deal of smuggling of Oriental immigrants into the country that way anymore." The battle against migrant illegality, radical nationalism, and labor militancy transformed the U.S.-Canadian boundary from an imaginary line on maps and atlases to a lived reality in the Pacific Northwest. In the process, it established territorial sovereignty as the rightful prerogative of the nation-state in which technologies and practices like border patrol and checkpoints, immigration detention and deportation, and travel and identification documents became standard, even natural, expressions of state sovereignty that would be brought to bear against new foreign threats and to elaborate future borders. "No, we don't and won't have as much trouble along the Canadian border as we will along the Mexican border," Commissioner Weedin explained. Indeed, he predicted in 1924 that, "The Mexican border will be the big problem of the future."[125]

Epilogue and Conclusion

BOUNDED NATIONS AND BOUNDLESS MARKETS

> THE GREATEST TRADE AND COMMERCE that will ever be had in this world is awaiting some city on the Pacific that is willing, able, wise, and foresighted enough to reach and secure it. This idea is not an opinion, it is reality. Already this trade amounts to hundreds of millions a year; but that is only a beginning. The China Club can secure most of this trade for Seattle if it will sincerely strive to secure it. That trade is not only between China (especially South China) but also between the Philippines, Japan, and the United States.[1]

> But this [domestic] field, as vast it is, is nothing compared with the vaster foreign field in which Seattle merchants will soon be pushing their trade. The teeming millions of the Orient, are, for all purposes of trade, Seattle's near neighbors. The trade of China, which is for the most part in British hands, is now estimated at $130,000,000 annually, and it can securely be said that it is yet in its infancy. The development of this vast empire has but begun, and, though the China trade has been the stake for which nations have waged war through a dozen centuries, it is as nothing compared with what it will be in the near future.[2]

THE FIRST DECLARATION WAS PRINTED in a letter to Seattle China Club members in 1925. The second was penned by a Washington State pioneer in 1890. These almost identical paeans to the "Oriental trade," separated by some thirty-five years, might be considered an earlier version of what historian Bruce Cumings has called "rimspeak"—a discourse that rendered Euro-American capitalist penetration of the Asia-Pacific a natural, even inevitable, outcome of a shrinking world.[3] As the two passages suggest, the intervening years of unfulfilled promises did little to diminish the obsession with the "China markets" and faith in its transformative power to turn Seattle into a vital hub for transpacific commerce and trade. Nor did the intense backlash against Asian immigrants and the border buildup it initiated do much to slow the pursuit of Asian markets. In fact, a huge surge in foreign trade with Asia was witnessed in this age of exclusion, which integrated Seattle and its surrounding hinterlands more tightly into the orbit of Pacific commerce. The proliferation of boundaries was thus, paradoxically, accompanied by intensifying transnational flows of people, goods, and capital that collapsed space and time, paving the way for a more unified global marketplace. Embodying one of the central contradictions of the global age, bounded nations that imagined themselves as discrete, inviolable spaces remained firmly committed to working toward "a global realm with no limits."[4]

The dialectics of globalization, I argue, reworked the logic of race in new and important ways during this period, shifting the terms of inclusion and exclusion to accommodate the expansionist imperatives of global capitalism. The rhetoric of international goodwill, cross-cultural understanding, and bridging the divide between East and West—pieces of a protomulticulturalism, if you will—increasingly came up in the context of promoting international trade with Asia and was therefore inextricably intertwined with the globalization of trade and finance. This cosmopolitan capitalism, which manipulated racial and cultural differences to gain an advantage in a highly competitive world economy, gestured toward the racial liberalism that was to come in the postwar era.

THE SEATTLE CHINA CLUB

On a fall evening in 1916, leading citizens of Seattle—financiers, industrialists, merchants, educators, and policy makers—gathered at the upscale New Washington Hotel in downtown Seattle to hear a presentation from Julean Arnold, the commercial attaché in China for the United States Department of Commerce.[5] As the distinguished guests dined on Peking duck, pineapple chicken, and steamed rice, Arnold rattled off facts and figures about the Asia trade, paying tribute to its vast potential. For example, he projected China's foreign trade growing from a little over a billion dollars to sixty-five billion in the next several decades and believed that if Seattle was strategic about it, the emerald city could capture a substantial share of this expanding trade and commerce. He insisted that "no other city is as well favored to take the initiative . . . in building up trade between the two countries." Concluding his presentation, Arnold noted the following: "The people of the United States have seen China in the past through the eyes of Europe." But he contended

FIGURE 6.1. The original members of the China Club of Seattle, September 9, 1916. The Wing Luke Museum.

that "[t]he United States is now a Pacific power and we must understand China and the Orient by seeing them directly across the ocean."[6] His presentation was persuasive: By the end of the night, a number of members of the audience pledged to support his proposal to start the China Club—an organization wholly devoted to encouraging foreign trade between the United States, China, and Asia more broadly.

The years of frustration and disappointment experienced by the likes of Chin Gee Hee, Charles Takahashi, and James J. Hill apparently did little to debunk the myth of the China markets. Thomas Burke, for one, who witnessed the ups and downs of the Oriental trade firsthand as Hill's lawyer and partner, went on to double down on his patron's failed vision, helping to launch the China Club in 1916. As the club's first president, Burke tapped into his extensive political and social networks to bring together a veritable who's who of finance, banking, trading, shipping, and education in Seattle. Inaugural members included, among others, D. W. Hartzell, president of the Northwest Trading Co., William Pigott, founder of the Seattle

Steel and Seattle Car Manufacturing Co., J. E. Chilberg, president of the Scandinavian-American Bank, Richard Ballinger, former U.S. secretary of the interior, Ross Piles, secretary of the Foreign Trade Bureau of Seattle, and Dr. Henry Suzzallo, president of the University of Washington. Burke was, of course, no slouch himself, having been a former State Supreme Court chief justice and at the time of the start of the China Club, the president of the Seattle Chamber of Commerce and the president of the Associated Chambers of Commerce on the Pacific coast.

The China Club opened to great fanfare in September 1916. As to be expected, the business community in Seattle and elsewhere on the Pacific coast was effusive in its praise: "The new organization will become a valuable force, not only in stimulating the trade of Seattle with the great country of China, but in promoting friendly contact between America and the Orient."[7] The club's vision also happened to intersect with the interests of the state, for it dovetailed neatly with America's "Open Door" policy in China, and thus drew the endorsement of government officials and policy makers as well. Both the offices of the secretary of commerce and the secretary of state sent formal letters of congratulations in 1916. In his letter, E. T. Williams, chief of the Far East division of the State Department, wrote glowingly: "I am glad to hear of this enterprising action of the Seattle businessmen. It is a step in the right direction. The future possibilities of our trade with China are very great, and this is, it appears to me, the psychological moment for action."[8]

The talk of the China trade's great promise only served to magnify what was at stake for Seattle and generated a sense of urgency among members of the China Club: "The commerce has grown so rapidly that it has aroused San Francisco, England, Japan, and Germany and the China Club will have the battle of its life to secure for Seattle the largest share of the increase of this commerce."[9] In this global competition, only those cities and nations willing to take vigorous and concerted action—that is, those willing to exploit their competitive advantage to the fullest—would prevail. As Thomas Burke sternly warned, "For, unless we are able to do that, we might as well give up the race before we have begun, and settle down to the habits and customs of a third or fourth rate provincial town."[10] Burke himself had no intention of consigning Seattle to backwater status. Under his leadership, the China Club worked aggressively on a number of different fronts and on both sides of the Pacific to capture the Oriental trade for Seattle. On the domestic side, the club leveraged the considerable political clout of its members to lobby local and national governments for improving maritime infrastructure, increasing trade subsidies, and relaxing shipping regulations. While not all of this lobbying was successful, it did result in certain tangible gains including upgrades to the Seattle harbor, construction of new grain elevators and warehouses, and slightly lower transpacific shipping rates.

At the same time, club officials understood that if their project were to be successful they would have to forge direct ties with the governments, businesses, and consumers of the Asia-Pacific: "Emphasis has been laid by Mr. Arnold on the fact that the Far Eastern trade of this country cannot flourish until we go over to China after it and establish our organizations there."[11] Acting on this advice, the China Club, in collaboration with the Seattle Chamber of Commerce, sent a delegation of Seattle financers, industrialists, and traders to China, Japan, and Korea, respectively, to gauge their potential industrial capacities. Thomas Burke led one such economic mission to Southeast China in 1916, where his group was given a tour of its countryside, seaports, factories, and offices. They were part of a burgeoning American presence in southern China. The previous year, prominent American businessmen and educators in Nanking, with the support of the American consul and local Chinese officials, had established the Chinese American Association. Its stated purpose was to "stimulate friendly intercourse between Chinese and American citizens." However, the business-heavy roster suggests that it was mostly commercial-related intercourse that the organization had in mind.[12]

These transpacific missions reignited old bonds dating back to Seattle's early days. In 1924, Burke's old friend Chin Gee Hee, who, if you recall, left for China to establish a railroad line in his home province, invited him and the Seattle China Club to come to the opening of the port in his district. Since his departure from Seattle, Chin Gee Hee had been hard at work on two closely related nation-building projects: the construction of the Sun Ning Railroad and the establishment of a port in the southern part of Guangdong province. In his letter of invitation in 1924, Chin wrote: "[S]ee for yourself just what such a port would mean to the business world of not only China and the U.S. but to the entire countries of the globe." Appealing to U.S. commercial interests, he explained how the port's opening "will enable the Chinese people to ship to China direct without having to have all cargoes first landed on British soil." Designed to compete with British Hong Kong, Chin explained "it will be the gateway to all of China and the U.S. will always have it within their control."[13]

Yet, as much as the "China market" was a product of material processes—constituted from newly developed consumer markets, trade partnerships, and so forth—it was also called into being through a discursive project that constructed Seattle as a natural gateway to the Asia-Pacific. "Naturally from its situation upon the sea coast, the Pacific Northwest, inhabited as it is by a commercial people, is brought into close commercial relations with the people of the Orient," Thomas Burke declared. "It is as certain as that tomorrow's sun will rise that the Pacific Ocean is soon to become the theatre of a mighty commerce. By virtue of our unrivaled resources, energy and enterprise, and of our commanding position on that ocean . . . this country is bound to become the dominating commercial power of that great sea." "Nothing," he contended, "could be more natural than that a commerce should spring up between the countries served by that great highway."[14] There was, of course, nothing "natural" about this vision: Transportation corridors, trade routes, and overseas markets were just some of the things that had to be constructed, artificially as it were, for his vision to come to fruition. This discourse, nevertheless, continued to loom large in China Club–sponsored speeches and writings. As a piece of club literature stated in 1925, "Seattle is 800 miles nearer the Orient than San Francisco and this, as you all know, is a permanent condition and makes the natural entry port to the trade of the Orient."[15]

The enormous growth in trade between Seattle and Asia in the immediate years following the club's formation served to substantiate this discourse, giving reality to the fiction that Seattle was simply fulfilling its destiny as the great gateway to the Asia-Pacific. Exports from Seattle to China and Japan—that is, the Oriental trade—grew from $40 million in 1916 to $168 million in 1919. Imports showed similar trends, increasing from $117 million in 1916 to $268 million in 1919. By 1922, the Asia trade constituted about half of Seattle's total foreign trade.[16] If you include Hawai'i, Alaska, and the Philippines in this figure, it rose close to two-thirds.[17] These formal and informal colonial markets existed as part of a series of interconnected overseas markets in which Seattle became a principal node. Cotton, grain, lumber, and wheat were among the commodities most actively being traded to Asia and the South Pacific. Not coincidentally, these were the same commodities that early Asia-market pioneers James J. Hill, Chin Gee Hee, and Charles Takahashi had worked so hard to cultivate in overseas markets several decades earlier. It appears that a new generation of Asia-market enthusiasts were now benefiting from their earlier efforts.

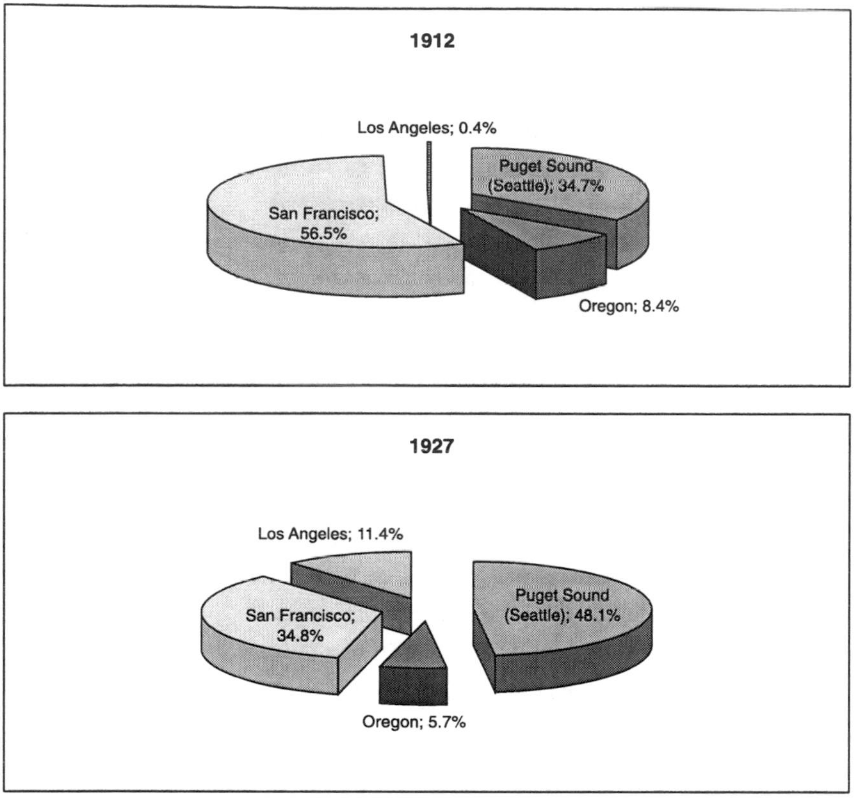

TABLE 6.1 Share of China Trade among U.S. West Coast Port Cities.

Despite the fact that this was supposed to be an inevitable outcome—Seattle becoming a leading transpacific city—the China Club was quick to seize credit for it. The club celebrated its ten-year anniversary in 1926 by toasting an important milestone for the city and by singling out the club's role in achieving it: That was the year when Seattle overtook San Francisco to become the leading port for the China trade on the West Coast. "As the Pacific Coast's leading seaport and as the port of entry to the Orient, the China Club believes Seattle's commercial future is connected in a most vital way with the future of China and the degree to which this city is able to cement its contacts with the Chinese in a friendly, understanding and constructive way. In this field of activity the China Club of Seattle stands alone and has a record of achievement for the ten years of existence which has met with the unqualified endorsement and admiration of the best interests of the city."

The strategy to open overseas markets and for informal empire in Asia incorporated the logic of an incipient multiculturalism that signaled a shift from white supremacy and settler colonialism to racial liberalism and transnational capitalism. The two, in fact, went hand in hand.[18] This is by no means to suggest a clean break from the racial past, of racial pogroms, riots, and exclusion.[19] As historian Thomas Holt has observed, the staying power of racism stems, in part, from the fact that "it is never entirely new": "Shards and fragments of its past incarnations are embedded in the new."[20] In the Pacific Northwest, the racial past lived on in the continued exploitation and subordination of racialized foreign bodies, signifying the persistent existence of racial domination and hierarchy. Nevertheless, there were important changes to the racial phenomenon and to the ideological work that it performed. Race was rearticulated in such a way to support Seattle's global aspirations. The China Club's mission statement hinted at this racial reworking: "The mission of the China Club of Seattle is to increase the awareness, understanding and appreciation of developments in Chinese culture, history, philosophy, and current affairs. We believe it is important to enhance the means for social and commercial interchange between our respective cultures."

In this section, I discuss how this embrace of cultural diversity followed from an imperial impulse to open Asia to global capitalism. As an early form of corporate liberal multiculturalism, it rendered Euro-American capitalist penetration of Asia and the Open Door ideology underpinning it innocuous, even benevolent. As Julean Arnold insisted in 1916, China and the rest of Asia welcomed "American capital, American materials, and American engineering skills," the Chinese people wanting "to see the American flag on the Pacific in a large and permanent way."[21] The strategy was developed as a corollary to the Open Door policy that was enunciated at the turn of the twentieth century, which largely eschewed the practice of opening foreign markets at gunpoint (in Asia, anyway) and instead called for less coercive measures. The Open Door, which called for equal access to Chinese markets among the world's major powers, was designed both to "get the American foot solidly into a market always fantasized as unfathomable and to hold China together at that critical level between competence and impotence."[22] The policy was premised on the belief that American businesses, if given a chance, could dominate just about anywhere, and is the reason some scholars have given as to why the United States was not as keen on a territorial empire.

I am not suggesting here that we can simply reduce multiculturalism to a capitalist ploy, a reductive economism, if you will. It was more complicated and more organic than that, born out of a liberal internationalism that saw the future comity of nations as being inextricably bound up with free trade and market liberalization.[23] That is to say, it was embedded in an "American way of looking at the world," an American "weltanschauung" as historian Bruce Cumings calls it, in which the spread of free markets was conflated with the spread of peace and prosperity.[24] Thomas Burke made these connections explicitly, highlighting the core principles of an emerging liberal world order, in an address he gave as president of the Seattle Chamber of Commerce to welcome a distinguished delegation of Japanese to Seattle in 1909: "In our day commerce is the great peacemaker and peace preserver. Every business transaction that goes to make up foreign trade is a bond of peace, a hostage to the world for the maintenance of the peace of nations."[25] The cultural logic of this still inchoate American internationalism reconfigured race in new and important ways, laying the foundation for the transition to racial liberalism.

The study of postwar racial liberalism has produced some terrific scholarship yielding important insights.[26] But, in my view, it has not paid enough attention to the material realities—that is, the changes to the global political economy—that went together with the postwar ascendance of racial liberalism. How, for example, the emergence of a liberal (and later neoliberal) world order reconfigured race, and whiteness more specifically, I believe, is still an open question. Nor has it, on a related issue, been sufficiently sensitive to regional and geographical variations, often equating the black-white experiences of the South and, more recently, of the North, with that of the nation. In doing so, scholars have missed sight of how racial liberalism, being wedded to specific political, economic, and cultural contexts, developed along regional lines and along a different set of racial axes. By providing a brief description of the multiculturalism of Seattle's corporate elite and the way it was deployed to perpetuate an empire of capital in Asia in the decades before World War II, this section suggests new places, both within and beyond the nation's borders, to look for the origins of postwar racial liberalism.

Americans with actual experience in China believed that the lack of competency in Chinese culture and language posed a serious obstacle for American businesses in China. In 1920, Julean Arnold lamented the fact that even students from elite institutions of higher learning in America "could not name or write correctly four of the most important cities in China." He asserted plainly that, "[t]he Chinese know more about us than we do about them."[27] And it was why he spent so much time, when stateside, trying to convince college and university presidents to add courses in Asian history, culture, and languages to their curricular. "If the American people are quite seriously interested in the marvelous trade potentialities which present themselves in China, they should without further delay create facilities here for such a study,"[28] he exhorted. He suggested they, "[e]ncourage the boys and girls in our schools to study Oriental history, literature, and geography." Arnold recommended that Henry Suzzallo, president of the University of Washington, establish a department of Chinese; the university, not coincidentally, became one of the major American centers for area studies during the Cold War.[29]

The Seattle China Club tried to address this cultural deficiency by appointing prominent educators and scholars, including Henry Suzzallo, Herbert Gowen, Frank B. Cooper, and M. M. Skinner, to the club's executive committee. Dr. Suzzallo was elected the first vice president of the China Club. Professor Gowen was the first chair of the Department of Oriental Studies, forerunner to the Jackson School of International Studies, at the University of Washington, and was later a part of Robert Park's Race Relations Survey team studying the "Oriental problem" on the Pacific coast.[30] Cooper was superintendent of Seattle schools and was a pioneer of sorts as one of the first American educators to add rudimentary Asian language learning to public school curricula. He was selected to be a delegate to the first Pan Pacific Conference on Education organized by the U.S. Department of Education in Honolulu, Hawai'i in 1921, its stated goal being to "bring all nations and peoples about the Pacific Ocean into closer friendly and commercial contact and relationship."[31] Skinner was professor of the College of Business Administration in the newly created department of foreign trade at the University of Washington. In 1921, the University of Washington, with financial support from the Seattle Chamber of Commerce and the China Club, granted Skinner a leave of absence from the university so that he could take up the post as head of the department of economics at Canton Christian College in China. In addition to his official duties at the college, he traveled and taught throughout China, visiting colleges and universities in Hankow, Peking, Shanghai, and Wuchang, "in the interest of a movement to organize commercial courses in leading mission colleges."[32] To put it more bluntly, Skinner was working feverishly, as one Chinese student journal noted, "to sell Seattle and the University of Washington to China."[33]

These cultural and scholarly exchanges began with the visit of W. K. Chung, the former commissioner of education of Canton, in November 1916. As the first formal guest of the Seattle China Club, the distinguished Chinese scholar and educator lectured on the "value of education as a forerunner of trade development."[34] Present at the event was Henry Suzzallo, Frank Cooper, and Herbert Gowen, who each individually affirmed the content of Chung's address during the question and answer time. In a joint venture with the University of Washington and the Seattle Chamber of Commerce, the Seattle China Club also conducted a student exchange program with China during this time. In 1925, the China Club lobbied Congress to allow China to send 10,000 students each year to the Pacific Northwest. Hoping to train native intermediaries who could facilitate trade and commerce between China and the United States, under the club's proposal, exchange students were required to take courses on trade as part of their education. J. C. Herbsman, executive secretary of the China Club, claimed that, "We will get back 10 for one of all that this plan costs us in time and effort."[35]

While believing these efforts to be salutary, Thomas Burke was convinced that the best way of raising up a new generation of Chin Gee Hees was to draw directly from the U.S. population of Chinese: Chinese Americans: "By our making selection of about 20 bright young Chinese men from this country who read, write, and understand both languages . . . [they] can be the go-between." "In such a manner, we will always have at our fingers end, men who can be relied upon to have a good idea of the trade workings on both sides of the water and in both languages, and this is the very thing that is causing many American companies a tremendously heavy loss, and threatening to drive three out of five of the Exporting and Importing companies to the wall."[36] Throwing their support behind Burke's proposal, Seattle's captains of industry endowed fifteen scholarships for such training, beginning in 1918. For its part, the University of Washington set up a specific academic track for these scholarship students that combined language training with an education in industrial and trade policy. Speaking at the National Foreign Trade Convention in May 1920, Clancy Lewis of the Manufacturers' Association of Washington made special mention of this scholarship program: "These Chinese students are conducting themselves in an admirable manner. They are showing their worth as students, and we realize and appreciate the fact that those men are going to be the contact between the commerce of at least the Northwestern section of the Pacific and China in the years to come."[37]

Immigration reform was also a key piece to this elite brand of corporate worldliness, going together with the program of cultural exchange and outreach. Without looking to overturn the exclusion laws on the books, the Seattle China Club and the Chamber of Commerce pressed U.S. officials to loosen immigrant regulations and to streamline bureaucratic procedures so as to make the bloated system less cumbersome for some Asian immigrants. One of the changes they sought most was to a policy that subjected exempt Chinese immigrants—merchants, teachers, students, and visitors—to the same set of draconian regulations and procedures that were applied to Chinese laborers:

> It is our opinion that there is a misconception on the part of authorities of the fundamental purpose and intent of the Chinese Exclusion Law. This law, and the Treaty upon which it is based, were aimed solely at the exclusion of Chinese laborers, all other classes being admissible as of right; whereas, the manner of its administration indicates an official belief that the purpose of the law is the exclusion of all Chinese with exception of certain privileged classes which are admitted as a matter of grace, and these applicants are faced with regulations which do not apply to immigrants generally and are in disregard of rights which are theirs in common with those of the most favored nation.[38]

For years, the U.S. Immigration Service in Seattle and elsewhere on the West Coast, as a matter of practice, had treated all Chinese immigrants, irrespective of their class status, as if they were laborers, until they could prove otherwise, posing difficulties for Chinese merchants, scholars, and students looking to enter or visit the country. Herbert Gowen made the case that such "[a]n iron-bound policy of exclusion can only keep apart, and that against the course of nature and against the interests of both sides of the Pacific"; he also argued that "commerce is developed with the Orient itself through the presence of Oriental agents here."[39]

The issue over exempt Asians came up again in the debate over the National Origins Act in the early 1920s. One of its key proposals, to bar admission to those immigrants "ineligible to citizenship," would have barred Asian immigrants from entering the country regardless of class status, effectively ending exemptions for Chinese and Japanese merchants and businessmen. The China Club and the Seattle Chamber of Commerce lobbied heavily against the legislation, pointing to the deleterious impact it would have on economic relations with the Far East. Despite their efforts, the National Origins Act became law in 1924, with the principal sponsor being a congressman from the State of Washington, no less. Addressing the trustees at the Carnegie Endowment for International Peace in New York City in 1925, Thomas Burke spoke out against the new law: "The immigration question, with all due respect to the Congress, was most unhappily handled." While affirming the plenary power of the federal government over immigration regulation, he thought nevertheless that the "end which the Congress aimed ar could have been attained by kindly methods and by maintaining friendly and neighborly relations with Japan. But that course was not followed."[40]

Yet, this high-minded rhetoric aside, the package of reforms the China Club advocated was never about challenging the status quo on immigration. Being mainly concerned with the reform's impact on commercial exchange and the expansion of markets, the China Club's immigration reform agenda was extremely narrow, one that reflected a distinct class bias.[41] The Club's proposals were, to be sure, a retreat from overt xenophobia and racism but, by affirming the state's plenary power to admit, exclude, and deport aliens based on a hierarchy of racial desirability, they continued to uphold the principle of racial exclusion enshrined in U.S. immigration and naturalization law. For instance, Burke thought it was both reasonable and good to limit the number of Asian immigrants entering the country. "In accordance with the policy of this country Japanese laborers and laborers from other Oriental countries are excluded from the United States," he explained in a 1919 speech. ". . . . This is a recognized right of every sovereign country. When exercised in a friendly and humane spirit no nation can complain of it."[42] Thus, on this score, Burke and the China Club were in complete agreement with anti-Asian restrictionists and nativists. Built into this broad consensus were shared assumptions about the nation, its racial and cultural character, and the threat posed to it by accepting too many inassimilable foreigners. But whereas restrictionists and nativists saw a future flood in a trickle, Seattle's elite, viewing Asian immigration as a necessary evil, thought that the nation could accept a small number of Asian foreigners without it having "an appreciable effect in altering the American type."[43] So when it came to the National Origins Act, it was not that they opposed the quota system per se but the fact that it would not allow for Asian immigration at all, keeping out those people who "help to keep up and develop trade."[44]

. . .

In 1925, delegates to the National Foreign Trade Convention in Seattle opened their proceedings by hailing the inauguration of a new era in Pacific relations in which the heterogeneous peoples and nations of the Far East, Europe, North America, and the Pacific would be joined together through international cooperation, mutual understanding, and a shared prosperity.[45] As a precursor to a future discourse of globalization, this talk of an integrated humanity, as Fernando Coronil has so eloquently written, "set in motion the belief that the separate histories, geographies, and cultures that have divided humanity are now being brought together by the warm embrace of globalization, understood as a progressive process of planetary integration."[46] Ironically, convention delegates cast this vision of a unified Pacific just as the United States had passed legislation to bar half of the world's population, and nearly all of the people of the Pacific, from entering the United States. Such were the creative tensions and contradictions of a globalization born of colonial modernity.

Focusing on the western U.S.-Canadian borderlands, this book has attempted to show how seemingly contradictory impulses—globalization and nationalization, inclusion and exclusion, mobility and immobility, and cosmopolitanism and parochialism—worked mutually, even dialectically, to forge an "American lake," a Pacific region aligned and configured by U.S. imperial power in the late nineteenth and early twentieth centuries. These dialectical strategies of U.S. imperial rule that simultaneously erected and erased boundaries, compelled and impeded movement, and denied and celebrated difference have perplexed scholars about the exact nature of America's empire for more than a generation, with the debates over whether or not it was a formal or informal empire and whether or not it was exceptional, still raging.[47] Yet, regardless of how we choose to label this American empire, its impact was undeniable, felt far and wide across the Pacific, in the new global divisions of labor and capital it structured, in the new legal and administrative classifications of people and territories it produced, and in the new boundaries of racial segregation it delineated, which were all underwritten by new relations of domination.

But as much as empire builders tried to control and manage the processes of imperial integration, the project fissured and fractured under the weight of its numerous contradictions. Indeed, the very agents that made this integration a possibility also brought the "contradiction between the Pacific as Euro-American invention and its Asian content," into sharp relief.[48] There were the Asian laborers who refused to be deployed and relocated for work; there were the Chinese and Japanese middlemen and brokers who engaged Euro-American imperial power through selective appropriation to strengthen, with varying success, their individual and their nation's position within this regional formation; and there were the South Asian radicals who traversed the circuits of empire to offer competing alternatives to an imperial modernity. They were the living embodiments of the contradictions and tensions at work in the region's creation, a world forged out of conflicting forces emanating from multiple locations and through different actors across the Pacific. As such, the imperial formation of the Pacific world portended the central contradictions and struggles of a future age: our present.

NOTES

INTRODUCTION

1. "Uniting of the Orient and the Occident," *Seattle Times*, Aug. 31, 1896.

2. *Report of Royal Commission on Chinese Immigration: Report and Evidence* (Ottawa, 1885), 155–60.

3. For a recent intervention in borderland studies that calls for a wider, hemispheric approach among its practitioners, see Jeremy Adelman and Stephen Aron, "From Borderlands to Borders: Empires, Nation-States, and the Peoples in Between in North American History," *American Historical Review* 104 (June 1999): 814–841. On the U.S.-Canadian borderlands, see Ken Coates and John M. Findlay, eds. *Parallel Destinies: Canadians, Americans, and the Western Border* (Seattle: University of Washington Press, 2002); Benjamin Johnson and Andrew R. Graybill, *Bridging National Borders in North America: Transnational and Comparative Histories* (Durham: Duke University Press, 2010); Sheila McManus, *The Line Which Separates: Race, Gender, and the Making of the Alberta-Montana Borderlands* (Lincoln: University of Nebraska Press, 2005). For a selection of the rich literature on the U.S.-Mexican borderlands, see Neil Foley, *White Scourge: Mexicans, Blacks, and Poor Whites in Texas Cotton Culture* (Berkeley: University of California Press, 1997); Linda Gordon, *The Great Arizona Orphan Abduction* (Cambridge: Harvard University Press, 2000); Samuel Truett, *Fugitive Landscapes: The Forgotten History of U.S.-Mexico Borderlands* (New Haven: Yale University Press, 2006); Alicia Schmidt Camacho, *Migrant Imaginaries: Latino Cultural Politics in the U.S.-Mexico Borderlands* (New York: New York University Press, 2008); Katherine Benton-Cohen, *Borderline Americans: Racial Division and Labor War in the Arizona Borderlands* (Cambridge: Harvard University Press, 2009).

4. Richard Drinnon, *Facing West: The Metaphysics of Indian-Hating and Empire-Building* (Norman: University of Oklahoma Press, 1997). See also Matthew Frye Jacobson, *Barbarian Virtues: The United States Encounters Foreign Peoples at Home and Abroad, 1876–1917* (New York: Hill and Wang, 2000); and Rob Wilson,

Reimagining the American Pacific: From South Pacific to Bamboo Ridge and Beyond (Durham: Duke University Press, 2000).

5. See Gerald Horne, *The White Pacific: U.S. Imperialism and Black Slavery in the South Seas After the Civil War* (Honolulu: University of Hawaii Press, 2007), 6. On this point, also Oscar Campomanes, "New Formations of Asian American Studies and the Question of U.S. Imperialism," *Positions: East Asia Cultures Critique* 5 (1997): 523–550.

6. Henry Yu, "Los Angeles and American Studies in a Pacific World of Migrations," *American Quarterly* 56:3 (Sept., 2004): 531–543. For recent efforts to re-orient U.S. history to the Pacific, see Bruce Cumings, *Dominion from Sea to Sea: Pacific Ascendancy and American Power* (New Haven: Yale University Press, 2009); Gary Y. Okihiro, *Island World: A History of Hawai'i and the United States* (Berkeley: University of California Press, 2008).

7. On how struggles over Asian migration in the Anglophone world spawned new migration and border controls, see Aristide Zolberg, "The Great Wall against China: Responses to the First Immigration Crisis, 1885–1925," in *Migration, Migration History, History: Old Paradigms and New Perspectives,* ed. Jan Lucassen and Leo Lucassen (Bern: Peter Lang, 1999); Erika Lee, *At America's Gates: Chinese Immigration During the Exclusion Era, 1882–1943* (Chapel Hill: University of North Carolina Press, 2003); Adam McKeown, *Melancholy Order: Asian Migration and the Globalization of Borders* (New York: Columbia University Press, 2008); and Marilyn Lake and Henry Reynolds, *Drawing the Global Colour Line* (Cambridge: Cambridge University Press, 2008).

8. On how the illegal Mexican alien and the southern boundary were mutually constructed, see George J. Sanchez, *Becoming Mexican-American: Ethnicity, Culture, and Identity in Chicano Los Angeles, 1900–1945* (Oxford: Oxford University Press, 1995), 38–62; Mae M. Ngai, *Impossible Subjects: Illegal Aliens and the Making of Modern America* (Princeton: Princeton University Press, 2004), 56–90; Joseph Nevins, *Operation Gatekeeper: The Rise of the "Illegal Alien" and the Making of the U.S.-Mexico Boundary* (New York: Routledge, 2002); Nicholas De Genova, *Working the Boundaries: Race, Space, and "Illegality" in Mexican Chicago* (Durham: Duke University Press, 2005); Kelly Lytle Hernandez, *Migra! A History of the U.S. Border Patrol* (Berkeley: University of California Press, 2010); and Rachel St. John, *Line in the Sand: A History of the Western U.S.-Mexico Border* (Princeton: Princeton University Press, 2011).

9. On how efforts to discipline and control imperial subjects was ultimately brought to bear on "domestic" spies and subversives, see Alfred McCoy, *Policing America's Empire: The United States, the Philippines, and the Rise of the Surveillance State* (Madison: University of Wisconsin Press, 2009).

10. Ann Laura Stoler and Frederick Cooper, "Between Metropole and Colony: Rethinking a Research Agenda," in *Tensions of Empire: Colonial Encounters in a Bourgeois World,* ed. Ann Laura Stoler and Frederick Cooper (Berkeley: University of California Press, 1997), 1–56.

11. On the global/local nexus, see Henri Lefebvre, *The Production of Space,* trans. Donald Nicholson-Smith (Oxford: Blackwell, 1991). On ways the nation facilitated

global integration, and vice versa, see Aihwa Ong, *Flexible Citizenship: The Cultural Logics of Transnationality* (Durham: Duke University Press, 1999); Saskia Sassen, *Territory, Authority, Rights: From Medieval to Global Assemblages* (Princeton: Princeton University Press, 2006).

12. See Lake and Reynolds, *Drawing the Global Color Line.*

13. "Oriental Immigration," *The Outlook*, Jan. 14, 1911.

14. Amy Kaplan, *The Anarchy of Empire in the Making of U.S. Culture* (Cambridge: Harvard University Press 2003), 15. David Noble has also identified these two seemingly contradictory impulses as representing the hallmarks of an American empire. See his, *Death of a Nation: American Culture and the End of Exceptionalism* (Minneapolis: University of Minnesota Press, 2002).

15. William Appleman Williams, *Tragedy of American Diplomacy* (New York: World Publishing Company, 1959). A generation of "New Left" scholars expanded on the notion of the "Open Door," showing how the ideology arose from the problem of overproduction and the attending domestic crises it produced in the late nineteenth century. See Walter LaFeber, *The New Empire: An Interpretation of American Expansion, 1860–1898* (Ithaca: Cornell University Press, 1963). On America's China policy during this period, see Thomas McCormick, *The China Market: America's Quest for Informal Empire* (Chicago: Quadrangle Books, 1967); and Marilyn Young, *Rhetoric of Empire: American China Policy, 1895–1901* (Cambridge, 1969: Harvard University Press). On how the logic of expanding market relations continues to define American power in the world, see Ellen Meiksins Wood, *Empire of Capital* (New York: Verso, 2003).

16. Tony Ballantyne, *Orientalism and Race: Aryanism in the British Empire* (New York: Palgrave, 2002), 14.

17. Arif Dirlik, "Introduction: Pacific Contradictions," in What Is in a Rim? Critical Perspectives on the Pacific Region Idea, ed. Arif Dirlik (Lanham: Rowman and Littlefield, 1998), 9.

18. Jane Burbank and Frederick Cooper, Empires in World History: Power and the Politics of Difference (Princeton: Princeton University Press, 2010).

19. Michael Geyer and Charles Bright, "World History in a Global Age," American Historical Review 100:4 (Oct., 1995), 1053.

20. On the Spanish construction of the earlier Pacific world, see O.H.K. Spate's three-volume study, *The Spanish Lake*, vol. 1: *Monopolists and Free Booters;* vol. 2: *Paradise Lost and Found;* vol. 3 (Minneapolis: University of Minnesota, Press 1979, 1983, 1988).

21. Dennis Flynn and Arturo Giraldez argue that a "highly integrated global economy has existed since the sixteenth century," locating its origins in the Manila galleon trade. Dennis O. Flynn and Arturo Giraldez, "Cycles of Silver: Global Economic Unity through the Mid-Eighteenth Century," *Journal of World History* 13 (Fall 2002): 393; "Born with a 'Silver Spoon': The Origin of World Trade in 1571," *Journal of World History* 6 (Fall 1995): 201–21. For the history of the Manila Galleon trade, see William Lytle Schurz, *The Manila Galleon* (New York: E.P. Dutton, 1939).

22. Countering Eurocentric interpretations of East Asian history, Takeshi Hamashita argues that, "East Asia entered modern times not because of the coming of European powers but because of the dynamism inherent in the traditional, Sinocentric tributary system." Moreover, he argues that even as European powers made deeper inroads into the region in the nineteenth century, they did so through a "Sinocentric regional order," making their way to East Asia "via Islamic, Indian, and Southeast Asian spheres." See his chapter, "The Intra-regional System in East Asia in Modern Times," in *Network Power*, ed. Peter J. Katzenstein and Takashi Shiraishi (Ithaca: Cornell University Press, 1997), 113–135.

23. On British expansion into the Pacific in the eighteenth and early nineteenth centuries, see Alan Frost, *The Global Reach of Empire: Britain's Maritime Expansion in the Indian and Pacific Oceans, 1764–1815* (Carlton, Victoria: Miegunyah Press, 2003).

24. Dirlik, "Introduction: Pacific Contradictions," in *What is in a Rim*, 4.

25. Ibid., 15–16.

26. See Epeli Hau'ofa, *We Are the Ocean: Selected Works* (Honolulu: University of Hawai'i Press, 2008), 33. Malama Meleisea has criticized the one-sided paradigm of discovery that is strictly preoccupied with the words and actions of Euro-American colonizers and calls for Pacific histories that take into the account the responses of the islands people of the Solomons, Fiji, Tonga, and Hawai'i. See her essay, "Discovering Outsiders," in *The Cambridge History of Pacific Islanders*, eds. Donald Denoon, Stewart Firth, Jocelyn Linnekin, Karen Nero, and Malama Meleisea (Cambridge: Cambridge University Press, 1997), 119–151. On Pacific Islanders' resistance to Euro-American colonization, see Noenoe K. Silva, *Aloha Betrayed: Native Hawaiian Resistance to American Colonialism* (Durham: Duke University Press, 2004); Vicente M. Diaz, *Repositioning the Missionary: Rewriting the Histories of Colonialism, Native Catholicism, and Indigeneity in Guam* (Honolulu: University of Hawai'i Press, 2010).

27. While the concept of an Atlantic world has received sustained scholarly attention—so much so, that one of its practitioners David Armitage declared that "We are all Atlanticists now"—the Pacific has gone largely ignored. See his essay, "Three Concepts of Atlantic History," in David Armitage and Michael J. Braddick, eds. *The British Atlantic World, 1500–1800* (New York: Palgrave MacMillian, 2002); Paul Gilroy, *The Black Atlantic: Modernity and Double Consciousness* (Cambridge: Harvard University Press, 1992); David Hancock, *Citizens of the World: London Merchants and the Integration of the British Atlantic Community, 1735–1785* (Cambridge: Cambridge University Press, 1995); Daniel T. Rodgers, *Atlantic Crossings, Social Politics in a Progressive Age* (Cambridge: Harvard University Press, 1998).

28. Archeological findings show that the first peoples to settle the Pacific Northwest crossed the Bering Strait from Siberia twenty thousand years ago. Jean Barman, *The West Beyond the West: A History of British Columbia* (Vancouver: University of British Columbia Press, 1996), 13–31. On the concept of the "contact zone," where colonizers and the colonized met on new terrain to fashion new

identities and social formations, see Mary Louise Pratt, *Imperial Eyes: Travel Writing and Transculturation* (New York: Routledge, 1992).

29. Daniel Wright Clayton, *Islands of Truth: The Imperial Fashioning of Vancouver Island* (Vancouver: University of British Columbia Press, 2000).

30. On interracial sex and marriage during the fur trade, see Adele Perry, *On the Edge of Empire: Gender, Race, and the Making of British Columbia, 1849–1871* (Toronto: University of Toronto Press, 2001); Sykvia Van Kirk, *Many Tender Ties: Women in Fur-Trade Society, 1670–1870* (Norman: University of Oklahoma Press, 1980); and Jennifer S. Brown, *Strangers in the Blood: Fur Trade Company Families in Indian Country* (Vancouver: University of British Columbia Press, 1980).

31. On the importance of indigenous Hawaiian labor to the economic development of the Pacific Northwest, see Janice K. Duncan, *Minority without a Champion: Kanakas on the Pacific Coast, 1788–1850* (Oregon: Oregon Historical Society, 1972); Tom Koppel, *Kanaka: The Untold Story of Hawaiian Pioneers in British Columbia and the Pacific Northwest* (Vancouver: University of British Columbia Press, 1995); Jean Barman and Bruce Watson, *Leaving Paradise: Indigenous Hawaiians in the Pacific Northwest, 1787–1898* (Honolulu: University of Hawaii Press, 2006). On how the Kanakas were part of changing labor regimes that accompanied expanding capitalist relations in the North American West, see Howard Lamar's seminal essay, "From Bondage to Contract: Ethnic Labor in the American West, 1680–1890," in Steven Hahn and Jonathan Prude, eds., *The Countryside in the Age of Capitalist Transformation: Essays in the Social History of Rural America* (Chapel Hill: University of North Carolina Press, 1985), 293–324.

32. Cole Harris, *The Resettlement of British Columbia: Essays on Colonialism and Geographic Change* (Vancouver: University of British Columbia Press, 1997), 60. On early Native-European encounters in the Pacific Northwest, also see, Perry, *On the Edge of Empire* (Toronto: University of Toronto Press, 2001); Alexandra Harmon, *Indians in the Making: Ethnic Relations and Indian Identities around the Puget Sound* (Berkeley: University of California Press, 2000), 13–71. On the role of disease in the European conquest of the Pacific, see David Igler, "Diseased Goods: Global Exchanges in the Eastern Pacific Basin, 1770–1850," *American Historical Review* 109 (June 2004): 693–719.

33. While the Spanish had claimed the entire Pacific coast in the sixteenth century, their sovereign reach did not extend beyond the Sonoran desert in what is today Northern Mexico. Following the rise of the fur trade, Spain attempted to exert sovereignty further north but by this time it was too late. See Warren L. Cook, *Flood Tide of Empire: Spain and the Pacific Northwest, 1543–1819* (New Haven: Yale University Press, 1973).

34. The fur trade, as historian Gary Okihiro reminds us, was also "key to the development of the other shore, the Atlantic Northeast, where banks financed the undertaking, shipyards launched the ships, suppliers outfitted the expeditions, factories manufactured the glass, cloth, and metal items exchanged for the furs and pelts of North America's west coast, and investors received the final products from Asia along with their profits." Okihiro, *Island World*, 147.

35. Harris, *Resettlement of British Columbia*, 271.

36. G.E. Baker ed., *The Works of William H. Seward* (New York: Redfield, 1853–1884), 250.

37. Williams, *Tragedy of American Diplomacy;* LaFeber, *The New Empire.*

38. For the most recent articulations of these views, see Niall Ferguson, *Colossus: The Rise and Fall of the American Empire* (New York: Penguin, 2005); and Michael Hardt and Antonio Negri, *Empire* (Cambridge: Harvard University Press, 2001).

39. Ann Laura Stoler thinks that debating the American empire on these terms—formal verses informal, territorial verses non-territorial—has missed the larger point; that empires are by nature "moving targets." Ann Laura Stoler, "On Degrees of Imperial Sovereignty," *Public Culture* 18:1 (2006): 141.

40. Ann Laura Stoler with David Bond, "Refractions of Empire: Untimely Comparisons in Harsh Times," *Radical History Review* 95 (Spring 2006): 95.

41. Ibid.

42. This study has been, in part, guided by the question of how to bring the insights of Patricia Limerick, Richard White, William Cronon and other New Western Historians with those of William Appleman Williams, Walter LaFeber, and Amy Kaplan. For a sample of the New Western History; see Patricia Limerick, *The Legacy of Conquest: The Unbroken Past of the American West* (New York: W.W. Norton, 1988); Richard White, *"It's Your Misfortune and None of My Own": A New History of the American West* (Norman: Oklahoma University Press, 1993); William Cronon, George Miles, and Jay Gitlin, eds., *Under an Open Sky: Rethinking America's Western Past* (New York: W.W. Norton, 1993). On critical accounts of U.S. imperialism, see Williams, *Tragedy of American Diplomacy*; LaFeber; *The New Empire;* Amy Kaplan and Donald Pease, eds. *Cultures of United States Imperialism* (Durham: Duke University Press, 1993).

43. Richard Drinnon was perhaps the first scholar to establish a direct link between continental expansion and U.S. imperialism in the Pacific and wars in Asia, see his, *Facing West.*

44. Long before transnational and global histories were in vogue, Eric Wolf insisted that rather than treating concepts such as nation, society, and culture as static and bounded entities, we conceive of them instead as "bundles of relationships" constantly being remade in global fields of interaction and exchange. See Eric R. Wolf, *Europe and the People without a History* (Berkeley: University of California Press, 1982), 3–4. For calls to "internationalize" U.S. history and American Studies, see Ian Tyrell, "Making Nations/Making States: American Historians in Context of Empire," *Journal of American History 86* (1999): 2025–44; Michael Geyer and Charles Bright, "Where in the World is America? The History of the United States in the Global Age," in *Rethinking American History in a Global Age*, ed. Thomas Bender (Berkeley: University of California Press, 2002), 63–99; Shelley Fisher Fishkin, "Crossroads of Culture: The Transnational Turn in American Studies," *American Quarterly* (2004): 17–58.

45. See William Cronon, *Nature's Metropolis: Chicago and the Great West* (New York: W.W. Norton, 1992). On the city and suburb, see Robert O. Self, *American*

Babylon: Race and the Struggle for Postwar Oakland (Princeton: Princeton University Press, 2003). These works were, of course, inspired by Raymond William's classic formulation in *Country and City* (Oxford: Oxford University Press, 1975).

46. For sociological studies of the global city, see Saskia Sassen, *The Global City: New York, London, Tokyo* (Princeton: Princeton University Press, 2001); Neil Brenner, *New State Spaces: Urban Governance and the Rescaling of Statehood* (Oxford: Oxford University Press, 2004).

47 Bright and Geyer, 1995, 1,049.

48. On the emergence of the "White Pacific," see Horne, *The White Pacific* and Lake and Reynolds, *Drawing the Global Colour Line.* On the spatial dimensions of American empire, see Neil Smith, *American Empire: Roosevelt's Geographer and the Prelude to Globalization* (Berkeley: University of California Press, 2003); Don Mitchell, *The Lie of the Land: Migrant Workers and the California Landscape* (Minneapolis: University of Minnesota Press, 1996).

CHAPTER ONE

1. For a critique of Asian American history's captivity to the nation-state, see Lisa Lowe, *Immigrant Acts: On Asian American Cultural Politics* (Durham: Duke University Press, 1996). On how a wider imperial frame may yield new insights into the "origins" of Asian American history, see Moon-Ho Jung, *Coolies and Cane: Race, Labor, and Sugar in the Age of Emancipation* (Baltimore: John Hopkins University Press, 2006).

2. John K. Fairbanks, *Trade and Diplomacy on the China Coast: The Opening of the Treaty Ports, 1842–1854* (Cambridge: Harvard University Press, 1953).

3. George E. Baker ed., *The Works of William H. Seward*, vol. I (New York, 1853), 248.

4. Ballantyne, Orientalism and Race, 15.

5. Philip Kuhn, *Chinese among Others: Emigration in Modern Times* (Lanham: Rowman & Littlefield, 2008).

6. Michael Geyer and Charles Bright, "World History in a Global Age," *The American Historical Review* 100:4 (Oct., 1995): 1049.

7. James G. Swan, *The Northwest Coast: Or, Three Years' Residence in Washington Territory* (New York, 1857), 402.

8. Letter from James J. Hill to Thomas Burke, Apr. 4, 1898, University of Washington Special Collections (hereafter UWSC), Thomas Burke Papers, Accession #2808, Box #8, Folder 4.

9. Frederic James Grant, *Washington, the Evergreen State, and Seattle, Its Metropolis* (Seattle: Crawford and Conover, 1890), 38

10. Carlos Arnaldo Schwantes, *The Pacific Northwest: An Interpretive History* (Lincoln: University of Nebraska Press, 1996), 200–24.

11. *Report of Royal Commission on Chinese and Japanese Immigration* (Ottawa, 1902), 162. On salmon canning in the Pacific Northwest, see Chris Friday,

Organizing Asian American Labor: The Pacific Coast Canned-Salmon Industry, 1870–1942 (Philadelphia,: Temple University Press, 1994); and Alicja Muszynski, *Cheap Wage Labour: Race and Gender in the Fisheries of British Columbia* (Montreal: University of Montreal Press, 1996).

12. White, *"It's Your Misfortune and None of My Own,"* 433.

13. Jean Barman, *The West beyond the West: A History of British Columbia* (Toronto: University of Toronto Press, 1991); Richard Rajala, *Up-Coast: Forests and Industry on British Columbia's North Coast, 1870–2005* (Victoria: Royal British Columbia Museum, 2006); and Dianne Newell, *The Development of the Pacific Salmon-Canning Industry: A Grown Man's Game* (Montreal: University of Montreal Press, 1989).

14. R. E. Gosnell, "A Greater Britain on the Pacific," *Westward Ho: British Columbia Magazine* 2:1 (Jan., 1908): 10.

15. Daniel L. Pratt, "The Need of Oriental Labor in the Northwest," *The Westerner* 7:6 (1907), 3–5.

16. Pratt, "The Need of Oriental Labor in the Northwest," 3–5.

17. Hamashita, "The Intra-Regional System in East Asia in Modern Times."

18. Kuhn, *Chinese among Others*, 108.

19. On the Chi'ng emigration policy and how it evolved in response to Western imperial encroachment in the nineteenth century, see Shih-Shan Henry Tsai, *China and the Overseas Chinese in the United States, 1868–1911* (Fayetteville: University of Arkansas Press, 1983).

20. On the global institutions, networks, and practices underpinning Chinese labor migrations to North America, see Madeline Y. Hsu, *Dreaming of Gold, Dreaming of Home: Transnationalism and Migration between the United States and South China, 1882–1943* (Stanford: Stanford University Press, 2000); Adam McKeown, *Chinese Migrant Networks and Cultural Change: Peru, Chicago, and Hawaii, 1900–1936* (Chicago: University of Chicago Press, 2001); and Jung-Fang Tsai, *Hong Kong in Chinese History: Community and Social Unrest in the British Colony, 1842–1913* (New York: Columbia University Press, 1995).

21. Hsu, *Dreaming of Gold*, 36.

22. Kuhn, *Chinese among Others*, 108.

23. Kuhn, 108. It is impossible to know exactly what proportions of these Chinese emigrants were self-paid passengers or debtors bound by credit tickets.

24. Robert Wynne, *Reaction to the Chinese in the Pacific Northwest and British Columbia* (New York: Arno Press, 1978), 41–172; and Lorraine Hildebrand, *Straw Hats, Sandals and Steels: The Chinese in Washington State* (Tacoma: Washington State American Revolution Bicentennial Commission, 1977), 11–21.

25. *Washington Standard*, Oct. 3, 1879.

26. See Alexander Saxton, *The Indispensable Enemy: Labor and the Anti-Chinese Movement in California* (Berkeley: University of California Pres 1971); Friday, *Organizing Asian American Labor;* and Harry Con, *From China to Canada: A History of the Chinese Communities in Canada* (Toronto: McClelland and Steward Limited, 1982).

27. Mae M. Ngai, *The Lucky Ones: One Family and the Extraordinary Invention of Chinese America* (New York: Houghton Mifflin Harcourt, 2010); and Lisa Mar, *Brokering Belonging: Chinese in Canada's Exclusion Era, 1885–1945* (Oxford: University of Oxford Press, 2010).

28. Robert Park, of the famed Chicago School of Sociology, coined the term *marginal man* to describe the liminal figure who was caught between two social worlds as a result of the migration process. See his, "Human Migration and the Marginal Man," *American Journal of Sociology* 33 (1928): 881–93. One of Park's students, Paul Siu, in an attempt to provide an alternative to the linear assimilationist paradigm, argued that the Chinese immigrant was more of a "sojourner" than a "marginal man" because of the social isolation caused by white racism. See Paul Chan Pang Siu, *The Chinese Laundryman: A Study of Social Isolation,* ed. John Kuo Wei Tchen (New York: New York University Press, 1987).

29. Gosnell, "A Greater Britain on the Pacific," 10.

30. Quoted in Donald MacKay, *The Asian Dream: The Pacific Rim and Canada's National Railway* (Vancouver: Douglas & McIntyre, 1986), 29.

31. Census of Canada, 1931. The demographic breakdown of British Columbia's population was as follows: Native Indians comprised close to 55 percent, European settlers made up about 35 percent, and people of Asian descent, primarily from China, accounted for the last 10 percent of the population.

32. The C.P.R. awarded the initial contract for laborers to Andrew Onderdonk, an American labor supplier, who had earlier furnished laborers, Chinese and white, for San Francisco's major public works projects. Soon after, however, the Chinese Six Companies as well as a number of independent Chinese contractors competed for this business. Yip Sang's boss, labor contractor Kwong On Wo, secured a lion share of the C.P.R. contracting business. See Con, *From China to Canada*, 13–29.

33. "Yip Sang: Biography 1845–1927," University of British Columbia Special Collections (hereafter UBC), Chinese Canadian Research Collection, Box 25, Folder 56.

34. Letter from H. J. Cambie to J. M. R. Fairbairn, Sept. 4, 1923, City of Vancouver Archives (hereafter CVA), PAM 1922–23.

35. Pratt, "The Need of Oriental Labor in the Northwest," 2.

36. Letter from H. J. Cambie to J. M. R. Fairbairn, Sept. 4, 1923, CVA, PAM 1922–23.

37. Letter from H. J. Cambie to J. M. R. Fairbairn; see previous footnote.

38. Letter from Thomas Daly to Edward Tilton, Chief Engineer and Superintendent, C.P.R., Jan. 31, 1882, UBC, Jack Petley Collections, Box #1, Folder #5.

39. While exact figures are unavailable for the C.P.R., we know that California's Central Pacific during the three-year period it exclusively employed Chinese labor to build its transcontinental railroad saved $5.5 million dollars, giving us a rough sense of the financial benefits of using Chinese labor. See Saxton, *The Indispensable Enemy*, 56–57.

40. Con, From *China to Canada*, 21–22.

41. On the history of anti-Chinese politics and law in British Columbia, see Patricia E. Roy, *A White Man's Province: British Columbia Politicians and Chinese*

and Japanese Immigrants, 1858–1914 (Vancouver: University of British Columbia Press, 1989); W. Peter Ward, *White Canada Forever: Popular Attitudes and Public Policy toward Orientals in British Columbia* (Montreal: McGill-Queen's University Press, 1978); and Kenneth Munro, "The Chinese Immigration Act, 1885: Adolphe Chapleau and the French Canadian Attitude," *Canadian Ethnic Studies* 19:3 (1987), 89–101.

42. Pratt, "The Need of Oriental Labor in the Northwest," 1–6.

43. Pratt, 1907, 3.

44. *Report of Royal Commission on Chinese and Japanese Immigration*, 161.

45. Gunther Peck, *Reinventing Free Labor: Padrones and Immigrant Workers in the North American West, 1880–1930* (Cambridge: Cambridge University Press, 2000), 80.

46. McKeown, *Chinese Migrant Networks*, 86.

47. See business and financial records of Wing Sang Co. and Yip Sang Co., CVA, Yip Family and Yip Sang Ltd. Fonds, Add. MSS. 1108.

48. See Paul Yee, "Sam Kee: A Chinese Business in Early Vancouver," in Robert A. J. McDonald and Jean Barman eds., *Vancouver Past: Essays in Social History* (Vancouver: University of British Columbia Press, 1986), 91.

49. William Lyon Mackenzie King, *Royal Commission Appointed to Investigate Into the Losses Sustained by the Chinese Population of Vancouver, B.C., on the Occasion of the Riots in That City in September 1907, Report*, (Ottawa, 1907).

50. Paul Yee, *Saltwater City: An Illustrated History of the Chinese in Vancouver* (Vancouver: Douglas & McIntyre 2006), 36.

51. "Correspondence Regarding Freight and Passenger Business," UBC, Yip Sang Company, Chung Collection, Box 107, Folder 4.

52. Letter from G. Jardine, manager of the Wallace Fisheries, to the Wing Sang Company, Nov. 7, 1919, UBC, Yip Sang Company, Chung Collection Box 105, Folder 9.

53. See files in UBC, Yip Sang Company, Chung Collection, Box 106.

54. "Fish Shipping Related Correspondence and Other Records," UBC, Yip Sang Company, Chung Collection, Box 105, Folder 8.

55. McCormick, *China Market;* David Walker, *Anxious Nation: Australia and the Rise of Asia, 1850–1939* (Brisbane: University of Queensland Press, 1999); and Patricia Roy, *The Oriental Question: Consolidating a White Man's Province, 1914–1941* (Vancouver: University of British Columbia Press, 2003).

56. Grant, *Washington, the Evergreen State, and Seattle, Its Metropolis*, 38.

57. Grant, 38.

58. Beth LaDow, *The Medicine Line: Life and Death on a North American Borderland* (New York: Routledge, 2001), 73, 76.

59. Quoted in Julius W. Pratt, *Expansionists of 1898: The Acquisition of Hawaii and the Spanish Islands* (Chicago: Quadrangle, 1964), 271.

60. "Commercial Relations of Pacific Northwest," UWSC, Thomas Burke Papers, Accession #1483-2, Box #32, Folder 5.

61. Bruce Cumings, "Rimspeak; or, the Discourse of the "Pacific Rim," in *What Is in a Rim?*

62. See Kurt E. Armbruster, *Orphan Road: The Railroad Comes to Seattle 1853–1911* (Pullman: Washington State University Press, 1999); Albro Martin, *James J. Hill and the Opening of the Northwest* (Minnesota: Minnesota Historical Society Press, 1991); and Michael P. Malone, *James J. Hill: Empire Builder of the Northwest* (Norman: University of Oklahoma Press, 1997).

63. Quoted in John Foster Carr, "Creative Americans: A Great Railway Builder," *Outlook* 87 (October 1907): 397.

64. Quoted in Howard Schonberger, "James J. Hill and the Trade with the Orient," *Minnesota History* 41 (Winter 1968): 178–90.

65. On the ways in which an American exceptionalism has been produced and sustained through historiographical methods and practices, see Ian Tyrell, "American Exceptionalism in an Age of International History," *American Historical Review* 96 (1991): 1,033–55.

66. While Chin Gee Hee's rise to fortune may have been extraordinary, it was not exceptional. A Chinese middling elite emerged in every major city in the Pacific Northwest. According to Todd Stevens, their path to becoming merchants followed a similar pattern in which English language skills and understanding the workings of the law, especially as it related to contracts, were essential. Todd Stevens, "Brokers between Worlds: Chinese Merchants and Legal Culture in the Pacific Northwest, 1852–1925" (PhD diss., Princeton University, 2003). See also, Jeff MacDonald and Margaret Wilson, "Port Townsend's Pioneer Chinese Merchants," *Landmarks* (Winter, 1983).

67. Willard G. Jue, "Chin Gee-Hee: Chinese Pioneer Entrepreneur in Seattle and Toishan"; "Chin Gee-Hee," UWSC, Willard Jue Collections, Accession #5191-1, Box #1, Folder #9.

68. "Account and Letter Book," UWSC, Willard G. Jue Papers, Accession No. 5191-001, Box #1, Folder 12.

69. Letter from Chin Gee Hee to G. H. Warren, general manager of North Pacific, March 14, 1895, UWSC, Willard G. Jue Papers, Accession No. 5191, Box #1, Folder 9.

70. Letter from Chin Gee Hee to G. H. Warren; see previous footnote.

71. Doug Chin, *Seattle's International District: The Making of a Pan-Asian American Community* (Seattle: University of Washington Press, 2001), 14.

72. The coalescing of an anti-Chinese movement in the mid-1870s in San Francisco also pushed Chinese migrants northward, adding to Chin Gee Hee's labor supply. Stevens, "Brokers between Worlds," 40–43.

73. These numbers are a bit deceiving because many Chinese laborers entered the country by claiming other categories during these years, which set up a confrontation with the federal government. On the demographic impact of Chinese exclusion, see Bill Ong Hing, *Making and Remaking Asian America through Immigration Policy, 1850–1990* (Palo Alto: Stanford University Press, 1993), 48; and Judy Yung, *Unbound Feet: A Social History of Chinese Women in San Francisco* (Berkeley: University of California Press, 1995).

74. The two primary ways Chinese gained admission after 1882 were either through the "paper son" scheme whereby the immigrant claimed to be an offspring

of a legal resident of the United States or by claiming the status of an exempt class including merchant, student, or diplomat. See Hsu, *Dreaming of Gold*, 55–89.

75. *Port Townsend Leader*, Sept. 30, 1903.

76. Quoted in *New York Times*, July 7, 1884.

77. Letter to Walter S. Chance, Supervising Special Agent, Washington, DC, Oct. 6, 1899, NARA, RG 85, Entry 9, File 52730, Folder 89.

78. *Port Townsend Leader*, Sept. 30, 1903.

79. E. W. Wright, ed., *Lewis & Dryden's Marine History of the Pacific Northwest* (Portland: Lewis & Dryden Printing Company, 1895), 300.

80. Thomas W. Prosch, "A Chronological History of Seattle from 1850 to 1897," typescript (Seattle, 1901), 291–92, UWSC.

81. *West Shore,* March 14, 1891.

82. Quoted in Jeff MacDonald and Margaret Wilson, "Port Townsend's Pioneer Chinese Merchants," *Landmarks* (Winter, 1983): 21.

83. *Port Townsend Leader*, Jan. 20, 1904. For Chinese smugglers, see Letter from Lee Toy to M. S. Hill, Deputy Collector, Blaine, Oct. 7, 1899 Washington, WNA, RG 85, Entry 9, File 52730, Folder 89.

84. *Port Townsend Leader*, March 6, 1969.

85. As Todd Stevens shows, Chinese merchants were extremely adept at using the legal system to their advantage. See Stevens, "Brokers between Worlds."

86. *Census Reports, Twelfth Census of the United States Taken in the Year of 1900.* Vol. 1, Part I, Population (Washington, DC: Government Printing Office, 1901).

87. "The Orientals in the Lumber Industry in the State of Washington," Survey of Race Relations Records, Box 28, Hoover Institution Archives, Stanford University.

88. On America's informal empire of capital in the late nineteenth century, see Williams, *The Tragedy of American Diplomacy;* LaFeber, *The New Empire;* and Wood, *Empire of Capital.*

89. The growing eastbound traffic of Pacific Northwest lumber generated surplus capacities on westbound trains. Trade with Asia was supposed to remedy this imbalance. See Joseph Gilpin Pyle, *The Life of James J. Hill,* Vol. 1 (Garden City: Doubleday, 1917), 52.

90. Hill's train cars were typically filled going east hauling Pacific Northwest lumber but were empty traveling back west. His solution was to identify exports out east that could be shipped to Asia. Pyle, 1917, 49–66.

91. Quoted in Carr, "Creative Americans: A Great Railway Builder," 397.

92. William F. Prosser, *A History of Puget Sound Country: Its Resources, Its Commerce and Its People* (New York: Lewis Publishing Company, 1903), 115.

93. On Chin Gee Hee's efforts to build a railroad in Taishan, see Hsu, *Dreaming of Gold*, 156–75.

94. Quoted in "Chin Gee-Hee," UWSC, 6.

95. On the myriad obstacles American investors in China faced during this period, see McCormick, *China Market.* On earlier efforts to tap the China markets by postrevolutionary elites, see John Kuo Wei Tchen, *New York before Chinatown:*

Orientalism and the Shaping of American Culture 1776–1882 (Baltimore: John Hopkins University Press, 1999).

96. On the anti-American boycotts, see Guanhua Wang, *In Search of Justice: The 1905–1906 Chinese Anti-American Boycott* (Cambridge: Harvard University Press, 2002).

97. David M. Pletcher, *The Diplomacy of Involvement: American Economic Expansion across the Pacific, 1784–1900* (Columbia: University of Missouri Press, 2001), 5.

98. Hsu, *Dreaming of Gold*, 156–75.

99. See Pletcher, *The Diplomacy of Involvement*, 217–21.

100. *West Shore*, March 14, 1891.

101. Frederic J. Grant, *History of Seattle, Washington: With Illustrations and Biographical Sketches of Some of Its Prominent Men and Pioneers* (New York: American Publishing and Engraving Company, 1891), 188.

102. Letter to Walter S. Chance, Oct. 6, 1899, NARA, RG 85, Entry 9, File 52730, Folder 89.

103. Andrew Graybill, "Texas Rangers, Canadian Mounties, and the Policing of the Transnational Industrial Frontier, 1885–1910," *Western Historical Quarterly* 35.2 (2004): 167–91.

104. Roy, *White Man's Province*, 125.

105. McKeown, *Melancholy Order;* and Lake and Reynolds, *Drawing the Global Colour Line*.

106. On the Foran Act, see Peck, *Reinventing Free Labor*, 82–114; and Aristide R. Zolberg, *A Nation by Design: Immigration Policy in the Fashioning of America* (Cambridge: Harvard University Press, 2006), 193–98.

107. Grant, *History of Seattle, Washington*, 188. What nativists failed to acknowledge was that many of these so-called illegal Chinese migrants were previous residents of the United States who moved to British Columbia for the time being only after the completion of the Northern and Southern Pacific Railways had left them without jobs. Furthermore, because there was no border to speak of, at least in any practical sense, it is unclear whether the Chinese even knew that they were crossing international boundaries into a different country.

108. "Fisherman's Union," UBC, Chinese Canadian Research Collection, Box #9, Folder 14.

109. On the contract and how it defined social relations in the age of emancipation, see Amy Dru Stanley, *From Bondage to Contract: Wage Labor, Marriage, and the Market in the Age of Slave Emancipation* (Cambridge: Cambridge University Press, 1998).

110. As far as white workingmen were concerned, the exploitation of Chinese labor threatened their very livelihood. More specifically, by accepting wages that no white man could live on, they charged the Chinese "coolie" posed a threat to "free" white laborers everywhere. See Lawrence Glickman, *A Living Wage: American Workers and the Making of Consumer Society* (Ithaca: Cornell University Press, 1997), 85–90. On the threat of white slavery and how it shaped a racialized class consciousness, see David R. Roediger, *The Wages of Whiteness: Race and the Making of the American Working Class* (New York: Verso, 1991), 65–92; and Gunther Peck,

"White Slavery and Whiteness: A Transnational View of the Sources of Working-Class Radicalism and Racism," in *Labor: Studies in Working-Class History of the Americas* 1:2 (June 2004): 41–63.

111. *Seattle Union Record*, Dec. 15, 1900.

112. On the politics of "coolie' labor, see Jung, *Coolies and Cane.*

113. Carlos Schwantes, "Protest in a Promised Land: Unemployment, Disinheritance, and the Origins of Labor Militancy in the Pacific Northwest, 1885–1886," *Western Historical Quarterly* 13 (1982): 377.

114. On the 1885–86 anti-Chinese riots, see Sarah Dougher, *Sent Out on the Tracks They Built: Sinophobia in Olympia, 1886* (Olympia: S. Dougher and N. McClure, 1998); James A. Halseth and Bruce A. Glasrud, "Anti-Chinese Movements in Washington, 1885–1886: A Reconsideration," in *The Northwest Mosaic: Minority Conflicts in Pacific Northwest History*, ed. James A. Halseth and Bruce A. Glasrud (Boulder: Pruett Publishing Co., 1977); Jules Karlin, "The Anti-Chinese Outbreak in Seattle," *Pacific Northwest Quarterly* 29 (1948); and Jules Karlin, "The Anti-Chinese Outbreak in Tacoma, 1885," *Pacific Historical Review* 23 (1954).

115. *Seattle Daily Call,* Nov. 19, 1885.

116. Letter from Chin Gee Hee to Chinese consul in San Francisco, Nov. 4, 1885, UWSC, Willard Jue Collections, Accession #5191-1, Box #1, Folder #9.

117. The 1886 anti-Chinese riot was recounted in the *B.C. Federationist*, Nov. 18, 1911.

118. "A History of Organized Labor in Vancouver and its Struggle against the Degradation of the Working Class," UBC, Harry Cowan Scrapbooks.

119. "Chinese Riots 1887, 1907," City of Vancouver Archives (hereafter CVA), J. S. Matthew Collections, Add. MSS. 54, 504-A-7, File 175.

120. Representing Dominion subjects as law-abiding as opposed to "rowdy and lawless Americans" was a way of articulating a distinct Canadian national identity during a time when the United States was emerging as an expanding continental power. See Tina Loo, *Making Law, Order, and Authority in British Columbia, 1821–1871* (Toronto: University of Toronto Press, 1994); and also Barman, *The West beyond the West*, 63–94.

121. Personal writings, Angus MacInnis Memorial Collections, UBC, Box#70, Folder 9.

122. "A History of Organized Labor in Vancouver and its Struggle against the Degradation of the Working Class," UBC, Harry Cowan Scrapbooks.

123. "Office Memorandum," Feb. 11, 1891, National Archives of Canada (Ottawa) (hereafter NAC), RG 7, Series G-1, File 22.

124. Lee, *At America's Gates*, 177.

125. Lee, 152.

126. "Restriction on Immigration," House Immigration Committee hearings, 63d Congress, 2d sess. (Washington, DC: Government Printing Office, 1914).

127. Some of the finest opium in North America was cultivated and produced in Victoria, British Columbia. To understand how opium use and trafficking became associated with the Chinese in Canada, see Carolyn Strange and Tina

Loo, *Making Good: Law and Moral Regulation in Canada* (Toronto: University of Toronto Press, 1997).

128. Letter to Walter S. Chance, Oct. 6, 1899, NARA, RG 85, Entry 9, File 52730, Folder 89.

129. Letter from Inspector Fisher to F. D. Huestis, March 17, 1900, United States, National Archives Pacific Alaska Region (hereafter NARA-PA), RG 36, Box #106, Folder 3.

130. *Seattle Union Record*, Oct. 19, 1901.

131. *Seattle Union Record*, June 22, 1901 and Oct. 19, 1901.

132. *Province*, Sept. 6, 1901.

133. "Digest of, and Comment Upon, Report of Immigrant Inspector Marcus Braun," Sept. 20, 1907, NARA, RG 85, Entry 9, File 51360, Folder 44-D.

134. On the various laws affecting Chinese immigration, see Lucy E. Salyer, *Laws Harsh as Tigers: Chinese Immigrants and the Shaping of Modern Immigration Law* (Chapel Hill: University of North Carolina Press, 1995).

135. Letter from the Chinese Inspector to F. D. Huestis, Oct. 13, 1898, NARA-PA, RG 36, Box #105, Folder 5.

136. Letter to Walter S. Chance, October 6, 1899, NARA, RG 85, Entry 9, File 52730, Folder 89.

CHAPTER TWO

1. Letter from superintendent to Vice President L. W. Hill, Feb. 28, 1906, UWSC, Northern Pacific Railway Company, Accession #4415, Reel 1.

2. Letter from superintendent to Vice President L.W. Hill, Feb. 28, 1906, UWSC, Northern Pacific Railway Company, Accession #4415, Reel 1.

3. Quoted in Edward Janes Carpenter, *America in Hawaii: A History of United States Influence in the Hawaiian Islands* (Boston: Small, Maynard & Company, 1899), 152. U.S. imperialists, like Alfred Thayer Mahan and Theodore Roosevelt, also pushed for the annexation of Hawai'i for geopolitical reasons, viewing it as an important coaling station in the Pacific, vital to a nation looking to transform itself into a naval power. See Sadao Asada, *Culture Shock and Japanese-American Relations: Historical Essays* (Columbia: University of Missouri Press, 2007), 68–71.

4. Eiichiro Azuma, *Between Two Empires: Race, History, and Transnationalism in Japanese America* (Oxford: Oxford University Press, 2005), 23.

5. Williams, *Tragedy of American Diplomacy*; LaFeber, *The New Empire;* and McCormick, *China Market.*

6. Whitelaw Reid, *Problems of Expansion: As Considered in Papers and Addresses* (New York: The Century Co., 1900), 42.

7. Cumings, *Dominion from Sea to Sea*, 126–54.

8. Alfred Thayer Mahan argued that, for the United States to become a truly global power, it would need a two-ocean navy. See his *The Influence of Sea Power upon History: 1660–1783* (Boston: Little. Brown and Company, 1890).

9. For example, when the Boxer Uprising threatened U.S. commercial interests in China in the summer of 1900, President McKinley sent American troops based in Manila to Peking to crush the rebellion. See LaFeber, *The Clash: U.S.-Japanese Relations throughout History* (New York: W.W. Norton, 1997), 67. In this regard, these new naval bases were employed very much like railroads in the American West, where soldiers were quickly dispatched and transported to put down Native American uprisings.

10. LaFeber, *The Clash,* 41.

11. LaFeber, *The Clash,* 85–86.

12. Yukiko Koshiro, *Trans-Pacific Racisms: And the U. S. Occupation of Japan* (New York: Columbia University Press, 1999), 92–93.

13. Akira Iriye, *Pacific Estrangement: Japanese and American Expansion, 1897–1911* (Cambridge: Harvard University Press, 1972), 131.

14. Iriye, *Pacific Estrangement,* 132.

15. LaFeber, *The Clash,* 53–57.

16. Peter Duus, *The Abacus and the Sword: The Japanese Penetration of Korea, 1895–1910* (Berkeley: University of California Press, 1995), 254.

17. Azuma, *Between Two Empires,* 20.

18. Prosser, *A History of Puget Sound Country,* 220.

19. Koromo Kusawake, "The Early Pioneers," *The New Canadian: An Independent Organ for Canadians of Japanese Origin,* Aug. 12, 1977.

20. Betty Morita Shibayama interview, Oct. 27, 2003, Densho: The Japanese American Legacy Project.

21. Ninette Kelley and M. J. Trebilcock, *The Making of the Mosaic: A History of Canadian Immigration Policy* (Toronto: University of Toronto Press, 1998), 143.

22. Letter from General Superintendent Russell Harding to P. T. Downs, assistant superintendent, Spokane, Washington, June 7, 1900, UWSW, Northern Pacific Railway Company, Accession #4415, Reel 1.

23. Quoted in Clarence B. Bagley, *History of Seattle from the Earliest Settlement to the Present Time,* vol. 1 (Chicago: The S. J. Clarke Publishing Company, 1916), 261–62.

24. Connections and relationships with local officials and prefectures was important because, prior to the Second World War, they were the ones responsible for implementing and enforcing the nation's emigration policies. Japan would develop a centralized system of migration control during the occupation period. See Tessa Morris-Suzuki, *Borderline Japan: Foreigners and Frontier Controls in the Postwar Era* (Cambridge: Cambridge University Press, 2010), 41–45.

25. Yuji Ichioka, *The Issei: The World of the First Generation Japanese Immigrants, 1885–1924* (New York: Free Press, 1990), 53–64.

26. Letter from C. T. Takahashi to the Great Northern Railway, Jan. 18, 1903, UWSC, Northern Pacific Railway Company, Accession #4414, Reel 1.

27. Letter from William Remington to Russell Harding, Aug. 30, 1898, UWSC, Northern Pacific Railway Company, Accession #4415, Reel 1.

28. *Report of Royal Commission on Chinese and Japanese Immigration,* 414.

29. Ichioka, *The Issei*, 53–64.

30. Quoted from Kazuo Ito, *Issei: A History of Japanese Immigrants in North America*, Shinichiro Nakamura and Jean S. Gerard, trans. (Seattle: Japanese Community Service, 1973), 309.

31. Ito, *Issei,* 308. For a similar story of deception and resistance in the labor contracting process, see Mary Ota Higa interview, Dec. 17, 2004, Densho: The Japanese American Legacy Project.

32. Letter from C. T. Takahashi to the Great Northern Railway, Jan. 18, 1903, UWSC, Northern Pacific Railway Company, Accession #4414, Reel 1.

33. Letter from C. T. Takahashi to G.T. Slade, Oct. 11, 1906, UWSC, Northern Pacific Railway Company, Accession #4415, Reel 1.

34. Letter from C. T. Takahashi to the Great Northern Railway, Jan. 18, 1903, UWSC, Northern Pacific Railway Company, Accession #4414, Reel 1.

35. Rolf Knight and Maya Koizumi, *A Man of Our Times: A Life-History of a Japanese-Canadian Fisherman* (Vancouver: New Star Books, 1976), 44.

36. *Tacoma Daily News,* Jan. 16, 1899.

37. *Union Record,* Nov. 3, 1900.

38. This fear of Japan was revived in the 1980s and early 1990s, when Americans fretted over being eclipsed by Japanese economic power. See John W. Dower, *War without Mercy: Race and Power in the Pacific War* (New York: Pantheon, 1986).

39. *Union Record,* May 10, 1902 and Nov. 30, 1901.

40. *Union Record,* May 4, 1900.

41. *Union Record,* Nov. 30, 1901.

42. *Spokesman-Review,* June 14, 1900.

43. *Union Record,* May 3, 1902.

44. See Lee, *At America's Gates,* 64–68.

45. *Union Record,* July 22, 1905.

46. Western Labor Council Proceedings, May 23, 1900, UWSC, AFL-CIO-King County Labor Council of Washington, Accession $1940-1, Box #35.

47. *Union Record,* May 4, 1900.

48. *U.S. Report of the Commissioner General of Immigration, 1905,* 66.

49. Western Labor Council Proceedings, April 18 and 25, 1900, UWSC, AFL-CIO-King County Labor Council of Washington, Accession #1940-1, Box #35.

50. *Union Record,* Oct. 27, 1900.

51. On the *Herrenvolk* republicanism that informed the formation of the white working class, see Roediger, *The Wages of Whiteness,* 59–60.

52. *Seattle Post-Intelligencer,* Oct. 27, 1900.

53. Letter from Superintendent Russell Harding to the Oriental Trading Company, Jan. 22, 1903, UWSC, Northern Pacific Railway Company, Accession #4414, Reel 1.

54. Letter from G. T. Slade to H. A. Kennedy, Dec. 15, 1901, UWSC, Northern Pacific Railway Company, Accession #4415, Reel 1.

55. Letter from the general manager to G. T. Slade, July 19, 1903, UWSC, Northern Pacific Railway Company, Accession #4415, Reel 1.

56. For several years, Takahashi tried to convince the Great Northern and the Northern Pacific of the benefits of a single labor provider. In exchange, he offered to transfer the job fees that the firm normally collected from laborers to the two railroad companies. Mostly because of James Hill's intervention, the Northern Pacific agreed to the terms in 1904, making the Oriental Trading Co. the sole labor agent for both companies. See letter from C. T. Takahashi to the Great Northern Railway, Jan. 18, 1903, UWSC, Northern Pacific Railway Company, Accession #4414, Reel 1.

57. Letter from H. A. Kennedy to F. E. Ward, Mar. 5, 1903, UWSC, Northern Pacific Railway Company, Accession #4414, Reel 1.

58. Letter from the Oriental Trading Company to G. T. Slade, Aug. 13, 1906, UWSC, Northern Pacific Railway Company, Accession #4414, Reel 1.

59. Letter from G. T. Slade to H. A. Kennedy, June 24, 1903, UWSC, Northern Pacific Railway Company, Accession #4415, Reel 1.

60. Letter from C.T. Takahashi to G.T. Slade, June 7, 1906, UWSC, Northern Pacific Railway Company, Accession #4415, Reel 1.

61. *Seattle Union Record*, Sept. 28, 1907 and *American Reveille*, Sept. 12, 1907.

62. Letter from C. T. Takahashi to F. E. Ward, Oct. 10, 1905, UWSC, Northern Pacific Railway Company, Accession #4414, Reel 1.

63. Letter from Charles Takahashi to G. T. Slade, Aug. 11, 1906, UWSC, Northern Pacific Railway Company, Accession #4414, Reel 1.

64. Letter from the Law Office of Shank and Smith to F. E. Ward, Apr. 22, 1902, UWSC, Northern Pacific Railway Company, Accession #4415, Reel 1.

65. Letter from Inspector Samuel Walker to F. D. Huestis, May 6, 1899, United States, NARA-PA, RG 36, Box #106, Folder 3.

66. Fumiko M. Noji interview, April 22, 1998, Densho: The Japanese American Legacy Project.

67. Letter from Inspector Samuel Walker to F. D. Huestis, May 6, 1899, NARA-PA, RG 36, Box #106, Folder 3.

68. Letter from Walter S. Chance, June 4, 1899, NARA-PA, RG 36, Box #105, Folder 1.

69. William P. Dillingham, *The Immigration Situation in Canada* (Washington: GPO, 1910), 68.

70. William Lyon Mackenzie, *Report of the Royal Commission Appointed to Inquire into the Methods by Which Oriental Labourers Have Been Induced to Come to Canada* (Ottawa: GPB, 1908).

71. Letter from assistant general solicitor to F. E. Ward, general manager, Oct. 20, 1904, UWSC, Northern Pacific Railway Company, Accession #4415, Reel 1.

72. Letter from Charles Takahashi to F. E. Ward, Oct. 10, 1905, UWSC, Northern Pacific Railway Company, Accession #4415, Reel 1.

73. Letter from G. T. Slade to L. W. Hill, Feb. 28, 1906, UWSC, Northern Pacific Railway Company, Accession #4415, Reel 1.

74. On Japanese labor militancy in Hawai'i, see Gary Okihiro, *Cane Fires: The Anti-Japanese Movement in Hawaii, 1865–1945* (Philadelphia: Temple

University Press), 43–45; and Moon-Kie Jung, *Reworking Race: The Making of Hawaii's Interracial Labor Movement* (New York: Columbia University Press, 2006).

75. See Rick Baldoz, *The Third Asiatic Invasion: Migration and Empire in Filipino America, 1898–1946* (New York: New York University Press, 2011), 49–54; and JoAnna Poblete-Cross, "Intra-Colonial Lives: Puerto Rican and Filipino Sugar Plantation Labor Recruits to Hawai'i, 1900 to 1940" (PhD diss., University of California, Los Angeles, 2006).

76. Stoler, "On Degrees of Imperial Sovereignty," 140–41.

77. John Hays Hammond, "The Menace of Japan's Success," in *The World's Work: A History of Our Time* 10: 6,274.

78. President Roosevelt's geopolitical designs in Asia required friendly relations with Japan, and thus, when the San Francisco situation threatened to evolve into a foreign relations disaster, Roosevelt intervened swiftly and went as far as authorizing the military to protect the Japanese community in the city. This flare-up was part of a series of clashes with Japan in the early twentieth century. See LaFeber, *The Clash.*

79. Letter from American Consul Abraham E. Smith to Assistant Secretary of State, Sept. 19, 1907, NARA, RG 85, Entry 9, File 51388, Folder 5.

80. Letter from P. L. Prentis to Commissioner General of Immigration Frank P. Sargent, Aug. 22, NARA, RG 85, Entry 9, File 51686, Folder 17-A.

81. *Seattle Times*, Sept. 22, 1907. For similar reports on the Japanese influx to the region, see also *American Reveille* Sept. 24, 1907.

82. Letter from C. A. Turner to John Sargent, Sept. 14, 1907, NARA, RG 85, Entry 9, File 51630, Folder 44-B.

83. Letter from P. L. Prentis to Commissioner General of Immigration Frank P. Sargent, Aug. 22, 1907, NARA, RG 85, Entry 9, File 51686, Folder 17-A.

84. Letter from superintendent to Vice President L. W. Hill, Feb. 28, 1906, UWSC, Northern Pacific Railway Company, Accession #4415, Reel 1.

85. Letter from C. A. Turner to John Sargent, Sept. 14, 1907, NARA, RG 85, Entry 9, File 51630, Folder 44-B.

86. Rolf Knight and Maya Koizumi, eds. *A Man of Our Times*, 31. "Going to the river," was the shorthand for Japanese seasonal migration to the Fraser River. See Osawa Shigeru interview, May 10 and 16, 1968, UWSC, Accession #960, Tape 217-B.

87. Letter from P. L. Prentis to Commissioner General of Immigration Frank P. Sargent, July 23, 1908, NARA, RG 85, Entry 9, File 51930, Part 1.

88. Letter from H. A. Kennedy to F. E. Ward, Sept. 6, 1904, UWSC, Northern Pacific Railway Company, Accession #4414, Reel 1.

89. Dillingham, *The Immigration Situation in Canada*, 66.

90. See Dorothy B. Fujita-Rony, *American Workers, Colonial Power: Philippine Seattle and the Transpacific West, 1919–1941* (Berkeley: University of California Press, 2003); and Friday, *Organizing Asian-American Labor.*

91. On how American colonial policy constructed the new legal category of the U.S. national for their Filipino imperial subjects, see Ngai, *Impossible Subjects*, 96–126.

92. Ito, *Issei*, 700–01.

93. Export statistics were culled from U.S. customs reports published in the *Port Townsend Leader* over these years.

94. For details of the international trade traffic through Seattle, see the *Annual Reports* of the Seattle (Washington) Harbor Department produced during these years.

95. Prosser, *History of the Puget Sound Country*, 20.

96. James J. Hill, "The Future of Our Oriental Trade" in *World's Work* 10: 6,467.

97. The growing eastbound traffic of Pacific Northwest lumber generated surplus capacities on westbound trains. Trade with Asia was supposed to remedy this imbalance. See Pyle, *The Life of James J. Hill*, 52.

98. Henry Rosenthal, *Report on Japan, Corea, and China. Prepared for J. J. Hill* (St. Paul, 1893).

99. Schonberger, "James J. Hill and the Trade with the Orient."

100. Hill, "The Future of Our Oriental Trade," 6,467.

101. Letter from C. T. Takahashi to G. T. Slade, Aug. 11, 1906, UWSC, Northern Pacific Railway Company, Accession #4415, Reel 1.

102. Letter from James J. Hill to Thomas Burke, Mar. 28, 1898, USWC, Thomas Burke Papers, Accession #1483-2, Box 8, Folder 2.

103. Letter from James J. Hill to Thomas Burke, Mar. 28, 1898, USWC, Thomas Burke Papers, Accession #1483-2, Box 8, Folder 2.

104. "How the Unmerged Pacific Roads Now Stand," in *World's Work* 10: 4,846.

105. "How the Unmerged Pacific Roads Now Stand," in *World's Work* 10: 4,846. In 1901, James J. Hill had gained control of the Northern Pacific Railway and its terminus ending in Tacoma.

106. Azuma, *Between Two Empires*, 20.

107. *New Seattle Chamber of Commerce Record*, vol. I, Mar. 15, 1913.

108. *Port Townsend Leader*, Jan. 8, 1914. For details of his other shipments, see *Port Townsend Leader*, Sept. 25, 1913, Oct. 2, 1913, and Nov. 6, 1913.

109. *Town Crier*, May 10, 1913.

110. Ito, *Issei*, 700–01.

111. James J. Hill, *Highways of Progress* (Aurora: Bibliographical Center for Research, 2009), 183. James J. Hill attributed his lack of success in Asia to the inaction of the federal government and, more specifically, to its reluctance to subsidize a merchant marine in a time when the governments of their competitors were doing so. Hill also blamed his failure on a decision made by the Interstate Commerce Commission in 1904 that required American transportation companies to publish export and import rates, which, again, put them at a distinct disadvantage vis-à-vis their European competitors.

112. Ballantyne, *Orientalism and Race*, 9.

CHAPTER THREE

1. *Seattle Union Record*, Sept. 7, 1907.

2. *Seattle Times,* Sept. 22, 1907.

3. *Vancouver World*, Aug. 26, 1907.

4. *B.C. Saturday Sunset* (Vancouver), July 16, 1907.

5. Most of this colonial and postcolonial scholarship builds on the seminal text by Edward Said, *Orientalism* (New York: Vintage, 1979); see also Stoler and Cooper, "Between Metropole and Colony: Rethinking a Research Agenda," in *Tensions of Empire;* Ballantyne, *Orientalism and Race.* W. E. B. DuBois was one of the first scholars to alert us to the connections between whiteness and empire building. See W. E. B. DuBois, *Darkwater, Voices from within the Veil* (New York: Harcourt, Brace, and Howe, 1920).

6. On how anti-Chinese racism unified the white working class in California, see Saxton, *The Indispensable Enemy.* On the ways racial thinking pervaded the project of westward expansion, see Reginald Horsman, *Race and Manifest Destiny: The Origins of American Racial Anglo-Saxons* (Cambridge: Harvard University Press, 1981); and Anders Stephanson, *Manifest Destiny: American Expansionism and the Empire of Right* (New York: Hill and Wang, 1995). On the mutually constitutive processes of empire building and racial subjection and how they bound together the white settler world, see Lake and Reynolds, *Drawing the Global Colour Line;* Gerald Horne, *The White Pacific*; and John Fitzgerald, *Big White Lie: Chinese Australians in White Australia* (Sydney: University of New South Wales Press, 2007). For transnational studies of Asian migration and exclusion on slightly different spatial scales, see Matthew Guterl and Christine Skwiot, "Atlantic and Pacific Crossings: Race, Empire, and the 'Labor Problem' in the Late Nineteenth Century," *Radical History Review* 91 (Winter 2005): 40–61; and Erika Lee, "The 'Yellow Peril' and Asian Exclusion in the Americas," *Pacific Historical Review* 76:4 (2007): 537–62.

7. Dirlik, "Introduction: Pacific Contradictions," in *What is in a Rim,* 5. See also Rob Wilson, *Reimagining the American Pacific: From South Pacific to Bamboo Ridge and Beyond* (Durham: Duke University Press, 2000); and Oscar Campomanes, "New Formations of Asian American Studies and the Question of U.S. Imperialism."

8. On the inextricable connections between U.S. interventions abroad and the production of racialized identities at home, see Kaplan, *Anarchy of Empire;* Paul Kramer, *The Blood of Government: Race, Empire, the United States, and the Philippines* (Chapel Hill: University of North Carolina Press, 2006); and Paul R. Spickard, *Almost All Aliens: Immigration, Race, and Colonialism in American History and Identity* (New York: Routledge, 2007).

9. According to some scholars, contemporary trends in globalization signal the demise of the nation-state. See, for example, Arjun Appadurai, *Modernity at Large: Cultural Dimensions of Globalization* (Minneapolis: University of Minnesota Press, 1996). For more complex readings of the relations between the

global and the national, see Aihwa Ong, *Flexible Citizenship: The Cultural Logics of Transnationality* (Durham: Duke University Press, 1999); and Saskia Sassen, *Territory, Authority, Rights: From Medieval to Global Assemblages* (Princeton: Princeton University Press, 2006).

10. On the different regional constructions of race and labor, see Saxton, *The Indispensable Enemy;* David Montejano, *Anglos and Mexicans in the Making of Texas, 1836–1986* (Austin: University of Texas Press, 1987); and Grace Elizabeth Hale, *Making Whiteness: The Culture of Segregation in the South, 1890–1940* (New York: Pantheon, 1998).

11. Stuart Hall, "Race, Articulation, and Societies Structured in Dominance," in *Sociological Theories: Race and Colonialism* (Paris: UNESCO, 1980). See also, Barbara Fields, "Slavery, Race, and Ideology in the United States of America," *New Left Review* 181 (May/June 1990): 95–118; and Thomas Holt, *The Problem of Race in the 21st Century* (Cambridge: Harvard University Press, 2000).

12. See White, *"It's Your Misfortune and None of My Own,"* 433; and Peck, *Reinventing Free Labor.*

13. This process of cultural formation was akin to what Yen Le Espirtu has called "panethnicity" in which different ethnic groups were congealed together, frequently in new geographical settings and where no critical mass of a single group existed. See Yen Le Espirtu, *Asian American Panethnicity: Bridging Institutions and Identities* (Philadelphia: Temple University Press, 1992). On how this process unfolded in other colonial settings and contact zones, see Neil Foley, *The White Scourge;* Linda Gordon, *The Great Arizona Orphan Abduction* (Cambridge: Harvard University Press, 1999); Vicente Rafael, *White Love and Other Events in Filipino History* (Durham: Duke University Press, 2000); and Jung, *Coolies and Cane.*

14. Harris, *The Resettlement of British Columbia,* 160. Also see Perry, *On the Edge of Empire.*

15. On whiteness, see Roediger, *The Wages of Whiteness;* Alexander Saxton, *The Rise and Fall of the White Republic: Class Politics and Mass Culture in Nineteenth-Century America* (London: Verso Press, 1990); Noel Ignatiev, *How the Irish Became White* (New York: Routledge, 1995); Eric Lott, *Love and Theft: Blackface Minstrelsy and the American Working Class* (New York: Oxford University Press, 1995); Matthew Frye Jacobson, *Whiteness of a Different Color: European Immigrants and the Alchemy of Race* (Cambridge: Harvard University Press, 1999); Bruce Nelson, *Divided We Stand: American Workers and the Struggle for Black Equality* (Princeton: Princeton University Press, 2000); and Thomas Guglielmo, *White on Arrival: Italians, Race, Color, and Power in Chicago, 1890–1945* (New York: Oxford University Press, 2004). For critiques of whiteness, see Peter Kolchin, "Whiteness Studies: The New History of Race in America," *Journal of American History* 89:1 (February 2002): 154–73; and Eric Arnesen, "Whiteness and the Historians' Imagination," *International Labor and Working-Class History* 60 (Fall 2001): 3–32.

16. See minutes of the monthly meeting, December 1910, in Asiatic Exclusion League, *Proceedings of the Asiatic Exclusion League, 1907–1913* (New York: Arno Press, 1977). On the development of American Anglo-Saxon ideology, see

Reginald Horsman, *Race and Manifest Destiny: The Origins of American Racial Anglo-Saxonism* (Cambridge, Harvard University Press, 1981); and John Higham, *Strangers in the Land: Patterns of American Nativism, 1860–1925* (New Brunswick: Rutgers University Press, 1955).

17. *Everett Labor Journal*, May 6, 1910.

18. N. Lascelles Ward, "The Oriental Problem," National Archives of Canada (Ottawa), (hereafter NAC), Record Group (hereafter RG) 76, Series 1-A-1, Vol. 83, File 9309.

19. See Alexandra Harmon, *Indians in the Making: Ethnic Relations and Indian Identities around Puget Sound* (Berkeley: University of California Press, 1998); Paige Raibmon, *Authentic Indians: Episodes of Encounter from the Late-Nineteenth-Century Northwest Coast* (Durham: Duke University Press, 2005); and John Sutton Lutz, *Makuk: A New History of Aboriginal-White Relations* (Seattle: University of Washington Press, 2007).

20. See minutes of the monthly meeting, June 1908, in Asiatic Exclusion League, *Proceedings of the Asiatic Exclusion League.*

21. Ernest Crawford reprinted in *Everett Labor Journal,* May 6, 1910.

22. *B.C. Federationist* (Vancouver), Jan. 20, 1912. By "black races," the editorial was referring to South Asian immigrants from British India rather than people of African descent, although white nativists commonly conflated the ethnoracial status of Asian "coolies" with blacks in the American South. This association was unsurprising given that mid-nineteenth-century political debates over Asian "coolie" labor led inevitably to comparisons to African Americans and chattel slavery. On this relationship between coolies and chattel slavery, see Jung, *Coolies and Cane,* 11–38.

23. *Seattle Union Record,* Nov. 3, 1900.

24. *Seattle Union Record,* May 10, 1902.

25. Roger Rouse argues that the national has "always existed in dialectical tension with broader processes and connections operating beyond and across . . . borders." See Roger Rouse, "Thinking through Transnationalism: Notes on the Cultural Politics of Class Relations in the Contemporary United States," *Public Culture* 7 (no. 2, 1995): 353–402, esp. 358. Michelle Ann Stephens writes similarly about blackness, arguing that black consciousness emerged at the intersection of the national and the global. See Michelle Ann Stephens, *Black Empire: The Masculine Global Imaginary of Caribbean Intellectuals in the United States, 1914–1962* (Durham: Duke University Press, 2005), 5.

26. *Seattle Union Record,* Feb. 22, 1907. As historian Dana Frank argued, "To be a 'worker' in the Seattle AFL was to be not only a wage earner but also white. See Dana Frank, *Purchasing Power: Consumer Organizing, Gender, and the Seattle Labor Movement, 1919–1929* (Cambridge: Cambridge University Press, 1994), 9.

27. Peck, *Reinventing Free Labor* and Foley, *The White Scourge*. On how ethnic differences shaped the immigration and settlement experiences of southern and eastern Europeans in the North American West, see Micaela di Leonardo, *The Varieties of Ethnic Experience: Kinship, Class, and Gender among California Italian-Americans* (Ithaca: Cornell University Press, 1984); and Patricia K. Wood,

Nationalism from the Margins: Italians in Alberta and British Columbia (Montreal: McGill-Queen's University Press, 2002).

28. On non-English-speaking immigrants, see Philip Dreyfus, "The IWW and the Limits of Inter-Ethnic Organizing: Reds, Whites, and Greeks in Grays Harbor, Washington, 1912," *Labor History* 38:4 (Fall 1997): 450–70. On how sexuality and gender constructed a class of "suspect whites" in the Pacific Northwest, see Peter Boag, *Same-Sex Affairs: Constructing and Controlling Homosexuality in the Pacific Northwest* (Berkeley: University of California Press, 2003). Interethnic differences, however, never resulted in the explicit exclusion of European immigrants from the labor movement or concerted opposition to their migration. See John Rowe, *The Hard-Rock Men: Cornish Immigrants and the North American Mining Frontier* (New York: Barnes and Noble Books, 1974), 246.

29. See Carlos A. Schwantes, *Radical Heritage: Labor, Socialism, and Reform in Washington and British Columbia, 1885–1917* (Moscow: Idaho University Press, 1994). On how a sense of Britishness and pride in its symbols animated the making of a white working class in Britain and its colonies, see Alastair Bonnett, "How the British Working Class Became White: The Symbolic (Re)Formation of Racialized Capitalism," *Journal of Historical Sociology* 11 (Sept. 1998): 316–40; and Jonathan Hyslop, "The Imperial Working Class Makes Itself 'White': White Labourism in Britain, Australia, and South Africa before the First World War," *Journal of Historical Sociology* 12 (Dec. 1999): 398–421.

30. Washington State Federation of Labor, *Proceedings of the Annual Convention* (Tacoma, 1907), 23.

31. See Ballantyne, *Orientalism and Race*, 15–16.

32. Accounts of anti-Asian agitation and exclusion have been confined to national histories of individual white settler colonies, a paradigm that obscures the movements and linkages that connected these developments across space and time. See Roy, *The Oriental Question;* Ward, *White Canada Forever;* Maria De Lepervanche, *Indians in a White Australia: An Account of Race, Class, and Indian Immigration to Eastern Australia* (Sydney: G. Allen & Unwin, 1984); Elmer Clarence Sandmeyer, *The Anti-Chinese Movement in California* (Champaign: University of Illinois Press, 1991); Malcolm McKinnon, *Immigrants and Citizens: New Zealanders and Asian Immigration in Historical Context* (Wellington: Institute of Policy Studies, Victoria University of Wellington, 1996); and Walker, *Anxious Nation*. There are comparative studies of anti-Asian movements and policies but they generally do not take up the question of how they might be connected. See Charles Price, *The Great White Walls are Built: Restrictive Immigration to North America and Australasia, 1836–1888* (Canberra: Australian National University Press, 1974); Andrew Markus, *Fear and Hatred: Purifying Australia and California, 1850–1901* (Sydney: Hale & Iremonger, 1979); and Sean Brawley, *The White Peril: Foreign Relations and Asian Immigration to Australasia and North America, 1919–1978* (Sydney: University of New South Wales Press, 1995).

33. For this critique, see George Sanchez, "Race, Nation, and Culture in Recent Immigration Studies," *Journal of American Ethnic History* (Summer

1999): 66–83. See also Matthew Frye Jacobson, *Roots Too: White Ethnic Revival in Post-Civil Rights America* (Cambridge: Harvard University Press, 2006), 31–42; and David R. Roediger, *Working toward Whiteness: How America's Immigrants Become White: The Strange Journey from Ellis Island to the Suburbs* (New York: Basic Books, 2005).

34. See Robert A. Huttenback, *Racism and Empire: White Settlers and Colored Immigrants in the British Self-Governing Colonies, 1830–1910* (Ithaca: Cornell University Press, 1976); and Robert Davies, *Capital, State, and White Labour in South Africa, 1900–1960: An Historical Materialist Analysis of Class Formation and Class Relations* (Brighton: Harvester Press, 1979).

35. See Eric J. Hobsbawm, *The Age of Empire, 1875–1914* (New York: Vintage, 1989), 63.

36. Peter Richardson and Jean Jacques Van-Helten, "The Gold-Mining Industry in the Transvaal, 1886–1899," in *The South African War: The Anglo-Boer War, 1899–1902,* ed. Peter Warick (Harlow, 1980), 21.

37. Transvaal and Orange Free State Chamber of Mines, *The Mining Industry: Evidence and Report of the Industrial Commission of Enquiry, with an Appendix Containing the Letter of Chamber of Mines to the Commission, the Principal Laws of the Republic Affecting the Mining Industry, and Other Documents of Interest Appertaining to the Evidence Given at the Enquiry* (Johannesburg, 1897), 124.

38. *Report of Royal Commission on Chinese and Japanese Immigration,* 77.

39. *Report of Royal Commission on Chinese and Japanese Immigration,* 81–87.

40. *Report of Royal Commission on Chinese and Japanese Immigration,* 81.

41. Daniel T. Rodgers, *Atlantic Crossings: Social Politics in a Progressive Age* (Cambridge: Harvard University Press, 1998), 3.

42. James Riley quoted in Elaine Katz, *A Trade Union Aristocracy: A History of White Workers in the Transvaal and the General Strike of 1913* (Johannesburg: University of Witwatersrand Press, 1976), 64.

43. On the triangular relations between whites, Asians, and black Africans in South Africa, see Davies, *Capital, State, and White Labour in South Africa.*

44. Schwantes, *Radical Heritage.*

45. Walker, *Anxious Nation,* 41–44.

46. Lloyd Ross, *William Lane and the Australian Labour Movement* (Sydney: Forward Press, 1935), 71, 43–44.

47. Joseph Lee, "Anti-Chinese Legislation in Australasia," *Quarterly Journal of Economics* (Jan. 1889), 222–23.

48. On Australians looking to California for precedents, see Fitzgerald, *Big White Lie,* 38–39.

49. David Walker, "Shooting Mabel: Warrior Masculinity and Asian Invasion," *History Australia* 2 (Dec. 2005), 89.1–89.11

50. *Worker,* Jan. 3, 1907.

51. Benedict Anderson has emphasized the role of print capitalism in the constitution of nations, but for white workers, the printed word facilitated the imagining of communities that were not necessarily congruent with the boundaries of

nation-states. See Benedict Anderson, *Imagined Communities: Reflections on the Origin and Spread of Nationalism* (New York: Verso, 1991).

52. *Worker,* June 6, 1907.

53. Jonathan Hyslop, *The Notorious Syndicalist: J. T. Bain: A Scottish Rebel in Colonial South Africa* (Johannesburg: Jacana Media, 2004), 162–66. On the Australian influence on the South African labor movement, see also Katz, *Trade Union Aristocracy.*

54. See R. D. Dawe, *Cornish Pioneers in South Africa: "Gold and Diamonds, Cooper and Blood"* (St. Austell: Cornish Hillside Publications, 1998), 197.

55. On the British diasporic labor movement, see Hyslop, "The Imperial Working Class Makes Itself 'White,'" 398–421.

56. *B.C. Saturday Sunset,* July 16, 1907.

57. *B.C. Saturday Sunset,* July 16, 1907.

58. Marilyn Lake, "The White Man under Siege: New Histories of Race in the Nineteenth Century and the Advent of White Australia," *History Workshop Journal* 58 (Autumn 2004): 41–62.

59. Surendra Bhana, *Indentured Indian Emigrants to Natal, 1860–1902: A Study Based on Ships' Lists* (New Delhi: Promilla & Co., 1991).

60. *B.C. Federationist,* Jan. 20, 1912.

61. *B.C. Federationist,* Jan. 20, 1912.

62. *Worker,* June 6, 1907.

63. On the symbolic importance of Haiti in the white racial imagination in the Atlantic world, see Ada Ferrer, *Insurgent Cuba: Race, Nation, and Revolution, 1868–1898* (Chapel Hill: University of North Carolina Press, 1999), 48–50.

64. Washington State Federation of Labor, *Proceedings of the Annual Convention,* 23.

65. *Vancouver World,* Jan. 23, 1914.

66. *Seattle Union Record,* Sept. 14, 1907.

67. On the Asiatic Exclusion League, see Eldon R. Penrose, *California Nativism: Organized Opposition to the Japanese, 1890–1913* (San Francisco: R & E Research Associates, 1973), 16.

68. See minutes of the monthly meeting, Dec. 1907, in Asiatic Exclusion League, *Proceedings of the Asiatic Exclusion League.*

69. *Vancouver World,* Aug. 26, 1907.

70. Hugh Johnston, *The East Indians in Canada* (Ottawa: Canadian Historical Association, 1984); and also see Joan M. Jensen, *Passage from India: Asian Indian Immigrants in North America* (New Haven: Yale University Press, 1988).

71. Letter from the superintendent of immigration to Commissioner General of Immigration John H. Clark, Sept. 15, 1913, NARA, RG 85, Entry 9, File 51388, Folder 5.

72. *American Reveille,* May 23, 1907.

73. *American Reveille,* Sept. 7, 1907.

74. *American Reveille,* Sept. 6, 1907.

75. Robert E. Wynne, "American Labor Leaders and the Vancouver Anti-Oriental Riot," *Pacific Northwest Quarterly* 57 (Oct. 1966): 172–79; and Ken

Adachi, *The Enemy That Never Was: A History of the Japanese Canadians* (Toronto: McClelland and Steward, 1976).

76. *Seattle Union Record,* Sept. 7, 1907.

77. Roy, *White Man's Province*, 185–226. On the international implications of the riots, see Howard H. Sugimoto, "The Vancouver Riots and its International Significance," *Pacific Northwest Quarterly* 64 (1973): 163–74.

78. *Ottawa Free Press,* Sept. 10, 1907.

79. *American Reveille*, Sept. 11, 1907.

80. William Lyon Mackenzie King, *Reports by W. L. Mackenzie King, C. M. G. Deputy Minister of Labour, Commissioner Appointed to Investigate into the Losses Sustained by the Chinese Population of Vancouver, B.C., on the Occasion of the Riots in That City in September 1907* (Ottawa: King's Printer 1908); William Lyon Mackenzie King, *Reports by W. L. Mackenzie King, C. M. G. Deputy Minister of Labour, Commissioner Appointed to Investigate into the Losses Sustained by the Japanese Population of Vancouver, B.C., on the Occasion of the Riots in That City in September 1907* (Ottawa: King's Printer, 1908).

81. *Seattle Union Record*, Sept. 14, 1907; and *Everett Labor Journal*, Oct. 29, 1909.

82. Girindra Mukerji, "The Hindu in America," *Overland Monthly* 2 (1908): 301–08.

83. On the different immigrant regulations in the white settler world, see McKeown, *Melancholy Order.*

84. It should be noted that the agreement between the United States and Japan was not only in response to the riots in the Pacific Northwest, but was also related to events in California. The segregation of Japanese from white children in San Francisco schools in 1906 and concerns over the increasing number of Japanese farm settlements across the West generated intense anti-Japanese sentiments, which—combined with the anti-Asian riots in the Pacific Northwest—led President Roosevelt to seek a diplomatic solution with Japan. On the anti-Japanese movement in California, see Ichioka, *The Issei*, 71–72; and Roger Daniels, *The Politics of Prejudice: The Anti-Japanese Movement in California and the Struggle for Japanese Exclusion* (Berkeley: University of California Press, 1977).

85. Philip J. Deloria, *Playing Indian* (New Haven: Yale University Press, 1998), 184.

86. *American Reveille*, Sept. 13, 1907.

87. Quoted in Roy Ito, *Stories of My People: A Japanese Canadian Journal* (Hamilton: Nisei Veterans Association, 1994), 59.

88. On the relationship between Scandinavian workers and the labor movement, see Dreyfus, "The IWW and the Limits of Inter-Ethnic Organizing," 450–70.

89. *American Reveille,* Sept. 17, 1907. On racial conflicts between Scandinavian and South Asian immigrants in the Pacific Northwest, see minutes from the Sept. 1908 monthly meeting in Asiatic Exclusion League, *Proceedings of the Asiatic Exclusion League.*

90. *American Reveille,* Sept. 11, 1907.

91. *Vancouver World*, Sept. 10, 1907.

92. *Seattle Union Record,* Sept. 28, 1907; and *American Reveille,* Sept. 12, 1907.

93. *American Reveille,* Sept. 17, 1907.

94. *Seattle Union Record,* Sept. 17, 1097.

95. *American Reveille,* Sept. 24, 1907.

96. *American Reveille,* Sept. 24, 1907.

97. *American Reveille,* Sept. 12, 1907.

98. *American Reveille,* Oct. 22, 1907.

CHAPTER FOUR

1. *Vancouver World,* Jan. 12, 1908.

2. Letter from R. O. Montgomery to Richard McBride, July 27, 1915, NAC, RG 6, Series E, Vol. 524, File 251.

3. Letter from Charles H. Riley to inspector in charge, Portland, Oregon, Jan. 14, 1914, WNA, RG 85, Entry 9, File 53572, Folder 92.

4. On the history of the IWW in the Pacific Northwest, see Melvyn Dubofsky, *We Shall Be All: A History of the Industrial Workers of the World,* 2nd ed. (Urbana: University of Illinois Press, 1988). On their activities in the Pacific Northwest, see Robert L. Tyler, *Rebels of the Woods: The IWW in the Pacific Northwest* (Eugene: University of Oregon Press, 1967); and Mark Leier, *Where the Fraser River Flows: A History of the Industrial Workers of the World in British Columbia* (Vancouver: New Star Press, 1990).

5. See Gail Bederman, *Manliness and Civilization: A Cultural History of Gender and Race in the United States, 1880–1917* (Chicago: University of Chicago Press, 1995). On the racialized working-class manhood of the IWW, see Foley, *The White Scourge,* 92–117; and Todd DePastino, *Citizen Hobo: How a Century of Homelessness Shaped America* (Chicago: University of Chicago Press, 2003), 95–126.

6. On the development of nationalist institutions and organizations in British India and the Crown's responses to them, see Ramesh Majumdar, *History of the Freedom Movement in India,* 3 vols. (Calcutta: Firma K. L. Mukhopadhyay, 1962–1963); Richard Popplewell, *Intelligence and Imperial Defence: British Intelligence and the Defence of the Indian Empire, 1904–1924* (London: F. Cass, 1995); and James Campbell Ker, *Political Trouble in India, 1907–1917* (Delhi: Oriental Publishers 1973).

7. On the competing nationalist discourses in India, see Partha Chatterjee, *The Nation and Its Fragments: Colonial and Postcolonial Histories* (Princeton: Princeton University Press, 1993); and Prasenjit Duara, *Rescuing History from the Nation: Questioning Narratives of Modern China* (Chicago: University of Chicago Press, 1995), 205–27.

8. Translated copies of the *Ghadar,* CVA, MSS. 69, 509-D-7, File 1.

9. On revolutionaries in the diaspora, see Harish K. Puri, *Ghadar Movement: Ideology, Organization and Strategy* (Amritsar: Guru Nanak Dev University Press,

1983); and Arun C. Bose, *Indian Revolutionaries Abroad, 1905–1927* (New Delhi: Northern Book Centre, 2002).

10. "Note on the Anti-British Movement among Natives of India in America," as part of letter from the secretary to the government of India to His Majesty's undersecretary of state for India, Feb. 27, 1913, London, UK, India Office and Library Records (hereafter IOLR), Judicial and Public Department Proceedings (JPDP), File 12/1.

11. "Hindu Agitation," July 21, 1908, NAC, RG 2, Vol. 955, PC# 1619.

12. For Taraknath Das's earlier revolutionary activities in India, see a British intelligence profile of him in "Indian Agitation in America," Dec. 17, 1912, IOLR, JPDP, File 1014/1913.

13. See Niharranjan Ray, "From Cultural to Militant Nationalism: The Emergence of the Anushilan Samiti," in Buddhadeva Bhattacharyya, ed., *Freedom Struggle and Anushilan Samiti* (Calcutta: D. C. Ghatak, 1979).

14. This momentous international event—representing the first instance in modern times a non-Western power defeated a traditional European power in the field of battle—also gave rise to pan-Asianist thoughts and visions among South Asian nationalists in which Japan was feted as champion of Asian peoples. On pan-Asianism in the wake of Japan's military success, see Cemil Aydin, *The Politics of Anti-Westernism in Asia: Visions of World Order in Pan-Islamic and Pan-Asian Thought* (New York: Columbia University Press, 2007).

15. Tapan K. Mukherjee, *Taraknath Das: Life and Letters of a Revolutionary in Exile* (Bengal: Jadavpur University, 1998), 7–8.

16. Letter from Ellis de Bruler to the commissioner general of immigration, Jan. 11, 1911, WNA, RG 85, Entry 9, File 51388, Folder 5.

17. Copy of private memorandum concerning Hindu immigration, particularly with regard to the present agitation for the admission of wives and families of the Hindus now resident in Canada, Jan. 22, 1912, CVA, Mss. 69, 509-D-7, File 1.

18. Memorandum, for the secretary of state, April 7, 1913, WNA, RG 85, Entry 9, File 51388, Folder 5.

19. Hannah Arendt, *Men in Dark Times* (New York: Harcourt, Brace & World, 1967), 9.

20. Mukherjee, *Taraknath Das*, 7–8.

21. The planters in British Honduras offered one- to three-year contracts, paying twelve dollars a month in addition to free housing for nine-hour workdays. The wages were exceedingly low if we compare them to the wages South Asians were accustomed to receiving in British Columbia and Washington where they sometimes earned two dollars a day or more in some lumber mills. Department of the Interior, 1908. *The East Indians of British Columbia: A Proposal to Send Them to British Honduras*, NAC, pamphlet 3413.

22. U.S. Immigration Commission, *Annual Report*, (Washington: GPO, 1910), 105.

23. Letter from P. L. Prentis to Commissioner General of Immigration Frank P. Sargent, Jan. 8, 1908, NARA, RG 85, Entry 9, File 51388, Folder 5.

24. Puri, *Ghadar Movement*, 18.

25. "Notes on the Personal Views of J.A.W.," May 22, 1912, IOLR, JPDP, File 126/1913.

26. See "Circular No. 12 of 1912, Indian Agitation in America (Continuation of Circular No. 5 of 1908)," IOLR, JPDP, File 126/1913, 7.

27. At the time of Rahim's entry, Dominion immigration officials had found on his body letters from Taraknath Das and instructions on how to make explosives. See Circular No. 12 of 1912, "Indian Agitation in America," as part of a letter from the government of India to His Majesty's undersecretary of state for India, Feb. 27, 1913, IOLR, JPDP, File 12/1.

28. "Report of Proceedings at Meeting of Hindus Held in O'Brien Hall, Vancouver, BC," Sept. 29, 1913, NARA, RG 85, Entry 9, File 51388, Folder 5.

29. Circular No. 12 of 1912, "Indian Agitation in America," as part of a letter from the government of India to His Majesty's undersecretary of state for India, Feb. 27, 1913, IOLR, JPDP, File 12/1.

30. Mrinalini Sinha, *Colonial Masculinity: The 'Manly Englishman' and the "Effeminate Bengali" in the Late Nineteenth Century* (Manchester: Manchester University Press, 1995), 21. On efforts to "feminize" nationalists in Dutch Indonesia, see Frances Gouda, "Good Mothers, Medeas, or Jezebels: Feminine Imagery in Colonial and Anticolonial Rhetoric in the Dutch East Indies, 1900–1942," in Frances Gouda and Julia Clancy-Smith eds., *Domesticating the Empire: Race, Gender, and Family Life in French and Dutch Colonialism* (Charlottesville: University Press of Virginia, 1998).

31. On the efforts of Bengali middle-class reformers and intellectuals to recuperate Bengali masculinity, see John Rosselli, "The Self-Image of Effeteness: Physical Education and Nationalism in Nineteenth-Century Bengal," *Past and Present* 86 (Feb. 1988): 121–48. This strategy to recuperate national manhood was certainly not unique to India. On similar efforts among Egyptian nationalists, see Wilson Chacko Jacob, *Working Out Egypt: Effendi Masculinity and Subject Formation in Colonial Modernity, 1870–1940* (Durham: Duke University Press, 2010), 65–91.

32. "Copies of the Free Hindusthan," July 21, 1908, NAC, RG 2, Vol. 955, PC# 1619.

33. *Western Clarion*, Feb. 29, 1908. South Asian revolutionaries drew eclectically from a number of different intellectual traditions and sources—some indigenous, some international—to animate their anticolonial politics. American revolutionary luminaries—George Washington, Thomas Paine, Patrick Henry—and their writings and thoughts figured prominently in revolutionary discourse. In the United States, revolutionaries found inspiration in a nation born of rebellion against an empire—in fact, the very same empire they were squaring off with.

34. In a collaboration between the colonizers and the colonized, in which both groups benefited (though highly unevenly) from its projection, the Punjabi Sikh was held up as the masculine ideal of the warrior-hero that imputed South Asian Sikh identity with martial valor, physical confidence, and a self-sacrificing manhood. See Tony Ballantyne, *Between Colonialism and Diaspora: Sikh Cultural Formations in an Imperial World* (Durham: Duke University Press, 2006).

35. Sinha, *Colonial Masculinity*; and Gouda, "Good Mothers, Medeas, or Jezebels."

36. "Copies of the Free Hindusthan," July 21, 1908, NAC, RG 2, Vol. 955, PC# 1619. As someone who drew from a number of different traditions and sources to forge his anticolonial views, including Marxism and socialism, Das understood that British imperialism in India was, in part, about class exploitation.

37. Puri, *Ghadar Movement*, 47.

38. See "Circular No. 12 of 1912, Indian Agitation in America (Continuation of Circular No. 5 of 1908)," IOLR, JPDP, File 126/1913, 6.

39. Translation of "The Sansar," A Hindustani paper printed in Victoria, January 3, 1914, CVA, Mss. 69, 509-D-7, File 1.

40. Copy of letter from Malcolm Reid to the deputy minister of the interior regarding publication of the *Hindustani* and its connection with the International Congress of India, January 12, 1914, CVA, Mss. 69, 509-D-7, File 1.

41. Translated copies of the *Ghadar*, CVA, Mss. 69, 509-D-7, File 1.

42. Arun Coomer Bose, "Indian Nationalist Agitations in the U.S.A. and Canada till the arrival of Har Dayal in 1911," *Journal of Indian History* 43 (April 1965): 227–39.

43. Translated copies of the *Ghadar*, CVA, MSS. 69, 509-D-7, File 1.

44. Puri, *Ghadar Movement*, 42.

45. See Peter Campbell, "East Meets Left: South Asian Militants and the Socialist Party of Canada in British Columbia, 1904–1914" *International Journal of Canadian Studies* 20 (Fall 1999): 35–66; and also Hugh Johnston, The *Voyage of the Komagata Maru: the Sikh Challenge to Canada's Colour Bar* (New Delhi: Oxford University Press, 1979), 8.

46. Ferrer, *Insurgent Cuba*; Peter Zinoman, *The Colonial Bastille, A History of Imprisonment in Vietnam, 1862–1940* (Berkeley: University of California Press, 2001), 240–66.

47. For histories of Lala Har Dyal's political activities in the American West, see Puri, *Ghadar Movement*; and also Emily C. Brown, *Har Dayal: Hindu Revolutionary and Rationalist* (Tucson: University of Arizona Press, 1975).

48. U.S. Immigration Bureau Memorandum, April 4, 1914, WNA, RG 85, Entry 9, File 53572, Folder 92.

49. Copies of the declarations [from Sikhs regarding tyranny], December 13, 1914, CVA, Mss. 69, 509-D-7, File 1.

50. Translated letter of Ganga Ram, Oct. 20, 1916, NAC, RG 13, Vol. 1157, File 9133, Box 50.

51. See "Circular No. 12 of 1912, Indian Agitation in America (Continuation of Circular No. 5 of 1908)," IOLR, JPDP, File 126/1913.

52. Letter to the undersecretary of state of India, April 25, 1913, IOLR, JPDP, File 126/1913

53. Ranjit Hall interview, Aug. 13, 1984, Simon Fraser University Archives, East Indian Oral History Project.

54. Letter from the secretary of state to the viceroy, Home Department, April 1913, IOLR, JPDP, File 126/1913.

55. Mukherjee, *Taraknath Das*, 63.

56. "Translation Letter No. 2," Oct. 20, 1914, WNA, RG 85, Entry 9, File 53854, Folder 133-A/B.

57. *The Industrial Worker,* Nov. 31, 1912.

58. In addition to IWW activists, the *Industrial Worker* and other radical labor publicity circulated across borders in the Pacific Northwest. See Schwantes, *Radical Heritage*, 186–87.

59. *Industrial Worker,* Feb. 3, 1917.

60. Paul Phillips, *No Power Greater: A Century of Labour in British Columbia* (Vancouver: B.C. Federation of Labour and Boag Foundation, 1967), 46; and Andrew R. McCormack, *Reformers, Rebels, and Revolutionaries: The Western Canadian Radical Movement, 1899–1919* (Toronto: University of Toronto Press, 1977), 99. The transnational aspirations of the IWW was recognized in the opening moments of its founding convention when Canadian delegate John Riordan convincingly argued that the union be named the "Industrial Workers of the World" instead of the narrow, nation-based proposal of "Industrial Workers of America."

61. *Union Record,* May 4, 1900. The IWW, on the other hand, attributed workers' transience to the acute conditions of industrial capitalism, rejecting the notion that it was evidence of moral or personal failing, as some social reformers and labor leaders claimed. See Peck, *Reinventing Free Labor;* and Glickman, *A Living Wage.*

62. *Western Clarion,* Mar. 14, 1913. It should be noted that the Socialist Party's position regarding Asian immigrants was far from monolithic and was riddled with tensions and contradictions. There were a number of members who called for the end of racist union policies and who saw it, in the words of one Socialist organizer, "just as necessary to organize the colored races as the white." See *B.C. Federationist,* Oct. 31, 1907.

63. On how the prostitute emerged as the symbol of bondage in the age of emancipation, see Stanley, *From Bondage to Contract*, 218–63.

64. As one white labor activist noted, "Domestic service, house cleaning, sweeping, and a multitude of such duties that generally fall to the lot of widows, old women and girls are monopolized by Japs." Their unmanliness, moreover, was forcing white women into a life of immorality. See *Union Record,* Mar. 9, 1907.

65. *Industrial Worker,* June 29, 1909.

66. *Industrial Worker,* Aug. 26, 1909.

67. *Industrial Worker,* June 29, 1909.

68. *Industrial Worker,* April 22, 1909.

69. *Industrial Worker,* Aug. 26, 1909.

70. *Industrial Worker,* April 15, 1909.

71. *Industrial Worker,* May 20, 1909.

72. "Testimonial Meeting on the Oriental," Mar. 4, 1924, Hoover Institution Archives, Stanford University, Race Relations Survey, Box 24, Fold 16.

73. Beginning in the mid-1880s, Euro-American sugar planters in Hawai'i, confronted with the perennial problems of labor scarcity and cost, began to contract laborers from Japan. The thousands of Japanese who migrated to the islands

searching for new opportunities composed the largest group of the multiracial labor force assembled by the sugar planters and their labor agents. The Japanese, however, proved to be less than docile, employing resistance strategies that included sabotage, work slowdowns, and desertions. By the turn of the twentieth century, Japanese plantation workers moved beyond individualized forms of resistance and began to organize strikes and mount collective protests, proving their willingness to challenge the island's sugar oligarchy directly.

74. For a history of Japanese labor radicalism on the Hawaiian Islands, see Ronald Takaki, *Pau Hana: Plantation Life and Labor in Hawaii 1835–1920* (Honolulu: University of Hawaii Press, 1983); and Edward D. Beechert, *Working in Hawaii: A Labor History* (Honolulu: University of Hawaii Press, 1985).

75. *Industrial Worker*, May 20, 1909.

76. *Industrial Worker*, Aug. 26, 1909.

77. *Industrial Worker*, July 15, 1909.

78. *Industrial Worker*, Nov. 23, 1911.

79. For further details of the 1922 Chinese Seamen's Union strike in Hong Kong, see Josephine Fowler, *Japanese and Chinese Immigrant Activists: Organizing in American and International Communist Movements, 1919–1933* (New Brunswick: Rutgers University Press, 2007).

80. *Industrial Worker*, March 18, 1922.

81. Agnes Laut, *Am I My Brother's Keeper? A Study of British Columbia's Labor & Oriental Problems* (Toronto: Saturday Night, 1913), 36.

82. Laut, *Am I My Brother's Keeper?*, 36.

83. Campbell, "East Meets Left."

84. Letter from W. C. Hopkinson to W. W. Cory, Apr. 1, 1912, NAC, RG 7, G-21, Vol. 202, File 332, Part 6.

85. Laut, *Am I My Brother's Keeper?*

86. Letter from the chief, Military Intelligence branch to the Labor Department, attention Mr. Parker, WNA, RG 85, Entry 9, File 53854, Folder 133-A/B.

87. *B.C. Federationist*, Dec. 12, 1912.

88. *B.C. Federationist*, Dec. 12, 1912.

89. "Testimonial Meeting on the Oriental," Mar. 4, 1924. Hoover Institution Archives, Stanford University, Race Relations Survey, Box 24, Folder 16. The chairman of the meeting cautioned members about romanticizing their relationship with Asian workers. Indeed, "not a man in the hall and there must have been at least 150 men present had ever gotten acquainted with an Oriental while on the job."

90. *Industrial Worker*, Jan. 14, 1922.

91. DePastino, *Citizen Hobo*, 120. To see how the personhood of Theodore Roosevelt both reflected and produced racial manhood at the turn of the twentieth century, see Bederman, *Manliness and Civilization*, 170–216. On how these cultural ideas shaped the construction of a racialized working-class manhood, see Foley, *The White Scourge*, 92–117.

92. *Seattle Union Record*, Sept. 21, 1907.

93. *Industrial Worker*, Apr. 1, 1909.

94. *Industrial Worker*, Oct. 7, 1922.

95. "Testimonial Meeting on the Oriental," March 4, 1924, Hoover Institution Archives, Stanford University, Race Relations Survey, Box 24, Fold 16.

96. Laut, *Am I My Brother's Keeper?* 24.

97. Osawa Shigeru interview, May 10 and 16, 1968, UWSC, Accession #960, Tape 217-B.

CHAPTER FIVE

1. See Johnston, *The Voyage of the Komagata Maru.*

2. Confidential letter to A. Percy Sherwood, chief commissioner of police, Ottawa, Nov. 8, 1916, NAC, RG 13, Vol. 1157, File 9133, Box 50.

3. Letter from Malcolm Reid to W. D. Scott, Aug. 8, 1914, CVA Mss. 69-509-D-7 File 1.

4. On how imperial powers supported each other's empires, see Paul Kramer, "Empires, Exceptions, and Anglo-Saxons: Race and Rule between the British and United States Empires, 1880–1910," *Journal of American History* 88 (March 2002): 1315–53; and Anne Foster, *Projections of Power: The United States and Europe in Colonial Southeast Asia, 1919–1941* (Durham: Duke University Press, 2010).

5. On the struggles over Asian migration in the Anglophone colonial settler world, and how they established border control as a rightful prerogative of the nation-state, see Aristide Zolberg, "The Great Wall against China: Responses to the First Immigration Crisis, 1885–1925," in *Migration, Migration History, History: Old Paradigms and New Perspectives,* ed. Jan Lucassen and Leo Lucassen (Bern: Peter Lang, 1999); McKeown, *Melancholy Order;* and Lake and Reynolds, *Drawing the Global Colour Line.*

6. On the ways modern states deployed rationalizing technologies and practices—the census, surveys, and maps—to make societies legible for social control and engineering, see James C. Scott, *Seeing Like a State: How Certain Schemes to Improve the Human Condition Have Failed* (New Haven: Yale University Press, 1998). On the emergence of the U.S. national security state, see McCoy, *Policing America's Empire;* Christopher Capozzola, *Uncle Sam Wants You: World War I and the Making of the Modern American Citizen* (Oxford: Oxford University Press, 2008); and William Preston, Jr., *Aliens and Dissenters: Federal Suppression of Radicals, 1903–1933* (Cambridge: Harvard University Press, 1963). On the origins of British imperial intelligence gathering, see C. A. Bayly, *Empire and Information: Intelligence Gathering and Social Communication in India, 1780–1870* (Cambridge: Cambridge University Press 1996); and Priya Satia, *Spies in Arabia: The Great War and the Cultural Foundations of Britain's Covert Empire in the Middle East* (Oxford: Oxford University Press, 2008).

7. Letter from Oscar S. Straus to Secretary of State Elihu Root, Dec. 30, 1907, NARA, RG 85, Entry 9, File 51630, Folder 44.

8. *Port Townsend Leader,* July 31, 1907.

9. Letter from Inspector-in-Charge John H. Sargent to Commissioner General of Immigration Frank P. Sargent, Sept. 19, 1907, NARA, RG 85, Entry 9, File 51360, Folder 44.

10. Letter from John H. Sargent to Frank P. Sargent (see previous note).

11. "Digest of, and Comment Upon, Report of Immigrant Inspector Marcus Braun," Sept. 20, 1907, NARA, RG 85, Entry 9, File 51360, Folder 44-D.

12. Foley, *The White Scourge,* 47.

13. Letter from John H. Sargent to F. H. Larned, Sept. 24, 1908, NARA, RG 85, Entry 9, File 52999, Folder 26.

14. Marcus Braun, "How Can We Enforce Our Exclusion Laws?" *The Annals of the American Academy* 34:2 (Sept., 1909), 360–62.

15. Japanese and South Asian immigrants were made ineligible to citizenship in subsequent years. See Ian Haney-Lopez, *White by Law: The Legal Construction of Race* (New York: New York University Press, 1996), 56–77.

16. *Seattle Times,* Sept. 22, 1907; and *American Reveille,* Sept. 24, 1907.

17. *Vancouver World,* Aug. 26, 1907. To see how the Asiatic Exclusion League contributed to the making of this crisis, see minutes of the monthly meeting, September 1907, Asiatic Exclusion League, *Proceedings of the Asiatic Exclusion League.*

18. Bruno Ramirez with Yves Otis, *Crossing the 49th Parallel: Migration from Canada to the United States, 1900–1930* (Ithaca: Cornell University Press, 2001); and LaDow, *The Medicine Line.*

19. On aboriginal labor and migration in the Northwest Pacific coast, see Raibmon, *Authentic Indians*; Harmon, *Indians in the Making;* and Lutz, *Makuk.*

20. Scholars have focused on the San Francisco School Board's decision to segregate white and Japanese students to determine the cause of the Gentlemen's Agreement, while ignoring the role and impact of the riots in the Pacific Northwest. See Roger Daniels, *The Politics of Prejudice: The Anti-Japanese Movement in California and the Struggle for Japanese Exclusion* (Berkeley: University of California Press, 1977), 33–35, and 37–41.

21. Letter from Commissioner General of Immigration Frank P. Sargent to the commissioner of immigration, Montreal, Canada, September 10, 1907, NARA, RG 85, Entry 9, File 51686, Folder 17-A.

22. *American Reveille,* Sept. 24, 1907.

23. Letter from Charles Babcock to F. P. Sargent, Sept. 28, 1907, NARA, RG 85, Entry 9, File 51893/102, Part 1.

24. Letter from John H. Sargent to F. H. Larned, Oct. 2, 1909, NARA, RG 85, Entry 9, File 52999, Folder 26.

25. Letter from Inspector Charles Babcock to Inspector-in-Charge John H. Sargent, Nov. 4, 1908, NARA, RG 85, Entry 9, File 52999, Folder 26.

26. Letter from Seattle Commissioner of Immigration Ellis DeBruler to Commissioner General of Immigration Daniel J. Keefe, Dec. 3, 1909, NARA, RG 85, Entry 9, File 52999, Folder 26-A.

27. Letter from Commissioner General of Immigration Daniel J. Keefe to the secretary of commerce and labor, Dec. 10, 1909, NARA, RG 85, Entry 9, File 52999, Folder 26-A.

28. Letter from Everett Wallace to Commissioner General of Immigration Daniel J. Keefe, Dec. 6, 1909, NARA, RG 85, Entry 9, File 52999, Folder 26-B.

29. Letter from P. L. Prentis to Commissioner General of Immigration Frank P. Sargent, July 23, 1908, NARA, RG 85, Entry 9, File 51930, Part 1.

30. Letter from C. A. Turner to Inspector-in-Charge John H. Sargent, Sept. 14, 1907, NARA, RG 85, Entry 9, File 51630, Folder 44-B.

31. Letter from Immigrant Inspector Benjamin Hunter to Inspector-in-Charge John H. Sargent, Aug. 31, 1907, NARA, RG 85, Entry 9, File 51686, Folder 17-A.

32. Letter from Charles Babcock to Commissioner General of Immigration F. P. Sargent, Sept. 28, 1907, NARA, RG 85, Entry 9, File 51893, Folder 102; letter from H. C. Beach to F. D. Huestis, June 11, 1900, NARA – PA, RG 36, Box#107, Folder 2.

33. *Daily Colonist,* Sept. 11, 1909.

34. Letter from Henry M. White to the Commissioner General of Immigration Anthony Caminetti, Mar. 16, 1914, NARA, RG 85, Entry 9, File 52999, Folder 26-G.

35. *Vancouver World,* April 15, 1908.

36. Letter from Charles Babcock to Inspector-in-Charge John H. Sargent, Oct. 7, 1907, NARA, RG 85, Entry 9, File 51893, Folder 102, Part 1.

37. Richard Rajala, "Pulling Lumber: Indo-Canadians in the British Columbia Forest Industry, 1900–1998," *B.C. Historical News* 36:1 (2002/2003), 2–9.

38. Letter from John H. Clark to the Commissioner General of Immigration A. Caminetti, May 27, 1914, NARA, RG 85, Entry 9, File 51388, Folder 5.

39. Samuel Gompers, *The Samuel Gompers Papers, Vol. 5: An Expanding Movement at the Turn of the Century, 1898–1902,* ed. Stuart Bruce Kaufman, Grace Palladino, and Peter J. Albert (Champaign: University of Illinois Press, 1996), 28.

40. On the connections between white supremacy and anti-imperialism, see Michael Salman, *The Embarrassment of Slavery: Controversies over Bondage and Nationalism in the American Colonial Philippines* (Berkeley: University of California Press, 2001); and Eric Love, *Race over Empire: Racism and U.S. Imperialism, 1865–1900* (Chapel Hill: University of North Carolina Press, 2004).

41. Letter to the commissioner of immigration, Jan. 31, 1911, WNA, RG 85, Entry 9, File 51388/5, Subfile 1.

42. Memorandum for the Secretary, from Commissioner-General of Immigration Daniel J. Keefe, April 7, 1913, WNA, RG 85, Entry 9, File 51388, Folder 5.

43. Kaplan, *Anarchy of Empire,* 3. Also see, Ngai, *Impossible Subjects,* 100.

44. Mae Ngai makes this point very explicitly in her book, *Impossible Subjects.*

45. Letter from Daniel Keefe to commissioner of immigration, San Francisco, California, March 8, 1910, NARA, RG 85, Entry 9, File 51388, Folder 5.

46. *Vancouver Ledger,* June 6, 1903.

47. Report of Malcolm Reid, April 1, 1914, CVA, MSS. 69, 509-D-7, File 1.

48. "Restriction on Immigration," House Immigration Committee hearings, 63d Congress, 2d sess. (Washington, DC: Government Printing Office, 1914).

49. *Industrial Worker*, Dec. 19, 1912.

50. Marian Smith, "The INS at the U.S.-Canadian Border, 1893–1933: An Overview of Issues and Topics," *Michigan Historical Review* 26 (Fall 2000): 127–47.

51. As historian Linda Gordon has argued, "what made the West a land of opportunity was the chance to become white." See Gordon, *The Great Arizona Orphan Abduction*, 104. On whiteness in the multiracial West, see Saxton, *The Indispensable Enemy;* and Tomas Almaguer, *Racial Fault Lines: The Historical Origins of White Supremacy in California* (Berkeley: University of California Press, 1994).

52. William Lyon Mackenzie King, *Deputy Minister of Labor on Mission to England to Confer with the British Authorities on the Subject of Immigration from the Orient and Immigration from India in Particular,* report (Ottawa: King's Printer, 1908).

53. Jensen, *Passage from India*, 81–82.

54. Circular to boundary inspectors, Jan. 16, 1914, NAC, RG 76, Series I-A-1, Vol. 561, File 808722.

55. Ramirez, *Crossing the 49th Parallel*, 37.

56. Circular, immigration, Mar. 12, 1913, NAC, RG 76, Series I-A-1, Vol. 561, File 808722.

57. Letter to Superintendent of Immigration W. D. Scott, March 1, 1912, NAC, RG 76, Series 1-A-1, Vol. 578, File 817172.

58. On the rise of American nativism and its opposition to southern and eastern European immigration, see Higham, *Strangers in the Land.*

59. Letter to Superintendent of Immigration W. D. Scott, Mar. 1, 1912, NAC, RG 76, Series I-A-1, Vol. 578, File 817172.

60. *The Province*, Jan. 20, 1908.

61. Letter from G. L. Milne to W. D. Scott, NAC, RG 76, Vol. 387, File 536999, Part 1.

62. Adam McKeown, "Ritualization of Regulation: The Enforcement of Chinese Exclusion in the United States and China," *American Historical Review* 108 (April 2003): 379. See also, Salyer, *Laws Harsh as Tigers;* Ngai, *Impossible Subjects;* and Lee, *At America's Gates.*

63. Quoted in Kazuo, *Issei*, 87.

64. *American Reveille*, Oct. 17, 1907.

65. *The Province*, Dec. 4, 1913.

66. Nayan Shah, *Contagious Divides: Epidemics and Race in San Francisco's Chinatown* (Berkeley: University of California Press 2001), 187.

67. Letter from the Seattle Immigration Office to Commissioner General of Immigration Frank P. Sargent, May 18, 1908, NARA, RG 85, Entry 9, File 51893, Part 2.

68. "Digest of, and Comment Upon, Report of Immigrant Inspector Marcus Braun," NARA.

69. Letter from Superintendent of Immigration W. D. Scott to Medical Superintendent M. Chishild, Nov. 15, 1909, NARA, RG 85, Entry 9, File 51630, Folder 44-D.

70. Fumiko Uyeda Groves interview, June 16, 1998, Densho: The Japanese American Legacy Project.

71. "Restriction of Immigration of Hindu Laborers," House Immigration Committee hearings, 63d Congress, 2d sess. (Washington, DC: Government Printing Office, 1914).

72. "Industrial Relations," vol. 7 (Asiatic Smuggling), Final Report and Testimony, Commission on Industrial Relations, 64th Congress, 1st sess. (Washington, DC: Government Printing Office, 1916).

73. Letter from Immigrant Inspector P. L. Prentis to the Commissioner General of Immigration Frank P. Sargent, Aug. 22, 1907, NARA, RG 85, Entry 9, File 51686, Folder 17-A.

74. Memorandum to the Secretary of State Williams Jennings Bryan, June 12, 1914, NARA, RG 85, Entry 9, File 51388, Folder 5.

75. See Johnston, *The Voyage of the Komagata Maru.*

76. Confidential letter to A. Percy Sherwood, Chief Commissioner of Police, Ottawa, Nov. 8, 1916, NAC, RG 13, Vol. 1157, File 9133, Box 50.

77. Letter from R. O. Montgomery to Richard McBride, July 27, 1915, NAC, RG 6, Series E, Vol. 524, File 251.

78. Quoted in Puri, *Ghadar Movement,* 31.

79. For a description of the life and career of William Hopkinson, see Hugh Johnston, "The Surveillance of Indian Nationalists in North America, 1908–1918," *B.C. Studies* 1988 (78): 3–27; and also Johnston, *The Voyage of the* Komagata Maru, 1, 7, and 137.

80. "Indian Agitation on the Pacific Coast (especially in California): Proposed Grant of Annual Allowances for W. C. Hopkinson of the Canadian Immigration Department, for Obtaining Information," July 21, 1913, IOLR, JPDP, File 126/1913.

81. According to a communication intercepted by British intelligence, Har Dayal asked his anarchist friends at the Bakunin Club if they had heard about "what one of my men has done in India?" referring to the assassination attempt on Lord Hardinge. See "Circular No. 12 of 1912, Indian Agitation in America (Continuation of Circular No. 5 of 1908)," IOLR, JPDP, File 126/1913, 4.

82. "Confidential Memorandum: For Information of India Office," prepared by William Hopkinson, March 1913, IOLR, JPDP, File 126/1913. Hopkinson held the following positions: (1) inspector of Dominion Immigration Department, (2) Indian interpreter, (3) Dominion police officer, (4) special agent of the Canadian government (when in foreign territory), and (5) Hindu interpreter of the United States Immigration Department.

83. U.S. Immigration Commission, *Annual Report,* (Washington: GPO, 1910), 105.

84. See British intelligence profile of Hussain Rahim in "Indian Agitation in America," December 17, 1912, IOLR, JPDP, File 1014/1913.

85. "Circular No. 12 of 1912, Indian Agitation in America," as part of a letter from the secretary to the government of India to His Majesty's undersecretary of state for India, Feb. 27, 1913, IOLR, JPDP, File 12/1.

86. Letter from the Hindustani Association to the Canadian Immigration Department, NAC, RG 76, Vol. 561, File 808722, Part 1.

87. Letter from W. C. Hopkinson to Deputy Minister of the Interior W. W. Cory, March 26, 1913, IOLR, JPDP, File 6/1024.

88. Mukherjee, *Taraknath Das*, 59.

89. Jensen, *Passage from India*, 191.

90. Letter from Charles H. Reily to inspector in charge, Portland, Oregon, Jan. 14, 1914, NARA, RG 85, Entry 9, File 53572, Folder 92. Another U.S. immigration official reported in 1914 that "It is felt by this office that the prejudice existing among the Hindus against both the Canadian Immigration and our Service in British Columbia has reached such a stage that it will be necessary for our officers to take steps to protect themselves." Letter from the inspector in charge to the U.S. commissioner of immigration, Oct. 29, 1914, NARA, RG 85, Entry 9, File 53854, Folder 133-A/B.

91. See letter from the chief press censor for Canada to General W. Gwatkin, Jan. 6, 1916, NAC, RG 6, Series E, Vol. 524, File 251; letter to E. J. Chambers, Chief Press Censor of Canada, 1917, NAC, RG 6, Series E, Vol. 524, File 251; letter from the chief press censor of Canada to Deputy Postmaster General R. M. Coulter, Aug. 11, 1915, NAC, RG 6, Series E, Vol. 524, File 251.

92. See "Circular No. 12 of 1912, Indian Agitation in America (Continuation of Circular No. 5 of 1908)," IOLR, JPDP, File 126/1913, 14.

93. Letter from R. O. Montgomery to Richard McBride, July 27, 1915, NAC, RG 6, Series E, Vol. 524, File 251.

94. *The Province*, Jan. 31, 1916.

95. South Asian nationalist activists in Astoria, Oregon, alleged that the British vice consul was paying U.S immigration inspectors one hundred dollars per month for information. Letter from Charles H. Reilly to the inspector in charge, Portland, Oregon, Jan. 14, 1914, NARA, RG 85, Entry 9, File 53572, Folder 92.

96. Letter from the inspector in charge to the U.S. commissioner of immigration, Oct. 29, 1914, NARA, RG 85, Entry 9, File 53854, Folder 133-A/B.

97. "Restriction on Immigration," Hearings, House Immigration Committee, 63rd Congress, 2d Session (Washington, DC: GPO, 1914).

98. "Restriction on Immigration," (see previous note).

99. Letter from the inspector in charge to the U.S. commissioner of immigration, Oct. 29, 1914, NARA, RG 85, Entry 9, File 53854, Folder 133-A/B.

100. Letter from the chief, Military Intelligence branch to the Labor Department, attention Mr. Parker, WNA, RG 85, Entry 9, File 53854, Folder 133-A/B.

101. *Industrial Worker,* Feb. 20, 1913.

102. Schwantes, *Radical Heritage,* 186.

103. This figure represented approximately 15 percent of total IWW membership in North America. See Phillips, *No Power Greater*, 46; and McCormack, *Reformers, Rebels, and Revolutionaries*, 99.

104. Preston, *Aliens and Dissenters.*

105. On the way the state exploited the wartime hysteria over foreign radicalism to expand its policing powers, see Higham, *Strangers in the Land*, 194–285; Capozzola, *Uncle Sam Wants You*, 173–205; McCoy, *Policing America's Empire*, 293–346.

106. On the cultural representations of migrant wage workers in American culture, see DePastino, *Citizen Hobo*, 95–126; Frank Tobias Higbie, *Indispensable Outcasts: Hobo Workers and Community in the American Midwest, 1880–1930* (Champaign: University of Illinois Press, 2003); and Peter Boag, *Same-Sex Affairs: Constructing and Controlling Homosexuality in the Pacific Northwest* (Berkeley: University of California Press, 2003).

107. Kristofer Allerfeldt, *Race, Radicalism, Religion, and Restriction: Immigration in the Pacific Northwest, 1890–1924* (Santa Barbara: Prager, 2003), 95–152.

108. Preston Jr., *Aliens and Dissenters*, 61.

109. "IWW Deportation Cases," 82.

110. "IWW Deportation Cases," 82.

111. Quoted in Allerfeldt, *Race, Radicalism, Religion, and Restriction*, 136.

112. "IWW Deportation Cases," 12.

113. The Immigration Act of 1917 extended the period of deportability to five years. See Ngai, *Impossible Subjects*, 59.

114. "IWW Deportation Cases," 74–75.

115. McCormack, *Reformers, Rebels, and Revolutionaries*, 106; and Allerfeldt, *Race, Radicalism, Religion, and Restriction*, 116–17.

116. Angus MacInnis Memorial Collections, UBC, Box#70, Folder 9.

117. The Dominion had prior experience in the area, having earlier deployed the Royal Canadian Mounted Police (RCMP) on the boundary line to suppress labor dissent and activism across the border in its westernmost provinces. See Andrew Graybill, "Texas Rangers, Canadian Mounties, and the Policing of the Transnational Industrial Frontier, 1885–1910," *Western Historical Quarterly* 35:2 (2004): 167–91.

118. Rajani K. Das, *Hindustani Workers on the Pacific Coast* (Berlin, Walter DeGruyter, 1923), 88.

119. Barbara Ann Roberts, *Whence They Came: Deportation From Canada, 1900–1935* (Ottawa: University of Ottawa Press, 1988), 71–98.

120. Quoted in Cecilia Danysk, *Hired Hands: Labour and the Development of Prairie Agriculture, 1880–1930* (Toronto: McClelland & Stewart, 1995), 127.

121. "Ettor Deported," *American Employer* 1: 10 (May 1913): 604. Also see *New York Times*, "Canada Drives Ettor Out," Mar. 4, 1913.

122. *The Province*, Feb., 12, 1913; and *Industrial Worker*, Feb. 20, 1913.

123. Roberts, *Whence They Came*, 71–98. On the construction of deportation powers in Canada, see her "Shovelling Out the 'Mutinous': Political Deportations from Canada before 1936," *Labour/Le Travail* 18 (Fall 1986): 77–110.

124. Scott, *Seeing Like a State*.

125. Interview with Commissioner Weedin, Seattle Immigration station, Apr. 23, 1924, Hoover Institution Archives, Stanford University, Race Relations

Survey, Box 27, Folder 160. For genealogies of the U.S.-Mexico border, see Sanchez, *Becoming Mexican-American*, 38–62; St. John, *Line in the Sand*; and Hernandez, *Migra!*

EPILOGUE

1. Letter to members of the China Club, Oct. 15, 1925, UWSC, China Club of Seattle, Accession #1093, Box 1, Folder 7.

2. Grant, *Washington, The Evergreen State, and Seattle*, 38.

3. Cumings, "Rimspeak; or the Discourse of the "Pacific Rim."

4. Bruce Cumings, "Global Realm with No Limit, Global Realm with No Name," *Radical History Review* 57 (Spring 1993): 46–59. On this contradiction between the commitment to both boundless markets and bounded nations, see Noble, *Death of a Nation*; and Kaplan, *Anarchy of Empire*.

5. Julean Arnold was consul general at Hankow prior to being selected as part of the inaugural corps of commercial attaché for the U.S. Department of Commerce in 1916.

6. Frank F. Davis, "Broadening Our Chinese Trade," *Asia: Journal of the American Asiatic Association* 17 (March 1917): 40–45.

7. "Will Promote Understanding and Trade between America and China," *Seattle Chamber of Commerce Record*, Oct. 1, 1916, p. 5.

8. "Will Promote Understanding and Trade . . . " (see previous note).

9. Letter to the members of the China Club, Oct. 15, 1925, UWSC, China Club of Seattle, Accession #1093, Box #1, Folder 7.

10. Private writings, circa 1918, UWSC, Thomas Burke Papers, Accession #1483-2, Box 32, Folder 6.

11. Davis, "Broadening Our Chinese Trade," 43.

12. "Will Promote Understanding and Trade between America and China," p. 5.

13. Letter from Chin Gee Hee to Judge Thomas Burke, Aug. 22 and Sept. 10, 1924, UWSC, Thomas Burke Papers, Accession #1483-2, Box #3, Folder 31.

14. "Commercial Relations of Pacific N.W.," circa 1918, UWSC, Thomas Burke Papers, Accession #1483-2, Box #32, Folder 5.

15. Letters to members of the China Club, Oct. 15, 1925, UWSC, China Club of Seattle, Accession #1093, Box 1, Folder 6.

16. Richard C. Berner, *Seattle, 1921–1940: From Boom to Bust* (Seattle: Charles Press, 1992), 160–65.

17. In the *Seattle Port Warden Annual Reports*, U.S. colonial territories were categorized as domestic trading partners.

18. On the ways multiculturalism and the discourse of the "global" have been deployed to advance a neoliberal agenda in recent decades, see Nikhil Pal Singh, "Culture/Wars: Recoding Empire in an Age of Democracy," *American Quarterly* 50:3 (Sep. 1998), 471–522; Karen Ho, *Liquidated: An Ethnography of Wall Street*

(Durham: Duke University Press, 2009); and Katharyne Mitchell, *Crossing the Neoliberal Line: Pacific Rim Migration and the Metropolis* (Philadelphia: Temple University Press, 2004).

19. Newly arriving Filipinos, for example, faced nearly the same cycle of racial rioting, violence, and legal exclusion earlier Asian immigrants experienced. See Fujita-Rony, *American Workers, Colonial Power;* and Ngai, *Impossible Subjects,* 96–126.

20. Holt, *The Problem of Race in the Twenty-First Century,* 20. For a similar argument, see also, Etienne Balibar, "Is There a 'Neo-Racism'?" in *Race, Nation, Class: Ambiguous Identities,* ed. Etienne Balibar and Immanuel Wallerstein (London: Verso Press, 1991).

21. Davis, "Broadening Our Chinese Trade," 43.

22. See Cumings, *Dominion from Sea to Sea,* 139. The Open Door, as the author writes, was the "logical strategy of a rising power since colonies were another name for closed economic zones and the United States thought it could compete against anybody, anywhere."

23. On the core tenets of liberal modernity and how they guided America's role in the world following World War II, see Robert Latham, *The Liberal Moment: Modernity, Security, and the Making of Postwar International Order* (New York: Columbia University Press, 1997).

24. Cumings, *Dominion from Sea to Sea,* 139.

25. "Burke's Address of Welcome to the Visiting Japanese at a Banquet Given by the Seattle Chamber of Commerce in their Honor," Sep. 3, 1909, UWSC, Thomas Burke Papers, Accession #1483-2, Box #32, Folder 5. Burke would continue to make the case for this brand of liberal internationalism as a member of the board of trustees of the Carnegie Endowment for International Peace in New York City. It was perhaps fitting, then, that Thomas Burke spent his final moments making one last appeal for his internationalist vision. He collapsed into the arms of a board of trustee member before being able to finish his address.

26. On racial liberalism in the postwar era, see Michael Omi and Howard Winant, *Racial Formation in the United States: From the 1960s to the 1980s* (New York: Routledge, 1994); Mary Dudziak, *Cold War Civil Rights: Race and the Image of American Democracy* (Princeton: Princeton University Press, 2000); Penny Von Eschen, *Race against Empire: Black Americans and Anticolonialism, 1937–1957* (Ithaca: Cornell University Press, 1997); Nikhil Pal Singh, *Black is a Country: Race and the Unfinished Struggle for Democracy* (Cambridge: Harvard University Press, 2004); Thomas J. Sugrue, *Sweet Land of Liberty: The Forgotten Struggle for Civil Rights in the North* (New York: Random House, 2008). On the rise of postwar racial liberalism in Canada, see Patricia E. Roy, *The Triumph of Citizenship: The Japanese and Chinese in Canada, 1941–67* (Vancouver: University of British Columbia Press, 2008). On how racial liberalism eventually morphs into a neoliberal multiculturalism that legitimates globalization and the hypermobility of capital, see Jodi Melamed, "The Spirit of Neoliberalism: From Racial Liberalism to Neoliberal Multiculturalism," *Social Text* 89 (Winter 2006): 1–25.

27. Arnold recommended to the university president that the University of Chicago establish a department of China; see "Discussion and Comment," *The Far Eastern Republic* 2:10 (July 1920): 197.

28. Davis, "Broadening Our Chinese Trade," 42.

29. To what extent these efforts presaged area studies is an open question though the fact that the University of Washington emerges as a vital center for area studies during the Cold War is highly suggestive. For a probing history of area studies during the Cold War, see Bruce Cumings, "Boundary Displacement: Area Studies and International Studies During and After the Cold War," *Bulletin of Concerned Asian Scholars*, 29:1 (1997): 6–26.

30. On how the Chicago school of sociology constructed the "Oriental problem" before World War II, see Henry Yu, *Thinking Orientals: Migration, Contact, and Exoticism* (Oxford: University of Oxford Press, 2001).

31. Some of the topics of discussion at the conference included the "use of history and geography to stimulate and enlighten mutual understanding and respect among the nations of the Pacific; the ideals of democracy and the task of education in contributing to their realization; the actual educational systems of various Pacific lands and possible improvements to them." See E. O. Sisson, "The Pan Pacific Educational Conference," *Pacific Review* 2 (Dec. 1921): 455–62.

32. "Men and Events," *China Monthly Review* 23 (1922): 482.

33. "Club News," *The Chinese Student Monthly* 17 (Nov. 1921–June 1922): 53.

34. "China Club Entertains First Guest," *Seattle Chamber of Commerce Record*, Dec. 1, 1916, p. 8.

35. Letter to members of the China Club, Oct. 15, 1925, UWSC, China Club of Seattle, Accession #1093, Box 1, Folder 7.

36. "A Plan for the Formation of a Chinese Co.," circa 1918, UWSC, Thomas Burke Papers, Accession #1483-2, Box #3, Folder 34. On how Chinese brokers became the first hyphenated Chinese-Americans and Chinese-Canadians, see Mae Ngai, *The Lucky Ones*; Mar, *Brokering Belonging*.

37. National Foreign Trade Council, *Official Report of the Seventh National Foreign Trade Convention* (New York: National Foreign Trade Council, 1920), 126–27.

38. Letter from China Club to O. K. Davis, secretary, Foreign Trade Council, Apr. 21, 1922, UWSC, China Club China Club of Seattle, Accession #1093, Box 1, Folder 2.

39. Herbert H. Gowen, "The Problem of Oriental Immigration in the State of Washington," *Annals of American Academy of Political and Social Science* 34:2 (Sep. 1909): 109–17.

40. Conover, *Thomas Burke*, 75.

41. This class bias was reflected in almost every one of the China Club's proposals, including its petitions for improvements in facilities for immigrants: "The China Club for two years has been endeavoring to improve conditions in Immigration Stations for Chinese entering the United States. At present the stations, particularly on the Pacific Coast, are very limited in facilities, unsanitary, and the treatment

accorded, particularly first-class passengers is such that it discourages them from entering the United States at Pacific Coast ports." Letter from China Club to O. K. Davis, secretary, Foreign Trade Council, Apr. 21, 1922, UWSC, China Club China Club of Seattle, Accession #1093, Box 1, Folder 2.

42. Thomas Burke speech, "To the People of Seattle," Sep. 1919, UWSC, Japan America Society of Seattle Records, Accession #3686-001, Box 32, Folder 6.

43. Gowen, "Problem of Oriental Immigration," 115.

44. The countries of Asia were each allocated a quota of 100, but because the law denied admission to those immigrants defined as "ineligible to citizenship," they could only be put to use by non-Asian people of those nations. On this twisted outcome, see Ngai, *Impossible Subjects,* 27.

45. *Official Report of the Twelfth National Foreign Trade Convention,* Seattle, Washington, June 24, 25, 26, 1925 (New York: National Foreign Trade Council, 1925).

46. Fernando Coronil, "Towards a Critique of Globalcentrism: Speculations on Capitalism's Nature," *Public Culture* 12:2 (2000): 351–74.

47. On a thoughtful critique of this framing, see Stoler, "On Degrees of Imperial Sovereignty."

48. Dirlik, "Pacific Contradictions," 9.

BIBLIOGRAPHY

Archival Sources

Great Britain

British Library, London

India Office Records, Public and Judicial Department Files

Canada

Canadian National Archives, Ottawa, ON

Privy Council Office, Record Group 2

Secretary of State, Record Group 6

Governor General's Office, Record Group 7

Justice, Record Group 13

Immigration, Record Group 76

City of Vancouver Archives, Vancouver, BC

City Clerk's Correspondence

Henry Herbert Stevens Fonds

Major Matthews Collection

Robert Beaven Collection

Sam Kee Collection

Vancouver and District Trades and Labour Council Fonds

Yip Family and Yip Sang Ltd. Fonds

Simon Fraser University Archives, Burnaby, BC

Indo-Canadian Collection

Indo-Canadian Oral History Collection

University of British Columbia Special Collections, Vancouver, BC

Angus MacInnis Fonds

Chinese-Canadian Research Collection

Harry Cowan Collection

International Pacific Salmon Fisheries Commission Collection

Jack Petley Collection

Japanese–Canadian Research Collection
Wallace B. Chung and Madeline H. Chung Collection
Won Alexander Cumyow Fonds

United States
Densho, Japanese American Legacy Project, Seattle, WA
Betty Morita Shibayama Interview, Oct. 27, 2003
Mary Ota Higa Interview, Dec. 17, 2004
Fumiko M. Noji Interview, Apr. 22, 1998
Fumiko Uyeda Groves Interview, June 16, 1998
Hoover Institution Archives, Stanford, CA
Survey of Race Relations, Major Documents
Survey of Race Relations, Minor Documents
United States Immigration and Naturalization Service, Central Office, Washington, DC
Subject Files of the U.S–INS
United States National Archives and Records Administration
U.S. Immigration and Naturalization Service, Record Group 85 Washington, DC
U.S. Customs Service, Record Group 36, Pacific Northwest Region, Seattle, WA
University of Washington Special Collections, Seattle, WA
China Club of Seattle Records
Japanese Association of North American Records
Kihachi Hirakawa Papers
Shigeru Osawa Papers
Thomas Burke Papers
Watson Squire Papers
Western Labor Council Proceedings
Willard Jue Papers
Washington State Oral/Aural History Project, 1972–1977, Olympia, WA
Wing Luke Museum
Misao Sakamoto Oral History Interview Transcript, 1993
Theodore Tetsuji Makamura Oral History Interview Transcript, 1993
Alfred Dong Mar Oral History Interview Transcript, 1900
Jimmy Mar Oral History Interview Transcript, 2002

Newspapers and Periodicals

American Reveille
B.C. Saturday Sunset
B.C. Federationist
Daily Call
Daily Colonist
Everett Labor Journal
Industrial Worker

Overland Monthly
Port Townsend Leader
Province
Seattle Post–Intelligencer
Seattle Times
Seattle Union Record
Spokesman–Review
Tacoma Daily News
Tacoma News Tribune
Town Crier
The New Canadian
The Outlook
Washington Magazine
Washington Standard
West Shore
Western Clarion
Vancouver Magazine
Vancouver World
The Worker

Government Serial Publications

United States Department of Labor. *Annual Report of the Commissioner General of Immigration to the Secretary of Labor.*
United State Department of Labor. *Annual Report of the Secretary of Labor.*

Government Publications

United States Congress. House. "Industrial Relations," Vol. 7 (Asiatic Smuggling), Final Report and Testimony, Commission on Industrial Relations, 64th Congress, 1st Session. Washington, DC: GPO, 1916.
United States Congress. House. Committee on Immigration and Naturalization. "Hindu Immigration." Hearings, 63rd Congress, 2d Session. Washington, DC: GPO, 1914.
———. Committee on Immigration and Naturalization. "Immigration Restriction." Hearings, 63rd Congress, 2d Session. Washington, DC: GPO, 1914.
———. Committee on Immigration and Naturalization. "Restriction of Immigration of Hindu Laborers." Hearings, 63rd Congress, 2d Session. Washington, DC: GPO, 1914.
United States Department of Interior. *Tenth Census of the United States: 1890* Washington, DC.
———. *Eleventh Census of the United States: 1900* Washington, DC.
———. *Twelfth Census of the United States: 1910* Washington, DC.
———. *Thirteenth Census of the United States: 1920* Washington, DC.

Canada. *Report of Royal Commission on Chinese Immigration*. Ottawa: Order of the Commission, 1885.

Canada. *Report of Royal Commission on Chinese and Japanese Immigration*. Ottawa: King's Printer, 1902.

Canada, Department of the Interior. *The East Indians of British Columbia: A proposal to send them to British Honduras,* 1908.

Canada. Department of Labour. *Report by W. L. Mackenzie King, C. M. G. Deputy Minister of Labour, Commissioner, appointed to investigate into the losses sustained by the Chinese population of Vancouver, BC on the occasion of the riots in that city in September 1907.*

Canada. Department of Labour. *Report by W. L. Mackenzie King, C. M. G. Deputy Minister of Labour, Commissioner, appointed to investigate into the losses sustained by the Japanese population of Vancouver, BC on the occasion of the riots in that city in September, 1907.*

Canada. Department of Labour. *Report by W. L. Mackenzie King, C. M. G. Deputy Minister of Labour, Commissioner, on mission to England to confer with the British authorities on the subject of immigration from Orient and immigration from India in particular,* 1908.

Unpublished Manuscripts

Geiger, Andrea. "Cross–Pacific Dimensions of Race, Caste, and Class: Meiji–era Japanese Immigrants in the North American West, 1885–1928." PhD dissertation, University of Washington, 2006.

MacDonald, Alexander N. "Seattle's Economic Development, 1880–1910." PhD dissertation, University of Washington, 1959.

McLouglin, Peter Martin. "Japanese and the Labor Movement of British Columbia." Bachelor's thesis, University of British Columbia, 1951.

Meneely, Alexander Howard. "The Anti–Chinese Movement in the Northwest." Master's thesis, University of Washington, 1922.

Murayama, Yuzo. "The Economic History of Japanese Immigration to the Pacific Northwest, 1890–1920." PhD dissertation, University of Washington, 1982.

Sohi, Seema. "Echoes of Mutiny: Race, Empire, and Indian Anti-Colonialists in North America." PhD dissertation, University of Washington, 2008.

Stevens, Todd. "Brokers between Worlds: Chinese Merchants and Legal Culture in the Pacific Northwest, 1852–1925." PhD dissertation, Princeton University, 2003.

Tanaka, Stefan A. "The Nikkei on Bainbridge Island: A Study of Migration and Community Development." Master's thesis, University of Washington, 1977.

Wynne, Robert E. "Reaction to the Chinese in the Pacific Northwest and British Columbia, 1850–1910." PhD dissertation, University of Washington, 1964.

Books and Articles

Asiatic Exclusion League. *Proceedings of the Asiatic Exclusion League, 1907–1913*. New York: Arno Press, 1977.

Braun, Marcus. "How Can We Enforce Our Exclusion Laws?" *The Annals of the American Academy*, 34:2 (September, 1909): 360–62.
Das, Rajani K. *Hindustani Workers on the Pacific Coast.* Berlin: Walter de Gruyter, 1923.
Gompers, Samuel, and Herman Gustadt. *Meat vs. Rice: American Manhood against Asiatic Exclusion. Which Shall Survive?* San Francisco: Asiatic Exclusion League, 1906.
Grant, Frederic J. *History of Seattle, Washington: With Illustrations and Biographical Sketches of Some of Its Prominent Men and Pioneers.* New York: American, 1891.
———. *Washington, the Evergreen State, and Seattle: Its Metropolis* Seattle: Crawford and Conover, 1890.
Ito, Roy. *Stories of my People: A Japanese–Canadian Journal.* Hamilton: Nisei Veterans Association, 1994.
Kazuo, Ito. *Issei: A History of Japanese Immigrants in North America*, Shinichiro Nakamura and Jean S Gerard, trans. Seattle: Japanese Community Service, 1973.
Knight, Rolf, and Maya Koizumi, eds. *A Man of Our Times: A Life-History of a Japanese-Canadian Fisherman.* Vancouver: New Star Books, 1976.
Laut, Agnes C. *Am I My Brother's Keeper? A Study of British Columbia's Labor and Oriental Problem.* Toronto: Saturday Night, 1913.
Mackenzie, R. D. *Oriental Exclusion.* Chicago: University of Chicago Press, 1928.
Mukerji, Girindra. "The Hindu in America," *Overland Monthly* 2:4 (1908): 301–08.
Price, Andrew. *Port Blakely: The Community Captain Renton Built.* Seattle: Port Blakely, 1990.
Swan, James G. *The Northwest Coast: Or, Three Years Residence in Washington Territory.* New York: Harper & Brothers, 1857.
Washington State Federation of Labor. *Proceedings of the Annual Convention.* Tacoma: The Federation, 1907.

Secondary Sources

Adachi, Ken. *The Enemy that Never Was: A History of the Japanese Canadians.* Toronto: McClelland and Stewart, 1976.
Adelman, Jeremy, and Stephen Aron, "From Borderlands to Borders: Empires, Nation-States, and the Peoples in between in North American History," *American Historical Review* 104 (June 1999): 814–41.
Allerfeldt, Kristofer. *Race, Radicalism, Religion, and Restriction: Immigration in the Pacific Northwest, 1890–1924.* Santa Barbara: Prager, 2003.
Almaguer, Tomas. *Racial Fault Lines: The Historical Origins of White Supremacy in California.* Berkeley: University of California Press, 1994.
Anderson, Benedict. *Imagined Communities: Reflections on the Origin and Spread of Nationalism.* New York: Verso Press, 1991.
Anderson, Kay J. *Vancouver's Chinatown: Racial Discourse in Canada, 1875–1980.* Montreal: McGill-Queen's University Press, 1991.
Arnesen, Eric. "Whiteness and the Historian's Imagination." *International Labor and Working-Class History* 60 (2001): 3–32.
Asada, Sadao. *Culture Shock and Japanese-American Relations: Historical Essays.* Columbia: University of Missouri Press, 2007.

Avery, Donald. *Reluctant Host: Canada's Response to Immigrant Workers, 1896–1914*. Toronto: McClelland and Steward, 1995.

Azuma, Eiichiro. *Between Two Empires: Race, History, and Transnationalism in Japanese America*. Oxford: Oxford University Press, 2005.

Baker, G. E. ed. *The Works of William H. Seward*. New York: Redfield, 1853–1884.

Baldoz, Rick. *The Third Asiatic Invasion: Migration and Empire in Filipino America, 1898–1946*. New York: New York University Press, 2011.

Ballantyne, Tony. *Orientalism and Race: Aryanism in the British Empire*. London: Palgrave, 2002.

———. *Between Colonialism and Diaspora: Sikh Cultural Formations in an Imperial World*. Durham: Duke University Press, 2006.

Barman, Jean. *The West beyond the West: A History of British Columbia*. Toronto: University of Toronto Press, 1991.

Barman, Jean, and Bruce Watson. *Leaving Paradise: Indigenous Hawaiians in the Pacific Northwest, 1787–1898*. Honolulu: University of Hawaii Press, 2006.

Bederman, Gail. *Manliness and Civilization: A Cultural History of Gender and Race in the United States, 1880–1917*. Chicago: University of Chicago Press, 1995.

Belshaw, John. *Colonization and Community: The Vancouver Island Coalfield and the Making of the British Columbian Working-Class*. Montreal: McGill-Queen's University Press, 2002.

Berner, Richard C. *Seattle, 1921–1940: From Boom to Bust*. Seattle: Charles Press, 1992.

Boag, Peter. *Same-Sex Affairs: Constructing and Controlling Homosexuality in the Pacific Northwest*. Berkeley: University of California Press, 2003.

Bose, Arun C. *Indian Revolutionaries Abroad, 1905–1922*. Patna: Bharati Bhawan, 1971.

Brawley, Sean. *The White Peril: Foreign Relations and Asian Immigration to Australasia and North America, 1919–1978*. Sydney: University of South Wales Press, 1995.

Brown, Emily C. *Har Dayal: Hindu Revolutionary and Rationalist*. Tucson: University of Arizona Press, 1975.

Camacho, Alicia Schmidt, *Migrant Imaginaries: Latino Cultural Politics in the U.S.–Mexico Borderlands*. New York: New York University Press, 2008.

Campbell, Peter. "East Meets Left: South Asian Militants and the Socialist Party of Canada in British Columbia, 1904–1914." *International Journal of Canadian Studies* 20 (1999): 35–66.

Campones, Oscar. "New Formations of Asian American Studies and the Question of U.S. Imperialism." *Positions: East Asia Cultures Critique* 5 (1997): 523–50.

Capozzola, Christopher. *Uncle Sam Wants You: World War I and the Making of the Modern American Citizen*. Oxford: Oxford University Press, 2008.

Clayton, Daniel Wright. *Islands of Truth: The Imperial Fashioning of Vancouver Island*. Vancouver: University of British Columbia Press, 2000.

Coates, Ken, and John M. Findlay, eds. *Parallel Destines: Canadians, Americans, and the Western Border*. Seattle: University of Washington Press, 2002.

Cohen, Katherine Benton. *Borderline Americans: Racial Division and Labor War in the Arizona Borderlands*. Cambridge: Harvard University Press, 2009.
Con, Harry. *From China to Canada: A History of the Chinese Communities in Canada*. Toronto: University of Toronto Press, 1982.
Cook, Warren L. *Flood Tide of Empire: Spain and the Pacific Northwest, 1543–1819*. New Haven: Yale University Press, 1973.
Coronil, Fernando. "Towards a Critique of Globalcentrism: Speculation on Capitalism's Nature," *Public Culture* 2:2 (2000): 351–74.
Cronon, William. *Nature's Metropolis: Chicago and the Great West*. New York: W. W. Norton, 1992.
Cumings, Bruce. *Dominion from Sea to Sea: Pacific Ascendancy and American Power*. New Haven: Yale University Press, 2009.
———. *Parallax Visions: Making Sense of American-East Asian Relations*. Durham: Duke University Press, 2000.
Davies, Robert. *Capital, State, and White Labour in South Africa, 1900–1960: An Historical Materialist Analysis of Class Formation and Class Relations*. Brighton: Harvester Press, 1979.
De Genova, Nicholas. *Working the Boundaries: Race, Space, and "Illegality" in Mexican Chicago*. Durham: Duke University Press, 2005.
DePastino, Todd. *Citizen Hobo: How a Century of Homelessness Shaped America*. Chicago: University of Chicago Press, 2003.
Diaz, Vicente M. *Repositioning the Missionary: Rewriting the Histories of Colonialism, Native Catholicism, and Indigeneity in Guam*. Honolulu: University of Hawai'i Press, 2010.
Dirlik, Arif, ed. *What Is in a Rim? Critical Perspectives on the Pacific Region Idea*. Lanham: Rowman and Littlefield, 1998.
Dreyfus, Philip. "The IWW and the Limits of Inter-Ethnic Organizing: Reds, Whites, and Greeks in Grays Harbor, Washington, 1912." *Labor History* 38:4 (1997): 450–70.
Drinnon, Richard. *Facing West: The Metaphysics of Indian-Hating and Empire-Building*. Norman: University of Oklahoma Press, 1997.
Duara, Prasenjit. *Rescuing History from the Nation: Questioning Narratives of Modern China*. Chicago: University of Chicago Press, 1995.
Dubofsky, Melvyn. "The Origins of Western Working-Class Radicalism, 1890–1905." *Labor History* 7:2 (1966): 131–54.
———. *We Shall Be All: A History of the Industrial Workers of the World*, 2nd ed. Urbana: University of Illinois Press, 1988.
Duncan, Janice K. *Minority without a Champion: Kanakas on the Pacific Coast, 1788–1850*. Oregon: Oregon Historical Society, 1972.
Duus, Peter. *The Abacus and the Sword: The Japanese Penetration of Korea, 1895–1910*. Berkeley: University of California Press, 1995.
Fairbanks, John K. *Trade and Diplomacy on the China Coast: The Opening of the Treaty Ports, 1842–1854*. Cambridge: Harvard University Press, 1953.

Ficken, Robert. *Unsettled Boundaries: Fraser Gold and the British-American Northwest.* Pullman: Washington State University Press, 2003.
Fields, Barbara J. "Slave, Race, and Ideology in the United States of America." *New Left Review* 181 (May–June 1990): 95–118.
Findlay, John M., and Richard White, eds. *Power and Place in the North American West.* Seattle: University of Washington Press, 1999.
Fink, Leon. *Workingmen's Democracy: The Knights of Labor and American Politics.* Urbana: University of Illinois Press, 1983.
Fitzgerald, John. *Big White Lie: Chinese Australians in White Australia.* Sydney: University of New South Wales Press, 2007.
Foley, Neil. *The White Scourge: Mexicans, Blacks, and Poor Whites in Texas Cotton Culture.* Berkeley: University of California Press, 1997.
Fowler, Josephine. *Japanese and Chinese Immigrant Activists: Organizing in American and International Communist Movements, 1919–1933.* New Brunswick: Rutgers University Press, 2007.
Foner, Philip S., and Daniel Rosenberg, eds. *Racism, Dissent, and Asian Americans from 1850 to the Present: A Documentary History.* Westport: Greenwood Press, 1993.
Fujita Rony, Dorothy B. *Americans Workers, American Power: Philippine Seattle and the Transpacific West, 1919–1941.* Berkeley: University of California Press, 2003.
Frank, Dana. *Purchasing Power: Consumer Organizing, Gender, and the Seattle Labor Movement, 1919–1929.* Cambridge: Cambridge University Press, 1994.
French, Doris. *Faith, Sweat, and Politics: The Early Trade Union Years in Canada.* Toronto: McClelland and Stewart, 1962.
Friday, Chris. *Organizing Asian American Labor: The Pacific Coast Canned-Salmon Industry, 1870–1942.* Philadelphia: Temple University Press, 1994.
Frost, Alan. *The Global Reach of Empire: Britain's Maritime Expansion in the Indian and Pacific Ocean, 1764–1815.* Carlton: Victoria, 2003.
Gabaccia, Donna. "Worker Internationalism and Italian Labor Migration, 1870–1914." *International Labor and Working-Class* History 45 (Spring 1994): 63–79.
———. "Is Everywhere Nowhere? Nomads, Nations, and the Immigrant Paradigm of United States History." *Journal of American History* 86:3 (1999): 1,115–34.
Gerstle, Gary. *Working-Class Americanism: The Politics of Labor in a Textile City, 1914–1960.* Cambridge: Cambridge University Press, 1989.
Gilroy, Paul. *The Black Atlantic: Modernity and Double Consciousness.* Cambridge: Harvard University Press, 1992.
Glickman, Lawrence. *A Living Wage: American Workers and the Making of Consumer Society.* Ithaca: Cornell University Press, 1997.
Gordon, Linda. *The Great Arizona Orphan Abduction.* Cambridge: Harvard University Press, 1999.
Graybill, Andrew. "Texas Rangers, Canadian Mounties, and the Policing of the Transnational Industrial Frontier, 1885–1910," *Western Historical Quarterly* 35:2 (2004): 167–91.

Guterl, Matthew, and Christine Skwiot. "Atlantic and Pacific Crossings: Race, Empire, and the 'Labor Problem' in the Late Nineteenth Century." *Radical History Review* 91 (Winter 2005): 40–61.
Hall, Stuart. "Race, Articulation, and Societies Structured in Dominance," in *Sociological Theories: Race and Colonialism*. Paris: UNESCO, 1980.
Hamashita, Takeshi. "The Intra-Regional System in East Asia in Modern Times," in *Network Power*, eds. Peter J. Katzenstein and Takashi Shiraishi. Ithaca: Cornell University Press, 1997.
Hancock, David. *Citizens of the World: London Merchants and the Integration of the British Atlantic Community, 1735–1785*. Cambridge: Cambridge University Press, 1995.
Hardt, Michael, and Antonio Negri, *Empire*. Cambridge: Harvard University Press, 2001.
Harmon, Alexandra. *Indians in the Making: Ethnic Relations and Indians Identities around Puget Sound*. Berkeley: University of California Press, 1999.
Harris, Cole. *The Resettlement of British Columbia: Essays on Colonialism and Geographical Change*. Vancouver: University of British Columbia Press, 1997.
Harvey, David. *The Condition of Postmodernity: An Inquiry into the Origins of Cultural Change*. Oxford: Blackwell, 1989.
Hau'ofa, Epeli. *We Are the Ocean: Selected Works*. Honolulu: University of Hawai'i Press, 2008.
Higbie, Frank Tobias. *Indispensable Outcasts: Hobo Workers and Community in the American Midwest, 1880–1930*. Champaign: University of Illinois Press, 2003.
Higham, John. *Strangers in the Land: Patterns of American Nativism, 1860–1925*. New Brunswick: Rutgers University Press, 1955.
Hing, Bill Ong. *Making and Remaking Asian Americans through Immigration Policy, 1850–1990*. Stanford: Stanford University Press, 1993.
Hildebrand, Lorraine. *Straw Hats, Sandals and Steels: The Chinese in Washington State*. Tacoma: Washington State American Revolution Bicentennial Commission, 1977.
Hobsbawm, Eric J. *The Age of Empire, 1875–1914*. New York: Vintage, 1989.
Holt, Thomas C. *The Problem of Race in the 21st Century*. Cambridge: Harvard University Press, 2000.
Horne, Gerald. *The White Pacific: U.S. Imperialism and Black Slavery in the South Seas After the Civil War*. Honolulu: University of Hawaii Press, 2007.
Horsman, Reginald. *Race and Manifest Destiny: The Origins of American Racial Anglo-Saxons*. Cambridge: Harvard University Press, 1981.
Hyslop, Jonathan. *The Notorious Syndicalist: J. T. Bain: A Scottish Rebel in Colonial South Africa*. Johannesburg: Jacana Media, 2004.
———. "The Imperial Working Class Makes Itself 'White': White Labourism in Britain, Australia, and South Africa before the First World War." *Journal of Historical Sociology* 12 (Dec. 1999): 398–421.
Hsu, Madeline. *Dreaming of Gold, Dreaming of Home: Transnationalism and Migration between the United States and South China, 1882–1943*. Stanford: Stanford University Press, 2000.

Hu-DeHart, Evelyn. "Coolies, Shopkeepers, Pioneers: The Chinese of Mexico and Peru, 1849–1930." *Amerasia Journal* 15:2 (1989): 91–116.

———. "Chinese Coolie Labor in Cuba and Peru in the Nineteenth Century: Free Labor or Neoslavery." *Journal of Overseas Chinese* 2:2 (April 1992): 149–82.

Hunter, Tera W. *To 'Joy My Freedom': Southern Black Women's Lives and Labors after the Civil War.* Cambridge: Harvard University Press, 1997.

Huttenback, Robert A. *Racism and Empire: White Settlers and Colored Immigrants in the British Self-Governing Colonies, 1830–1910.* Ithaca: Cornell University Press, 1976.

Ichioka, Yuji. *The Issei: The World of the First Generation Japanese Immigrants, 1885–1924.* New York: Free Press, 1990.

Igler, David. "Diseased Goods: Global Exchanges in the Eastern Pacific Basin, 1770–1850," *American Historical Review* 109 (June 2004): 693–719.

Iriye, Akira. *Pacific Estrangement: Japanese and American Expansionism, 1897–1911.* Cambridge: Harvard University Press, 1972.

———. *Across the Pacific: An Inner History of American–East Asian Relations.* Chicago: Harcourt, Brace, 1967.

Jacobson, David. *Rights across Borders: Immigration and the Decline of Citizenship.* Baltimore: John Hopkins University Press, 1996.

Jacobson, Matthew Frye. *Whiteness of a Different Color: European Immigrants and the Alchemy of Race.* Cambridge: Harvard University Press, 1998.

———. *Barbarian Virtues: The United States Encounters Foreign Peoples at Home and Abroad, 1876–1917.* New York: Hill and Wang, 2000.

Jensen, Joan M. *Passage from India: Asian Indian Immigrants in North America.* New Haven: Yale University Press, 1988.

Johnston, Hugh. *The Voyage of the Komagata Maru: The Sikh Challenge to Canada's Colour Bar.* New Delhi: Oxford University Press, 1979.

———. *The East Indians in Canada.* Ottawa: Canadian Historical Association, 1984.

Jung, Moon-Ho. *Coolies and Cane: Race, Labor, and Sugar in the Age of Emancipation.* Baltimore: John Hopkins University Press, 2006.

Kaplan, Amy. *The Anarchy of Empire in the Making of U.S. Culture.* Cambridge: Harvard University Press, 2003.

Kaplan, Amy, and Donald Pease, eds. *Cultures of United States Imperialism.* Durham: Duke University Press, 1993.

Katz, Elaine. *A Trade Union Aristocracy: A History of White Workers in the Transvaal and the General Strike of 1913.* Johannesburg: University of Witwatersrand Press, 1976.

Ker, James Campbell. *Political Trouble in India, 1907–1917.* Delhi: Oriental Publishers, 1973.

Kolchin, Peter. "Whiteness Studies: The New History of Race in America." *Journal of American History* 89 (2002): 154–73.

Kramer, Paul. *The Blood of Government: Race, Empire, the United States, and the Philippines* (Chapel Hill: University of North Carolina Press, 2006).

Kuhn, Philip. *Chinese among Others: Emigration in Modern Times*. Lanham: Rowman & Littlefield, 2008.

Ladow, Beth. *The Medicine Line: Life and Death on a North American Borderland*. New York: Routledge, 2001.

LaFeber, Walter. *The New Empire: An Interpretation of American Expansion, 1860–1898*. Ithaca: Cornell University Press, 1963.

———. *The Clash: U.S.-Japanese Relations throughout History*. New York: W. W. Norton, 1997.

Lai, Walton Look. *Indentured Labor, Caribbean Sugar: Chinese and Indian Migrants to the British West Indies, 1838–1918*. Baltimore: John Hopkins University Press, 1997.

Lake, Marilyn, and Henry Reynolds. *Drawing the Global Colour Line: White Men's Countries and the International Challenge of Racial Equality*. Cambridge: Cambridge University Press, 2008.

Lamar, Howard. "From Bondage to Contract: Ethnic Labor in the American West, 1600–1890," in *The Countryside in the Age of Capitalist Transformation: Essays in the Social History of Rural America*, eds. Steven Hahn and Jonathan Prude. Chapel Hill: University of North Carolina Press, 1985, 293–324.

Latham, Robert. *The Liberal Moment: Modernity, Security, and the Making of a Postwar International Order*. New York: Columbia University Press, 1997.

Lee, Erika. "'The "Yellow Peril' and Asian Exclusion in the Americas." *Pacific Historical Review* 76:4 (2007): 537–62.

———. *At America's Gates: Chinese Immigration during the Exclusion Era, 1882–1943*. Chapel Hill: The University of North Carolina Press, 2003.

Lee, Robert G. *Orientals: Asian Americans in Popular Culture*. Philadelphia: Temple University Press, 1999.

Leier, Mark. *Where the Fraser River Flows: A History of the Industrial Workers of the World in British Columbia*. Vancouver: New Star Books, 1990.

Limerick, Patricia. *The Legacy of Conquest: The Unbroken Past of the American West*. New York: W. W. Norton, 1988.

Loo, Tina. *Making Law, Order, and Authority in British Columbia, 1821–1871*. Toronto: University of Toronto Press, 1994.

Lowe, Lisa. *Immigrant Acts: On Asian American Cultural Politics*. Durham: Duke University Press, 1996.

Lorey, David. *The U.S.–Mexican Border in the Twentieth Century*. Wilmington: Scholarly Resources, 1999.

Majumdar, Ramesh. *History of the Freedom Movement in India*, 3 vols. Calcutta: Firma K. L. Mukhopadhyay, 1962–1963.

Mar, Lisa. *Brokering Belonging: Chinese in Canada's Exclusion Era, 1885–1945*. Oxford: University of Oxford Press, 2010.

McCormack, Andrew R. *Reformers, Rebels, and Revolutionaries: The Western Canadian Radical Movement, 1899–1919*. Toronto: University of Toronto Press, 1977.

McCormick, Thomas. *China Market: America's Quest for Informal Empire*. Chicago: Ivan R. Dee, 1967.

McCoy, Alfred. *Policing America's Empire: The United States, the Philippines, and the Rise of the Surveillance State.* Madison: University of Wisconsin Press, 2009.

McKeown, Adam. *Melancholy Order: Asian Migration and the Globalization of Borders.* New York: Columbia University Press, 2008.

———. *Chinese Migrant Networks and Cultural Change: Peru, Chicago, Hawaii, 1900–1936.* Chicago: University of Chicago Press, 2001.

Meleisea, Malama. "Discovering Outsiders," in *The Cambridge History of the Pacific Islanders*, eds. Donald Denoon, Steward Firth, Jocelyn Linnekin, Karen Nero, and Malama Meleisea. Cambridge: Cambridge University Press, 1997.

Mitchell, Don. *The Lie of the Land: Migrant Workers and the California Landscape.* Minneapolis: University of Minnesota Press, 1996.

Montejano, David. *Anglos and Mexicans in the Making of Texas, 1836–1986.* Austin: University of Texas Press, 1987.

Mouat, Jeremy. "The Genesis of Western Exceptionalism: British Columbia's Hard-Rock Miners, 1895–1903." *Canadian Historical Review* 71:3 (September 1990): 317–45.

Mukherjee, Tapan K. *Taraknath Das: Life and Letters of a Revolutionary in Exile.* Bengal: Jadavpur University, 1998.

Muszynski, Alicja. *Cheap Wage Labour: Race and Gender in the Fisheries of British Columbia.* Montreal: McGill-Queen's University Press, 1996.

Neuman, Gerald. *Strangers to the Constitution: Immigrants, Borders, and Fundamental Law.* Princeton: Princeton University Press, 1996.

Nevins, Joseph. *Operation Gatekeeper: The Rise of the "Illegal Alien" and the Making of the U.S.-Mexico Boundary.* New York: Routledge, 2002.

Ngai, Mae. *Impossible Subjects: Illegal Aliens and the Making of Modern America.* Princeton: Princeton University Press, 2004.

———. *The Lucky Ones: One Family and the Extraordinary Invention of Chinese America.* New York: Houghton Mifflin Harcourt, 2010.

Noble, David W. *Death of a Nation: American Culture and the End of Exceptionalism.* Minneapolis: University of Minnesota Press, 2003.

Okihiro, Gary Y. *Island World: A History of Hawai'i and the United States.* Berkeley: University of California Press, 2008.

———. *Cane Fires: The Anti-Japanese Movement in Hawaii, 1865–1945.* Philadelphia: Temple University Press, 1992.

Ong, Aihwa. *Flexible Citizenship: The Cultural Logics of Transnationality.* Durham: Duke University Press, 1999.

Paasi, Anssi. *Territories, Boundaries, and Consciousness: The Changing Geographies of the Finnish-Russian Border.* New York: John Wiley, 1996.

Peck, Gunther. *Reinventing Free Labor: Padrones and Immigrant Workers in the North American West.* Cambridge: Cambridge University Press, 2000.

Perry, Adele. *On the Edge of Empire: Gender, Race, and the Making of British Columbia, 1849–1871.* Toronto: University of Toronto Press, 2001.

Phillips, Paul. *No Power Greater: A Century of Labour in British Columbia.* Vancouver: Boag Foundation, 1967.

Pletcher, David M. *The Diplomacy of Involvement: American Economic Expansion Across the Pacific, 1784–1900*. Columbia: University of Missouri Press, 2002.

Popplewell, Richard. *Intelligence and Imperial Defence: British Intelligence and the Defence of the Indian Empire, 1904–1924*. London: F. Cass, 1995.

Preston, William. *Aliens and Dissenters: Federal Suppression of Radicals, 1903–1933*. Cambridge: Harvard University Press, 1963.

Price, Charles. *The Great White Walls are Built: Restrictive Immigration to North America and Australasia, 1836–1888.* Canberra: Australian National University Press, 1974.

Prosser, William F. *A History of Puget Sound Country: Its Resources, Its Commerce and Its People.* New York: Lewis Publishing Company, 1903.

Puri, Harish K. *Ghadar Movement: Ideology, Organization and Strategy.* Amritsar: Garu Nanak Dev University Press, 1983.

Pyle, Joseph Gilpin. *The Life of James J. Hill*, vol. 1. Garden City: Doubleday, 1917.

Rafael, Vicente. *White Love and Other Events in Filipino History.* Durham: Duke University Press, 2000.

Raibmon, Paige. *Authentic Indians: Episodes of Encounter from the Late-Nineteenth Century Northwest Coast.* Durham: Duke University Press, 2005.

Rajala, Richard. *Up-Coast: Forests and Industry on British Columbia's North Coast, 1870–2005*. Victoria: Royal British Columbia Museum, 2006.

Ramirez, Bruno with Yves Otis. *Crossing the* 49th *Parallel: Migration from Canada to the United States, 1900–1930*. Ithaca: Cornell University Press, 2001.

Roberts, Barbara Ann. *Whence They Came: Deportation from Canada, 1900–1935*. Ottawa: University of Ottawa Press, 1988.

Roediger, David R. *The Wages of Whiteness: Race and the Making of the American Working Class.* London: Verso, 1991.

———. *Towards the Abolition of Whiteness: Essays on Race, Politics, and Working Class History.* New York: Verso, 1994.

Rodgers, Daniel T. *Atlantic Crossings: Social Politics in a Progressive Age.* Cambridge: Harvard University Press, 1998.

Rouse, Roger. "Thinking through Transnationalism: Notes on the Cultural Politics of Class Relations in the Contemporary United States." *Public Culture* 7:2 (1995): 353–402.

Ross, Lloyd. *William Lane and the Australian Labor Movement.* Sydney: Forward Press, 1935.

Rosseli, John. "The Self-Image of Effeteness: Physical Education and Nationalism in Nineteenth-Century Bengal," *Past and Present* 86 (Feb. 1998): 121–48.

Roy, Patricia E. *White Man's Province: British Columbia Politicians and Chinese and Japanese Immigrants, 1858–1914*. Vancouver: University of British Columbia Press, 1989.

Sahlins, Peter. *Boundaries: The Making of France and Spain in the Pyrenees*. Berkeley: University of California Press, 1989.

Salyer, Lucy E. *Laws Harsh as Tigers: Chinese Immigrants and the Shaping of Modern Immigration Law*. Chapel Hill: University of North Carolina Press, 1995.

Sanchez, George J. *Becoming Mexican-American: Ethnicity, Culture, and Identity in Chicano Los Angeles, 1900–1945*. Oxford: Oxford University Press, 1995.

———. "Race, Nation, and Culture in Recent Immigration Studies." *Journal of American Ethnic History* (Summer 1999): 66–83.

Sassen, Saskia. *Territory, Authority, Rights: From Medieval to Global Assemblages*. Princeton: Princeton University Press, 2006.

———. *Globalization and its Discontents: Essays on the New Mobility of People and Money*. New York: New Press, 1999.

Saxton, Alexander. *The Indispensable Enemy: Labor and the Anti-Chinese Movement in California*. Berkeley: University of California Press, 1971.

Schmidt-Camacho, Alicia. *Migrant Imaginaries: Latino Cultural Politics in the U.S.-Mexico Borderlands*. New York: New York University Press, 2008.

Schurz, William Lytle. *The Manila Galleon*. New York: E. P. Dutton, 1939.

Schwantes, Carlos A. *Radical Heritage: Labor, Socialism, and Reform in Washington and British Columbia, 1885–1917*. Moscow: University of Idaho Press, 1994.

———. *The Pacific Northwest: An Interpretive History*. Lincoln: University of Nebraska Press, 1996.

Scott, James C. *Seeing like the State: How Certain Schemes to Improve the Human Condition Have Failed*. New Haven: Yale University Press, 1998.

Shah, Nayan. *Contagious Divides: Epidemics and Race in San Francisco's Chinatown*. Berkeley: University of California Press, 2001.

Silva, Noenoe K. *Aloha Betrayed: Native Hawaiian Resistance to American Colonialism*. Durham: Duke University Press, 2004.

Sinha, Mrinalini. *Colonial Masculinity: The "Manly Englishman" and the "Effeminate Bengali" in the Late Nineteenth Century*. Manchester: Manchester University Press, 1995.

Smith, Neil. *American Empire: Roosevelt's Geographer and the Prelude to Globalization*. Berkeley: University of California Press, 2003.

Soja, Edward W. *Postmodern Geographies: The Reassertion of Space in Critical Social Theory*. London: Verso, 1989.

Spate, O. H. K. *Paradise Found and Lost*, vol. 3. Minneapolis: University of Minnesota Press, 1988.

———. *Monopolists and Free Booters*, vol. 2. Minneapolis: University of Minnesota Press, 1979.

———. *The Pacific Since Magellan*, vol. 1. Minneapolis: University of Minnesota Press, 1979.

Spickard, Paul. *Almost All Aliens: Immigration, Race, and Colonialism in American History and Identity*. New York: Routledge, 2007.

Stanley, Amy Dru. *From Bondage to Contract: Wage Labor, Marriage, and the Market in the Age of Slave Emancipation* Cambridge: Cambridge University Press, 1998.

Stoler, Ann Laura, "On Degrees of Imperial Sovereignty," *Public Culture* 18:1 (2006): 125–46.

Stoler, Ann Laura, with David Bond, "Refractions of Empire: Untimely Comparisons in Harsh Times," *Radical History Review* 95 (Spring 2006): 93–107.

Stoler, Ann Laura, and Frederick Cooper, eds. *Tensions of Empire: Colonial Cultures in a Bourgeois World*. Berkeley: University of California Press, 1997.

Takaki, Ronald. *Pau Hana: Plantation Life and Labor in Hawaii, 1835–1920*. Honolulu: University of Hawaii Press, 1983.

Thelen, David. "Of Audiences, Borderlands, and Comparisons: Toward the Internationalization of American History." *Journal of American History* 79 (1992): 432–62.

Torpey, John. *The Invention of the Passport: Surveillance, Citizenship, and the State*. Cambridge: Cambridge University Press, 2000.

Truett, Samuel. *Fugitive Landscapes: The Forgotten History of the U.S.-Mexico Borderlands*. New Haven: Yale University Press, 2006.

Tsai, Jung-Fang. *Hong Kong in Chinese History: Community and Social Unrest in the British Colony, 1842–1913*. New York: Columbia University Press, 1995.

Tyrell, Ian. "Making Nations/Making States: American Historians in Context of Empire." *Journal of American History* 86 (1999): 2025–44.

Walker, David. *Anxious Nation: Australia and the Rise of Asia 1850–1939*. Queensland: University of Queensland Press, 1999.

Ward, Peter W. *White Canada Forever: Popular Attitudes and Public Policy toward Orientals in British Columbia*. Montreal: McGill-Queen's University Press, 1978.

White, Richard. *"It's Your Misfortune and None of My Own": A New History of the American West*. Norman: University of Oklahoma Press, 1991.

Williams, William Appleman. *The Tragedy of American Diplomacy*. New York: W. W. Norton, 1959.

Wilson, Francis. *Labor in the South African Gold Mines*. Cambridge: Cambridge University Press, 1972.

Wilson, Rob. *Reimagining the American Pacific: From South Pacific to Bamboo Ridge and Beyond*. Durham: Duke University Press, 2000.

Wood, Ellen Meiksins. *Empire of Capital*. New York: Verso, 2003.

Wolf, Eric R. *Europe and the People without a History*. Berkeley: University of California Press, 1982.

Wood, Patricia K. *Nationalism from the Margins: Italians in Alberta and British Columbia*. Montreal: McGill-Queen's University Press, 2002.

Wynne, Robert. *Reaction to the Chinese in the Pacific Northwest and British Columbia*. New York: Arno Press, 1978.

Yee, Paul. *Saltwater City: An Illustrated History of the Chinese in Vancouver*. Vancouver: Douglas & McIntyre, 2006.

Young, Marilyn. *The Rhetoric of Empire: American China Policy, 1895–1901.* Cambridge: Harvard University Press, 1969.

Yu, Henry. "Los Angeles and American Studies in a Pacific World of Migrations." *American Quarterly* 56 (2004): 531–43.

———. *Thinking Orientals: Migration, Contact, and Exoticism.* Oxford: Oxford University Press, 2001.

Yung, Judy. *Unbound Feet: A Social History of Chinese Women in San Francisco.* Berkeley: University of California Press, 1995.

Zolberg, Aristide. "The Great Wall against China: Responses to the First Immigration Crisis, 1885–1925," in *Migration, Migration History, History: Old Paradigms and New Perspectives,* Jan Lucassen and Leo Lucassen, eds. Bern: Peter Lang Pub., 1997.

INDEX

AMERICAN CROSSROADS

Edited by Earl Lewis, George Lipsitz, George Sánchez, Dana Takagi, Laura Briggs, and Nikhil Pal Singh

1. *Border Matters: Remapping American Cultural Studies*, by José David Saldívar
2. *The White Scourge: Mexicans, Blacks, and Poor Whites in Texas Cotton Culture*, by Neil Foley
3. *Indians in the Making: Ethnic Relations and Indian Identities around Puget Sound*, by Alexandra Harmon
4. *Aztlán and Viet Nam: Chicano and Chicana Experiences of the War*, edited by George Mariscal
5. *Immigration and the Political Economy of Home: West Indian Brooklyn and American Indian Minneapolis, 1945–1992*, by Rachel Buff
6. *Epic Encounters: Culture, Media, and U.S. Interests in the Middle East1945–2000*, by Melani McAlister
7. *Contagious Divides: Epidemics and Race in San Francisco's Chinatown*, by Nayan Shah
8. *Japanese American Celebration and Conflict: A History of Ethnic Identity and Festival, 1934–1990*, by Lon Kurashige
9. *American Sensations: Class, Empire, and the Production of Popular Culture*, by Shelley Streeby
10. *Colored White: Transcending the Racial Past*, by David R. Roediger
11. *Reproducing Empire: Race, Sex, Science, and U.S. Imperialism in Puerto Rico*, by Laura Briggs
12. *meXicana Encounters: The Making of Social Identities on the Borderlands*, by Rosa Linda Fregoso
13. *Popular Culture in the Age of White Flight: Fear and Fantasy in Suburban Los Angeles*, by Eric Avila

14. *Ties That Bind: The Story of an Afro-Cherokee Family in Slavery and Freedom*, by Tiya Miles
15. *Cultural Moves: African Americans and the Politics of Representation*, by Herman S. Gray
16. *Emancipation Betrayed: The Hidden History of Black Organizing and White Violence in Florida from Reconstruction to the Bloody Election of 1920*, by Paul Ortiz
17. *Eugenic Nation: Faults and Frontiers of Better Breeding in Modern America*, by Alexandra Minna Stern
18. *Audiotopia: Music, Race, and America*, by Josh Kun
19. *Black, Brown, Yellow, and Left: Radical Activism in Los Angeles*, by Laura Pulido
20. *Fit to Be Citizens? Public Health and Race in Los Angeles, 1879–1939*, by Natalia Molina
21. *Golden Gulag: Prisons, Surplus, Crisis, and Opposition in Globalizing California*, by Ruth Wilson Gilmore
22. *Proud to Be an Okie: Cultural Politics, Country Music, and Migration to Southern California*, by Peter La Chapelle
23. *Playing America's Game: Baseball, Latinos, and the Color Line*, by Adrian Burgos, Jr.
24. *The Power of the Zoot: Youth Culture and Resistance during World War II*, by Luis Alvarez
25. *Guantánamo: A Working-Class History between Empire and Revolution*, by Jana K. Lipman
26. *Between Arab and White: Race and Ethnicity in the Early Syria- American Diaspora*, by Sarah M. A. Gualtieri
27. *Mean Streets: Chicago Youths and the Everyday Struggle for Empowerment in the Multiracial City, 1908–1969*, by Andrew J. Diamond
28. *In Sight of America: Photography and the Development of U.S. Immigration Policy*, by Anna Pegler-Gordon
29. *Migra! A History of the U.S. Border Patrol*, by Kelly Lytle Hernández
30. *Racial Propositions: Ballot Initiatives and the Making of Postwar California*, by Daniel Martinez HoSang
31. *Stranger Intimacy: Contesting Race, Sexuality, and the Law in the North American West*, by Nayan Shah

32. *The Nicest Kids in Town: American Bandstand, Rock 'n' Roll, and the Struggle for Civil Rights in 1950s Philadelphia*, by Matthew F. Delmont

33. *Jack Johnson, Rebel Sojourner: Boxing in the Shadow of the Global Color Line*, by Theresa Rundstedler

34. *Pacific Connections: The Making of the U.S.-Canadian Borderlands*, by Kornel Chang

35. *States of Delinquency: Race and Science in the Making of California's Juvenile Justice System*, by Miroslava Chávez-García

TEXT
11/14 Garamond Premier Pro
DISPLAY
Garamond Premier Pro
COMPOSITION
MPS Ltd
PRINTING AND BINDING
IBT Global

CPSIA information can be obtained at www.ICGtesting.com
Printed in the USA
LVOW11s0100131115

462376LV00001B/34/P

9 780520 271692